Back to Reason

Discourses in Ancient Near Eastern and Biblical Studies
Series Editor: Emanuel Pfoh, CONICET & National University of La Plata

This series presents different studies of interpretative discourses, cultural representations and historiographical ideologies about the societies of the ancient Near East, ancient Egypt and Biblical scenarios appearing during the 19th and 20th centuries. The aim is to expose, deconstruct and analyze the ways in which Oriental and Biblical societies, cultures and histories were shaped by Western scholarship (Assyriology, Egyptology, Biblical studies), but also by literature and film, while attending to the main ideologies of the historiographical contexts of the last two centuries.

Back to Reason
Minimalism in Biblical Studies

Niels Peter Lemche

SHEFFIELD UK   BRISTOL CT

Published by Equinox Publishing Ltd.

UK   Office 415, The Workstation, 15 Paternoster Row, Sheffield,
        South Yorkshire S1 2BX
USA   ISD, 70 Enterprise Drive, Bristol, CT 06010

www.equinoxpub.com

First published 2022

© Niels Peter Lemche 2022

All rights reserved. No part of this publication may be reproduced or transmitted in any form or by any means, electronic or mechanical, including photocopying, recording or any information storage or retrieval system, without prior permission in writing from the publishers.

British Library Cataloguing-in-Publication Data

A catalogue record for this book is available from the British Library.

ISBN-13 978 1 80050 187 4   (hardback)
         978 1 80050 188 1   (paperback)
         978 1 80050 189 8   (ePDF)
         978 1 80050 190 4   (ePub)

Library of Congress Cataloging-in-Publication Data

Names: Lemche, Niels Peter, author.
Title: Back to reason : minimalism in biblical studies / Niels Peter Lemche.
Description: Sheffield, South Yorkshire ; Bristol, CT : Equinox Publishing Ltd., 2022. | Series: Discourses in ancient near eastern and biblical studies | Includes bibliographical references and index. | Summary: "This study addresses the development of 'Minimalism' from its roots in the historical-critical paradigm and outlines an alternative theory which exposes and explains the intention behind the fallacy of using a story found in the Old Testament to simply invent the biblical concept of Israel"-- Provided by publisher.
Identifiers: LCCN 2022004301 (print) | LCCN 2022004302 (ebook) | ISBN 9781800501874 (hardback) | ISBN 9781800501881 (paperback) | ISBN 9781800501898 (epdf) | ISBN 9781800501904 (epub)
Subjects: LCSH: Bible--Hermeneutics. | Minimalism (Literature) | Bible--Criticism, interpretation, etc. | Israel--Biblical teaching.
Classification: LCC BS476 .L45 2022 (print) | LCC BS476 (ebook) | DDC 220.601--dc23/eng/20220304
LC record available at https://lccn.loc.gov/2022004301
LC ebook record available at https://lccn.loc.gov/2022004302

Typeset by Sparks – www.sparkspublishing.com

Contents

Preface	vii
Introduction	1
1 The Minimalist–Maximalist Controversy	8
2 The Road to Minimalism	62
3 Back to Reason	124
Bibliography	146
Index of Scripture References	177
Index of Modern Authors	178
Index of Subjects	183

Preface

The title of this book goes back to a conversation with Philip R. Davies when he stayed with me during the EABS-meeting in Copenhagen in 2003. Occasionally Philip and I had that kind of discussion, and they always left a happy memory and a lot of inspiration. Thus, when I had published my book on the Canaanites back in 1991 we met at the SBL International Meeting in Rome that summer and had a discussion on the roof of the Casa Valdese that lasted from early evening to sunrise. The main subject was: Now since the Canaanites of the Old Testament are the bad guys in a play, who are the good guys?! Reading Philip's *In Search of 'Ancient Israel'* will disclose some of the points we made during the discussion. The world is definitely not the same after Philip passed away in May, 2018.

Finally I managed to sit down and get the book written. It had to be done. We, the minimalists, are not getting any younger. Philip is no more, Thomas (Thompson) is eighty-two, Keith (Whitelam) also was honoured with his Festschrift some years ago. The reason why I had to write this report has to do with me being a part of this discussion continuously for more than fifty years. I have therefore been able to put the minimalist–maximalist discussion into a perspective which has eluded many of the combatants. Minimalism was not an odd fad which suddenly let its voice be heard around 1990. It had been in preparation for almost a generation before.

The initiative to getting the book written was taken by Dr. Emanuel Pfoh (Manu), whom I had already met – virtually – when he was still an undergraduate and participated in an e-learning course of mine. As a PhD student he spent half a year with me in Copenhagen. Now he decided that his old professor should not just fade away (old soldiers never die!) and provoked me to write the book.

Another student from the e-learning course was Dr. Jim West, who has worked his usual magic on my Danlish, turning it into something readable. So don't say that e-learning is a waste of time. Our friendship goes back many years, both online and in person. My thanks go to both Manu and Jim. Without their encouragement and help this book would never have been written.

And finally, my thanks to the publisher. It all went very fast that day in October 2020. Manu asked me to write the book, I wrote an abstract and sent it to the editor, and got a contract the very same day. I signed it and returned it and in the afternoon it was already on Equinox's homepage. When I signed the contract, I had not written one word, and the manuscript was due in August 2021. We have all learned something about the use of virtual media during the Covid-19 pandemic! The pandemic somehow also helped to produce the book as everything was closed down. Libraries could not be visited, and the university had become a foreign country. I therefore had to do the writing without access to any library except my own. If a title or two (or more) are missing, my readers will know the reason.

Niels Peter Lemche
Huaröd, Sweden, 22 April 2021

Introduction

When I was asked to write the story of biblical minimalism – or the story of "the Copenhagen School (of the Old Testament)"[1] – my first thought was: is there still somebody out there who is interested? Is it not like flogging a dead horse? So much has changed since we began the deconstruction of the classical historical–critical edifice called "ancient Israel" more than fifty years ago. Not so long ago at my department, when I, in a bad mood, said: "Everything is going back to the former bad habits of biblical scholarship!" my former PhD student Tilde Binger replied: "You are absolutely wrong! Nothing is as it used to be, everything has changed".

Maybe she is right; nothing is as it used to be. Maybe we, the members of the Copenhagen School, accomplished a definite turn of direction in our field after all, although this specimen of "cultural memory" is not going to deal with all of the consequences of the changes caused by over fifty years of recent modern critical scholarship. First of all, such a review would be extremely boring, even redundant. Second, it would break all limits and somewhat cover up what was at stake – to "obscure history with facts" as it were. The changes primarily happened within the study of biblical historiography, and as a consequence in the study of ancient history. Other segments of academia are following, not least, in recent times, prophetical studies, but they still have a long way to go before they really catch up with the conclusions based on biblical historiography that we reached. The same can be said about the study of Psalms; although turning, for example, to Sigmund Mowinckel (1884–1965) today leaves the reader in a somewhat mixed mood. On one hand it is all so very old-fashioned, but at the same time, and in a strange way, it is still fascinating. Mowinckel, like his teacher Hermann Gunkel (1862–1932), belong to the past, but they cast long shadows to the very present. The same can be

---

[1] There have been many "Copenhagen Schools", and in many different areas. The most famous is, of course, Niels Bohr's school of nuclear physics. There is no reason to compete with that venerable institution. But then we have had the Copenhagen schools in linguistics and in sociology with Louis Hjelmslev at its centre. Furthermore, it should be noted that the name of the "Copenhagen School" was not chosen by its members; it was an epithet attached to a group of scholars by others, although it is impossible to say when it appeared for the first time.

said about scholars specializing in historical matters such as Albrecht Alt (1883–1956) and Martin Noth (1902–1968). They made sense of the story about Israel as related by Old Testament historiographers and came a long way in the process of freeing the study of Israel in ancient times from the rationalistic paraphrase of the biblical narratives of previous generations of biblical scholars, but they were still heavily influenced by the master narrative and transformed them into "history", sometimes without realizing the consequence of their own approach. But, as already said, like Mowinckel and Gunkel they belong to the past, although modern students might often benefit from reading their contributions.[2]

Biblical minimalism, which is discredited today in some parts of biblical scholarship, really builds on these great scholars of the past. It is, on the other hand, just as apparent that scholars from the Anglo-Saxon tradition, especially from North America, of the early and middle of the twentieth century are conspicuous by their absence. A scholar such as William Foxwell Albright and his students will have a major role to play in the discussion which follows, but it would be wrong to say that the minimalists learned much, if anything, from them. They are of course still prominent on the North American scene where many of the students of the students of Albright are still active, but contrary to their self-assuredness they have little impact outside of their own circle. It is one of the questions to be taken up here, as to why this is so, and it is not always very edifying reading.[3]

---

[2] It is the old adage repeated over and over again: Read Alt and read Noth, not books and articles about Alt and Noth! Alas, not so much has been translated from German into English: a minor selection of Alt's most famous articles from his *Kleine Schriften zur Geschichte des Volkes Israel* (Alt 1953b and 1959), are included in an English translation in Alt 1989; and Noth's *Textbuch* (Noth 1950a; ET Noth 1960a). Practically nothing of what they wrote about the ancient Near East is available in English, making it much easier to disguise how well oriented they were in fields other than the Old Testament. Thus Noth's famous book on the Israelite amphictyony, *Das System der Zwölf Stämme Israels* (Noth 1929), was never translated into English in spite of being the foundation for a whole generation's interpretation of the origins of ancient Israel.

[3] The monograph by Burke Long, *Planting and Reaping Albright: Politics, Ideology, and Interpreting the Bible* (Long 1997), explains what the program of Albright and his students really was about, in those days often called the "Baltimore School". It is an interesting study making it clear how consciously the members of this circle worked to secure the edifice laid down by their master, Albright himself. A highly critical study of Albright's politics, including his obvious sympathy for Zionism, by Brooke Sherrard, *American Biblical Archaeologists and Zionism: The Politics of Historical Ethnography* (Sherrard 2011), was never published, I am tempted to say "of course". I will return later on to the assertion that all archaeology in modern Israel is state of the art. Technically it may be true for most of it, but definitely not as far as interpretation goes.

Due to its nature, the aim of this book is not to present new ideas; or at least this is not the primary task. Though, at the end of this survey I will present a revised version of my studied opinion that the Old Testament is a Hellenistic book, which might be seen as the logical conclusion to ideas that have been like a red thread woven throughout my academic career. It has first and foremost to do with the quest for the origins of the Israelite twelve-tribe system which was central to the reconstruction of early Israelite history when I entered the field of Old Testament studies around sixty years ago. It was an integral part of the instructions of practically all young students because, on the one hand, it evidently addressed a very conspicuous motif in the historiography of early Israel in the Old Testament, while on the other, although the product of historical–critical scholarship, it was inoffensive to all sectors of biblical scholarship, liberal as well as conservative. It was simply the ruling paradigm in its time. The history of the decline of this paradigm will be extensively covered, not because it is part of the minimalist debate in recent years, but because it is instrumental in perceiving what happened after 1970.

The following main part will cover the various issues relating to the biblical version of Israel's history which has been the focus of the debate concerning the historiography of Israel in the Old Testament leading to the change in understanding of the character of this historiography and of its intentions. Few scholars of the older generation have indeed asked questions about intentions but have instead focused on historical issues. Generally, the idea has been to trace the history of ancient Israel as it really happened, making the most of the concept of Leopold von Ranke, "*wie es eigentlich gewesen*".[4] We may also say that from the beginning of historical–critical scholarship scholars have been obsessed with the issue of historicity. Based on source criticism developed as a historical method in Germany at the beginning of the nineteenth century by such historians as Barthold Georg Niebuhr (1776–1831), Leopold von Ranke (1795–1886), and Johann Gustav Droysen (1808–1884) the task of the student of historiography in the Old Testament was to sort out what was historical and what were later inventions and additions. The obsession was to find out what was the original source or the primary source and present this as the foundation on which to build historical reconstructions. Secondary

---

[4] "As it really was". Leopold von Ranke wrote "wie es eigentlich gewesen" and not "wie es eigentlich gewesen war" as claimed by a few North-American biblical scholars with a limited knowledge of German. It should be noted that when Leopold von Ranke coined the expression "eigentlich" did not primarily mean "really" but "essentially". The difference in meaning is not without importance for the development of historical thinking since von Ranke's own time. There is much more of the romantic idea of understanding history in the expression chosen by von Ranke. Cf., e.g., Gilbert 1987, and Griffin, 1993.

additions to the original text were evaluated as part of later speculations and reflections on the witness of the original text, representing secondary additions to the original document that were less important for the historian's task. In this way the final version of, say, the books of Samuel and Kings, was primarily a mine from which to dig out the lumbers of treasure, alias historical information, that could be considered primary evidence of events of the past, with much too little attention given to the intentions of the final editions of these books.

This form of textual analysis has been dubbed "revelation archaeology" by Bernd Jørg Diebner.[5] Behind "archaeological" investigation we find the hope to prove that the narrative cleansed of its secondary elements could be dated as closely as possible to the events described in the text, making it almost the product of an eyewitness to the events described in it. In retrospect the result of this approach could, at times, be hilarious – as when scholars for years discussed who might have been the author of the history of David's succession in the second book of Samuel and the first chapters of the first book of Kings, with David's priest Abiathar being one of the primary candidates because the story about the succession must have been written by an eyewitness.[6] In those days nobody really paid attention to the question of how an author supposed to have lived in the tenth century BCE in far-away Jerusalem could have mastered the novelistic qualities of later Hellenistic biographical composition.

Mario Liverani has, in his *Oltre la Bibbia*, presented an example of the problem.[7] His story of ancient Israel is divided into two parts: the first named

---

[5] Cf. Diebner 1984a. When all has been said about the "Copenhagen school" it should not be forgotten that a similar change of perspective occurred in other places, as at the University of Heidelberg centering around Diebner and his journal *Dielheimer Blätter*. It never became known in the same way as the "Copenhageners" most likely because of language problems: It was all published in German, inaccessible to many (most) North-American scholars.

[6] The classic presentation of this way of evaluating this narrative is Leonhard Rost 1926, reprinted in Rost 1965, 119–253.

[7] Mario Liverani 2003; ET Liverani 2005. In many ways Reinhard G. Kratz presents a similar approach to the question of the relation between the real Israel and the Israel of literature in his *Historisches und biblisches Israel: Das Überblick zum Alten Testament* (Kratz 2013; revised English translation Kratz 2015). In both cases, Liverani as well as Kratz, we see the distinction proposed by Philip R. Davies (Davies 1992) between three "Israels" to be operative: 1) The Israel of history: The Israel which was once in the real world of ancient Palestine; 2) the Israel of the Bible: The Israel which only exists in the narratives of the Old Testament, and 3) ancient Israel: The Israel which has been constructed by modern scholars by combining historical Israel with biblical Israel. Kratz sees historical "Israel" as represented in the Persian and Early Hellenistic periods in non-biblical documents including inscriptions, and a gradual growth of "biblical Israel" hand-in-hand with the beginning

"a normal history", the second "an invented history". The first part includes a not very exciting reconstruction of the history of ancient Israel, which might be reckoned a kind of rationalistic paraphrase – it is as a matter of fact rather conventional, the date of its appearance taken into consideration. The second part goes beyond the text as it is preserved in the Old Testament and here Liverani asks questions about the intention behind the description of Israel's ancient history. Thus, the story of the Patriarchs reflects concerns relating to problems between people returning from exile and the local inhabitants of Israel's land who had no experience of exile. The conquest of Canaan relates to problems between those who returned and those considered foreigners in their land. The biblical judges had to answer for problems relating to being a nation without kings, while the story of David and Solomon had to do with the establishment of a kingdom as a substitute for a kingless society. The invention of the temple of Solomon corresponds to the idea of a priestly rule, while the law may be considered the self-identification of "Israel", i.e., Judaism.

In this way Liverani's approach to the biblical history of Israel is similar to a method he had employed before, in his study of the gruesome story in Judges 19–21.[8] He goes behind the present text in order to find the motives behind its present form. Judges 19–21 is not a historical record from the time of the Judges but more likely a composition addressing problems of a much later date between, especially, the two tribes of Judah and Benjamin. As Liverani sees it, historical texts are essentially propaganda, exposing the interests of the authors. This approach has won him many supporters in Near Eastern studies at large, and it has been interesting to see how this worked out, when he turned to biblical studies, beginning with a study of the story of the ascension of King Joash in 2 Kings 11–12 (Liverani 1974).

However, the most recent histories of Israel in ancient times seem practically immune to such an approach. If we review two of the latest, by Christian Frevel and by Ernst Axel Knauf and Philippe Guillaume published almost simultaneously,[9] not much echoes recent developments in the study of Israel's history, and basically the traditional rationalistic censuring of biblical histo-

---

formation of biblical literature. A third option is to follow Garbini 2008 who sees the emergence of biblical historiography as a response to the influence from the Greeks: Simply to promote a "Hebrew" alternative to the governing Greek religio-historical paradigm.

[8] Liverani 1979b (ET: Liverani 2004, 160–92).

[9] Christian Frevel 2016, and Ernst Axel Knauf and Philippe Guillaume 2016. Nothing has changed in Ernst Axel Knauf and Hermann Michael Niemann 2021. I received a copy of this book when the present treatment was too far advanced to allow a more serious discussion.

riography leaves the remaining text as direct evidence of what happened in ancient Palestine. We may speak of various grades of rationalistic paraphrase, but it is still rationalistic paraphrase. In the case of Knauf and Guillaume this is very obvious: It is biblical Israel they study, but what is this "biblical Israel"? Where should we search for it? In the Bible of course. Elsewhere there is nothing or very little. The most conservative textbook, that by Ian Provan, V. Philip Long, and Tremper Longman III, is methodologically speaking, not far removed from Knauf's and Guillaume's volume, even if Knauf's and Guillaume's reconstruction of the pre-history of Israel is much more refined and critical of the biblical tradition than the one found in Provan, Long and Longman.[10] Apart from a series of corrections to earlier, mainly German histories of Israel, Knauf and Guillaume seems more or less satisfied with repeating previous ideas. Very little discussion about how to read the Old Testament historically is present – they seem to accept what is here, when there is just a slight possibility that it really happened. Very much the same can be said about Frevel's version of Israel's history, although he includes a lengthy discussion of methodology, including a short paragraph on "minimalism" and "maximalism" (Frevel 2016, 20–2). This paragraph is, however, substandard. Frevel does not seem to understand what it is all about and only mentions one point: the insistence of minimalists that nothing in the historiography of the Old Testament can be taken for granted without external evidence, in contrast to the maximalists who will accept anything that is not disproven by external evidence. Furthermore, his reference to this paragraph does not include a single reference to anything published by a "minimalist". This is hardly a satisfying state for a serious discussion, but after this disappointing couple of new "histories", I am happy to refer to Lester L. Grabbe's in many ways classic approach, in his *Ancient Israel*, not because Grabbe shall have the last word but because he meticulously presents "what is on the table" and also includes a more informed paragraph on the maximalist–minimalist controversy.[11] Neither should K.L. Noll have the last word, although his introduction to history represents a much more satisfying approach than either of the recent German versions.[12] The, perhaps, most satisfying handling of the discussion can be found in Megan Bishop Moore's and Brad E. Kelle's debate-book on *Biblical History and Israel's Past*, which already, in its

---

[10] Provan, Ian, V. Philip Long, Tremper Longman III 2003.

[11] Some good advice, if someone wants to obtain a better impression of recent studies of the history of Israel, is to look for a number of contemporary studies, such as Lester L. Grabbe 2007, 2nd edition, 2017), on the maximalist–minimalist debate cf. Grabbe, 2017, 24–25.

[12] K.L. Noll, 2002 (2nd enlarged edition 2013).

title, accepts the dichotomy between the Israel of history and the Israel of the Bible. If we use the North-American biblical scholarship popular expression "a balanced view" meaning a non-biased presentation, Moore's and Kelle's book certainly stands out.[13]

The next chapter will dig further into the discussion in these modern textbooks. Why is it necessary for Frevel to present such a distorted view of what biblical minimalism represents, and why does the competing history by Knauf and Guillaume not even mention the existence of the minimalists?[14] When Frevel's history and Knauf's and Guillaume's textbooks appeared the debate between minimalism and maximalism had been going on for more than twenty years. Both positions were therefore well-known. Therefore, it must have been a deliberate choice by Frevel to present his distorted discussion of the subject – as it certainly also was for Knauf and Guillaume and Niemann to totally ignore it.

---

[13] Megan Bishop Moore and Brad E. Kelle 2011.
[14] Neither does Knauf and Niemann 2021. Maybe I am mistaken but Knauf's actions look more and more like a *damnatio memoriae* of his opponents.

1 The Minimalist–Maximalist Controversy

At the end of the introduction I asked apropos the modern histories of Israel by Christian Frevel (2016) and by Ernst Axel Knauf and Philippe Guillaume (2016): Why are there no references, or only very indirect ones, to the developments in biblical studies over the last generation caused by the so-called "biblical minimalism"? I will try to answer this question in the following chapters. I pointed to a logical mistake committed by Christian Frevel in his history published as recently as 2016, which is so obvious that there must be an explanation for it. The total silence in Ernst Axel Knauf's and Philippe Guillaume's and now also Ernst Axel Knauf and Michael Niemann's volumes is a different matter. Evidently the three authors have chosen to totally ignore positions which, to them, may be considered "disturbing" or "uncomfortable", showing an attitude of "*Ich will nicht mehr wissen*" ("I will not know more") which has been quite common also or particularly within German biblical scholarship for more than a generation.[1] The logical mistake is clearly that there is no balance between a position that demands that something must rely on known evidence; such as in the case of Israel's history where external evidence whether textual (inscriptions) or material (archaeological) is slight, and the maximalist position that claims that everything must be trusted until proven false. The minimalist position is the correct one, as only information in the Bible which can be connected to external evidence may be the subject of a falsification process and therefore useful for a discussion of historical matters. The maximalist position is the one commonly found in biblical studies: If we have some information in the Bible that cannot be connected to external evidence, it is the assertion of the biblical historiographer that it

---

[1] Some earlier studies by Knauf have been more interesting in their openness to recent developments, especially his *Die Umwelt des Alten Testaments* (Knauf 1994). In its sophisticated approach to studying history, his article "From History to Interpretation" (Knauf 1991) also compares badly with the type of history present in his and Guillaume's textbook. As to the idea of not wishing to know more, cf. the highly informative study by Lester L. Grabbe on "The 'Comfortable Theory', 'Maximal Conservatism', and Neo-fundamentalism Revisited" (Grabbe 2002). As an afterthought it is absolutely astonishing how much of biblical studies falls within this category of not comfortable theory.

really happened. And here we have to remember the old Roman adage: *Unus testis nullius testis*, "one witness is no witness". Before something turns up which can change the status of this assertion, making it into a hypothesis, it remains an assertion. Further elaborations on this assertion remain assertions, ending in a web of assertions, a kind of house of cards, not likely to be part of the falsification process.

As an illustration of this we may here mention three different cases:

First we have the story in 2 Kings 18–19 of the Assyrian King Sennacherib's attack on Jerusalem in 701 BCE. The historicity of the event as such is clear as Sennacherib's annals also agree with the description of the attack in 2 Kings: The Assyrian king led a campaign to Palestine and besieged Jerusalem in this very year of 701 BCE.[2] The opening of the description in 2 Kings 18:13–16 is an echo of Sennacherib's version of the event. There are a number of differences and some things have been glossed over, such as the demand from Sennacherib that Hezekiah's daughters should be handed over to Sennacherib. These are minor details. There can be no doubt that the basic story of Sennacherib's attack in 2 Kings rests on historical facts. Thus it is clear from the Assyrian account as well as the Old Testament's that Sennacherib did not conquer Jerusalem but left Palestine after having received his tribute from Hezekiah, although he had already devastated the whole country, a fact that can be corroborated by archaeological facts: The country was destroyed through and through. All other cities in the area were demolished, whereas Jerusalem was spared. The fate of Lachish is paradigmatic in the form it is shown on the reliefs describing Sennacherib's conquest of the city put up in his palace.[3] The description of what happened after the tribute was paid by Hezekiah and the miraculous deliverance of Jerusalem which follows in 2 Kings 18 and 19, is a spinoff of the basic information about the campaign of that year with a very dubious historical content. Other things are at stake in this addition that encompasses the rest of 2 Kings 18 and most of 2 Kings 19.[4] However, these stories are evidence of how freely a biblical historiographer was able to deal with information available to him: The Assyrian version in some form close to the one which has been handed down to us.

---

[2] A translation of Sennacherib's version can be found in different places, the Assyrian text, with translation, thus in Luckenbill 2005 [1924], 32-4. A translation by A. Leo Oppenheim can be found in Pritchard 1955, 287-8, and by Mordechai Cogan in Hallo and Younger 2000, 302–304.

[3] Today displayed in the British Museum, but cf. the splendid publication by David Ussishkin, *The Conquest of Lachish by Sennacherib* (Ussishkin 1982).

[4] Elaborating on this theme cf. Lemche 2003b.

Second, we have the note in 1 Kings 14:25–26 and elaborated in 2 Chronicles 12:1–9 about the campaign of Pharaoh Shishak against Jerusalem in King Rehoboam's fifth regnal year. The notes in 1 Kings and 2 Chronicles are often related to a famous Egyptian inscription which tells about Pharaoh Shoshenq's campaign in Palestine in the second part of the tenth century BCE.[5] This Pharaoh seems to have "visited" almost every place of interest in the country – apart from Jerusalem and other places part of biblical Judah – which are not mentioned at all. King Shishak – or Shoshenq – without doubt conducted this campaign, and his inscription was legible – partly even today – for those who could read Egyptian hieroglyphs at the Bubastite Portal gate located within the great temple of Karnak in Egypt. A study of Palestinian cities included in this list shows a campaign that embraced the coastal plain, Galilee, and part of the Jordan Valley, but left the area ascribed to the Kingdom of Judah untouched. Although the Egyptian evidence seems to confirm the historicity of the campaign mentioned in 1 Kings 14:25–26, the presence of the external evidence creates more problems for the biblical story than if it had not been there: The evidence could be interpreted as a deliberate attempt from the side of the biblical historiographer to usurp a tradition about this Egyptian campaign by making Jerusalem its main target. In this manner a historical note is left in a grey zone where the event, the campaign of Pharaoh Shishak, really took place but the details of his plundering of Jerusalem are pure invention, which disturbs the impression of the period in 1 Kings arguing that the Kingdom of Judah was an entity to be reckoned with. Obviously it was not. The campaign may have been directed against the Kingdom of Israel, "the forgotten kingdom" to use Israel Finkelstein's expression, which was really a political entity of some importance which may be traced back to at least the Amarna period when Lab'aya ruled at Shechem.[6] However, this kingdom was "forgotten" by biblical historiographers and not part of the story about ancient Israel as related by the biblical historiographers.

Finally, we have in 2 Kings 22–23, the description of the reforms carried out by King Josiah of Judah, supposed to have been in 623 BCE. A variant of this narrative can be found in 2 Chronicles 34, which includes an evaluation of the importance of King Josiah very different from the one in 2 Kings. In 2 Kings Josiah is the hero king. He is stripped of most of his honour in the version of 2 Chronicles. Here his role as the great reformer of the temple cult in

---

[5] The list of names on the inscription which can be found in the Wikipedia article 'Bubastite Portal' is taken from Wilson 2005.
[6] On this Finkelstein 2006a and 2013b. Finkelstein's discussion of the campaign of Shishak can be found in Finkelstein 2013b, 41–4, 47–9.

Jerusalem has been transferred to King Hezekiah. King Josiah's reform has traditionally been considered one of the most important events in Israel's history, so-to-speak the beginning of monotheistic Judaism. There are a number of reasons for investing so much in the factuality of the events described in 2 Kings 22–23 but so far nothing has been found outside of the Old Testament that can confirm its historicity.[7] The historicity of this event is deemed a non-testified "fact". Without the reformation of the temple, normally called the deuteronomistic reform and related to the Book of Deuteronomy, and in general the deuteronomistic literature, not much is left for the defence of the historicity of the biblical version of Israel's pre-exilic history, or for the idea that the system of the twelve Israelite tribes originated before "Israel" was forced into exile, when some thousand people from Jerusalem and Judah was driven into exile in Babylon. We will return to the discussion later. Here it is only an example of what the so-called historical–critical scholars have been arguing for more than a century.

Returning to Christian Frevel's textbook, his dealing with Josiah's reform is another modern example of the lack of methodical reflection in biblical historical studies (Frevel 2016, 267–9).[8] His treatment includes both a critical assessment of what happened and a basic acceptance of the biblical version, and here we naturally are speaking about the version found in 2 Kings. It goes well with his characterization of the general attitude of the maximalist to the historical value of biblical texts that they can be used as evidence as long as they are not disproven by external facts. Although he does not describe himself as a maximalist, he will probably see himself as situated somewhere in the middle of the debate between minimalists and maximalists – a very crowded place it seems.

This is a position maintained by many modern biblical scholars who have forgotten what every soldier knows, that the worst position to choose in battle is the one in the middle of two warring parties. You don't get much praise from either side; rather you come under fire from both sides. We find notable scholars positioning themselves here, among those in recent times the Israeli archaeologist Israel Finkelstein, who belongs among scholars who consider the period between the fall of Samaria in 722 BCE and of Jerusalem in 587 BCE as pivotal in the formation of "Israelite" tradition.[9] It is also a defeatist position and a sign that the scholars defending it have given up the idea of

---

[7] I have, in several places, pointed at the basic lack of a historical background for this reform; thus in Lemche 2010a and 2010b. See now also Handy 2020.
[8] This must be seen in light of Frevel's first section, 2016, 17–40.
[9] Cf. thus Finkelstein and Silberman 2001, 251–95. In Finkelstein 2018, he is flirting with Hellenism but only as far as these books are concerned.

reforming their subject, i.e., having a part in the creation of new paradigms: *"Ich will nicht mehr wissen"*. A scholar does not create new knowledge by remaining caught in this position. The only way to get further is to have the audacity to propose something "new", even revolutionary, knowing that you will be the target of severe censoring from most scholars bound up with a traditional paradigm. This cannot be helped and is part of the "game" which is scholarship, whether biblical or not.[10] Of course it goes both ways. New proposals which may lead to new paradigms are not limited to the radical left; conservative scholars are just as likely to be active creating new conservative paradigms. In the middle, nothing happens.[11]

The tactics of those remaining in the middle, or even who present themselves as belonging here, has been described by Mario Liverani in his extensive review of Roland de Vaux's *Histoire ancienne d'Israël*.[12] Liverani described here the tactics used in de Vaux's history, which is only a fragment and was never finished because of its author's death in 1971 (Liverani 1976). De Vaux had planned to position himself as standing in the middle, placing on one side rather conservative scholars like Yehezkel Kaufmann,[13] with a position not far from the scholars belonging to the Albright circle. On the left de Vaux placed scholars of the German tradition – especially of Albrecht Alt and Martin Noth, with their questioning of the historicity of the biblical traditions about the patriarchs and the conquest.[14] In both cases de Vaux rejected a plain acceptance of historicity, but in spite of this he tried to place the patriarchs within a specific cultural and historical framework. The same procedure is followed in his discussion of the conquest tradition: Not a blind acceptance of the biblical record of these events but if anything a rationalistic retelling of

---

[10] Thomas Kuhn's description of how paradigms in science – including humanities – functions is mandatory reading. Cf. Kuhn 2012.

[11] In scholarship it is about the old Hegelian way of proceeding: Thesis + antithesis = synthesis. If nothing is fed into the existing paradigm, it will remain the same. New ideas are always legitimate proposals, not because they are to be accepted but because they question the status quo of the traditional paradigm. This is a very simple observation but nonetheless the alpha and omega of all scholarship. Even the study of the Bible is not an antiquarian humanistic discipline; it is a dynamic field of debate always changing, but it only changes when accepted opinions are questioned. For that reason the central position is a dead end, a place where nothing happens.

[12] Roland de Vaux 1971. It was planned as a complete history of ancient Israel, but at the author's death only a fragment of the second volume remained to be edited by the heirs of de Vaux (de Vaux 1973).

[13] Cf. for Yehezkiel Kaufman's position Kaufmann 1953.

[14] The respective positions of the Albrighteans and of Alt and Noth and their followers will be at the centre of the debate in the next chapter.

the biblical narrative. We can also say it this way: de Vaux never slavishly followed scholars on either side of him but always presented his own revaluation of other positions; thus when it came to the settlement of the Israelite tribes in Palestine, which in his view was a much more complicated affair than envisioned by Albright and his students – with at least four different theatres of conquest, and in the case of Martin Noth's hypothesis about the Israelite amphictyony: There was never any amphictyony,[15] which he for good reasons rejected, but because of his belonging to the centre he was never able to break out and formulate real alternatives to the two mainstream reconstructions of Israel's past in his time.

But this is not Liverani's principal point. His real objection is directed against de Vaux's description of Old Testament scholarship as divided between, on one side Kaufmann and Albright, and on the other Alt and Noth. When de Vaux's *Histoire* was published in 1971, these were no longer the two opposing frontlines in scholarship. The front had changed when George E. Mendenhall, in 1962, challenged the position of Albright on the conquest and proposed his theory of an inner-Palestinian revolutionary development (Mendenhall 1962). When we place Mendenhall on the left, de Vaux cannot any more be considered as belonging to the centre of scholarship, he has moved to the right. The centre position would now be the one occupied by Alt and Noth. It can be added, that as scholarship progressed, Mendenhall, and later also Norman K. Gottwald, who elaborated on his original idea (Gottwald 1979), began the journey to the centre of scholarship as new ideas emerged questioning their ideas as not soundly based neither in history, sociology, nor in methodology. When the scholars defamed as "minimalists" by their opponents emerged, Mendenhall and Gottwald became the new occupants of the central position, whereas all earlier positions moved to the right.

De Vaux's insistence of belonging to the middle became an increasing problem, not to him fifty years after he left this world, but to a scholar like Israel Finkelstein whose early career centred around an original reinterpretation of the archaeological evidence pointing to an Israelite conquest of Palestine at the beginning of the Iron Age, i.e., around 1200 BCE, but who also

---

[15] Cf. on the emigration of the Israelites, de Vaux 1978, 523–680, counting with separate settlements in southern Palestine (Judah, Simeon, and Levi), a second process in Transjordan (Reuben, Gilead-Gad, and Manasseh-Machir), one more in Central Palestine (Benjamin, and the House of Joseph), and finally one in northern Palestine (Asher, Naphtali, Zebulon, and Issachar). The hypothesis of the amphictyony is dismissed in a paragraph that simply says "The Twelve Tribes did not form an Amphictyony", de Vaux 1978, 700–16. The amphictyony, its rise and fall, will be the subject of discussion in the next chapter. A possible resurrection will be discussed in the last chapter.

included new sociological analyses of the world in which this conquest was supposed to have taken place.[16] From his later production it is clear that the turning point always was the question of the historicity of King David, when we compare the input of his two semi-popular books written in cooperation with Neil Asher Silberman (Finkelstein and Silberman 2001 and 2006). Comparing these two volumes makes it clear that the dissolution of the biblical image of the great King David – he merely becomes a chieftain, a kind of mafia boss, roaming the mountains of Judah in the tenth century – creates big problems for the very tradition of a united ancient Israel, because without David and following him Solomon and their mighty capital of Jerusalem, the traditional *Sitz im Leben* (historical place) of the tradition about the society of the twelve Israelite tribes in the time of the Davidic-Solomonic kingdom is no more.

The first blow to the historicity of the idea of the twelve tribes of ancient Israel was delivered when the hypothesis about the twelve-tribe league as the home of this tradition blew up. According to Noth, this was the place where the sacred traditions of early Israel, of its patriarchs and of the sojourn in and escape from Egypt were cultivated (Noth 1929). With the demise of the amphictyony, the origins of these traditions had to be moved down to a time where the unity of all Israelite tribes was in evidence, i.e. the time of David and Solomon. However, what happens when the biblical image of the great Israelite kingdom comprising all Israelite tribes vanishes into the thin air? Where then to place the idea of Israelite unity? Various candidates have been brought forward, such as the time of King Hezekiah, and especially the time of King Josiah. Now a different set of assumptions begins to appear, because neither Hezekiah's time nor Josiah's can be used as evidence of an Israelite polity embracing all twelve tribes. The idea of the twelve-tribe society is now

---

[16] Cf. Finkeslstein 1988. Finkelstein seemingly relied for a great part on the sociological analysis of Middle Eastern traditional culture as found in Lemche 1985, especially the idea of Middle Eastern society as a social continuum denying the traditional image among western observers of a bipartite or even tripartite society, divided between nomads, peasant, and city-dwellers, although we may now question how far he really adjusted to the social anthropological ideas found here. William G. Dever should have paid attention to this connection in his repeated criticism of Finkelstein, thus recently in Dever 2017, 194–210. In his critique Dever relies on the social anthropologist Philip Salzmann, and few other authorities, and on Michael Rowton's idea of a dimorphic society. Cf. Michael B. Rowton's studies on Near Eastern nomadism, of which perhaps the most important is Rowton 1974. Salzman is mentioned only in connection with his introduction to the volume he edited (Salzman 1980). Otherwise, Dever's only other anthropological source is Lancaster 1981 (1997). Although it is a good selection, it is still "arm-chair" anthropology, as the relevant chapter in Lemche 1985, 84–163. On Rowton, cf. Lemche 1985, 152–63.

situated not in a historical period where it was supposed to have existed, but in the cultural memory of certain circles which is not so easy to place in history.[17] The moment the idea of "Israel" is removed from history, we can no longer say with certainty that this idea originated in one period and not in another. There need not be any historical reality behind the notion of the twelve Israelite tribes. It can originate during the exile, in the Persian Period or in the Hellenistic Period as well, or it can be older. Its origin cannot be decided except in cases where the narratives about the twelve tribes of Israel can be dated. Maybe this is why Finkelstein is even now flirting with Hellenism in his recent collection of articles about Ezra and Nehemiah (Finkelstein 2018).[18]

Let the War Begin!

Minimalism[19]

Turning to the maximalist–minimalist controversy, we may ask: Who are these terrible minimalists? A generation ago the maximalists were the members of Albright's school, while the minimalists were represented by Albrecht Alt and Martin Noth (cf. Dever 1977, 77). Today the players in both roles have changed but the terminology is left unchanged. As an introduction to the discussion and at the same time as an indication of the climate of the ongoing debate, we will let two of the most vociferous critics of minimalism answer the question: Who are these minimalists who have created so much trouble for normal Bible readers really? Here follow two answers to the question, the first from Gary Rendsburg, the second from William G. Dever.[20]

---

[17] On the relationship between memory and history, see my forthcoming *Cultural Memory is not a Paper Tiger* which is based on the idea that cultural memory is not history – indeed memory never is – but represents what a literary elite believes is worth telling the ordinary people. It is a cultural *and* political weapon of mass instruction (see also Cubitt 2007). Cultural memory is often confused with *collective memory* which could be said to be the outcome of this mass instruction, i.e., the memory preserved among ordinary people.
[18] In practice it is also what Kratz proposes as the time when the idea of "biblical Israel" found a lasting expression, cf. Kratz 2015.
[19] I have written several contributions to the debate about minimalism as seen in the light of maximalism. I will in this place only refer to Lemche 2000, and to the condensed version in Lemche 2003a.
[20] Dever will play a main role in what follows, for the simple reason that he has written more about the subject than any other from his side. Several of his compatriots like Ronald Hendel or Richard Elliott Friedman will not be mentioned or only mentioned *en passant*.

Gary Rendsburg's answer to this question:

How could we possibly have come to this present state in the field of biblical studies? And who are these people, these minimalists? As I stated earlier, the pendulum of intellectual ideologies is constantly shifting, and the last thirty years have seen the decline of positive historicism and the rise of relativism and skepticism. In my estimation, what began as a healthy and constructive enterprise, questioning the teachings of our teachers, exploring new methods, and in many cases demanding more explicit evidence before jumping to conclusions, soon devolved into an unhealthy and deconstructive project, resulting in a classic case of throwing out the baby with the bath water. It is now clear that Albright overstated the case, but just because his vision of the conquest no longer holds that water, we need not discard the Israelite baby therewith. There clearly was an entity called Israel in the Early Iron Age, and there still is plenty of evidence to support that claim. To answer my second question, who are these people, these revisionists, these nihilists? What drives them? To give you the names of the four best known among them, they are Thomas Thompson, Philip Davies, Niels Lemche, and Keith Whitelam. Some of them are driven, as I indicated above, by Marxism and leftist politics. Some of them are former evangelical Christians who now see the evils of their former ways. Some of them are counterculture people, left over from the 60s and 70s, whose personality includes the questioning of authority in all aspects of their lives. But the two most important elements in the profile of these scholars are the following. First, almost without exception, these individuals have no expertise in the larger world of ancient Near Eastern studies. The luminaries whom I mentioned at the outset all had masterful control over a wide variety of languages and literatures, or they were the leading field archaeologists of their day. They made major contributions in the fields of Ugaritic studies, Assyriology, Egyptology, pottery analysis, stratigraphy, and so on. That is to say, their firsthand experience working with "real life" texts and "real life" material culture from the ancient world allowed these scholars to develop a true sense of how biblical texts were cut from the same cloth as ancient Near Eastern

---

In defense of this decision to mainly ignore them it has to be said that they have hardly contributed anything to the discussion which cannot be found in Dever's production apart from, maybe, the linguistic discussion (Hendel) and to some degree textual studies (Friedman).

texts. True, this group later would come under attack by what their detractors would term "parallelomania," and true some of these great scholars often went too far in making connections between the Bible and the ancient world. But at the same time, their extensive and direct familiarity with the history, religion, literature, and scribal traditions of the ancient Near East in general allowed them to see, correctly in my view, that the inner workings of the Bible correlate perfectly into this picture. By contrast, as my colleague Anson Rainey of Tel Aviv University has noted, Thompson, Davies, Lemche, and Whitelam have never excavated an Israelite or any other archaeological site and they have no experience in dealing with an archive of ancient Near Eastern texts such as those of Ebla, Mari, Nuzi, Amarna, Ugarit, and so on. In short, the academy has created an intellectual environment which permits the untrained to operate on an equal par with the trained.

Second, as you may have gathered, almost without exception, the scholars of this group are not Jewish. (Note that I do not call them Christians either, for most of them, I believe, would not classify themselves as such. Rather, they are part of the general secular world.) Now, at first glance, one might think that one's religious or ideological identification would have no effect on one's scholarship, and I too once naively thought this to be true. Frankly, I feel a bit of discomfort even mentioning the religious affiliations of individual scholars. For one would have hoped that such issues no longer mattered. But with the current group of revisionists, as I intimated earlier, ideology, not objective scholarship, governs. If it is not actual Marxism, it is leftist politics in general. If it is not revolution against the sins of one's youth, the sin being once having identified as an evangelical Christian, then the issue is anti-authority culture in general. Furthermore, and I do not hesitate to use the terms, these scholars are driven by anti-Zionism approaching anti-Semitism. By denuding Israel of any ethnic identity, and by denying the existence of Israel in the land at an early time, and by reading the Bible as a Zionist plot by 6th century Jews in Babylonia, the picture is very clear. Ironically, the world has shown signs of progressing away from the anti-Zionism ideology that dominated U.N. politics in the 1970s, but these scholars are stuck in that several-decades-old mud.[21]

---

[21] This quotation could for many years be found on this internet address: http://www.arts.mcgill.ca/programs/jewish/30yrs/rendsburg/index.html. It is now available here – in the context of a extensive lecture by Rendsburg: https://ldsfocuschrist2.wordpress.com/2007/04/04/current-state-of-biblical-studies-gary-rendsburg/ (accessed 26 April, 2021).

William G. Dever's reaction to the question of the identity of the minimalists – or, as he perhaps prefers to call them, the revisionists[22]:
They are:

- Philologians – with no pertinent texts
- Historians – with no history
- Theologians – with no empathy with religion
- Ethnographers – with no recognizable "ethnic groups", no training and no field experience
- Anthropologists – with no theory of culture and cultural change
- Literary critics – with little coherent concept of literary production
- Archaeologists – with no independent knowledge or appreciation of material culture remains (Dever 2001, 40).

I will return to these indictments, as William G. Dever calls the defamation of the minimalists and their so-called scholarship.

A note on revisionism

Wikipedia has an interesting listing of various forms of "revisionism" (https://en.wikipedia.org/wiki/Revisionism). It includes:

- *Historical revisionism*, the critical re-examination of presumed historical facts and existing historiography
- The "revisionists" school of thought in *Soviet and Communist studies*, as opposed to the Cold War "traditionalists" school
- *Historical negationism*, concerted denial of claims accepted by mainstream historians, may purport to be historical revisionism but its methodologies have no basis in historiography/profession of history
- *Revisionist School of Islamic Studies*, which questions whether the traditional accounts about Islam's early times are reliable historical sources

---

[22] "Revisionist" seems to be a favoured expression of scholars having different opinions from members of the Albright family (on this concept, cf. below). Thus John Van Seters in his memoirs refers to this label being placed on him and some of his colleagues, who are not members of Albright's family, cf. Van Seters 2018. It is interesting that this term began to appear around the same time as it became usual among new-Zionist historians to call their opponents who are critical of traditional Zionist claims "revisionists". Probably not a coincidence. See more on this development within Israeli historiography in Pappe 2014, 280–81.

- *Revisionism (Ireland)*, an issue in Irish historiography
- *Revisionism (Spain)*, a derogatory term used in Spanish historiographic debate
- *Revisionist Zionism*, a nationalist faction within the Zionist movement
- *Marxist revisionism*, a pejorative term used by some Marxists to describe ideas based on a revision of fundamental Marxist premises
- *Fictional revisionism*, the retelling of a story with substantial alterations in character or environment, to "revise" the view shown in the original work.

So it is a free-for-all to decide what Dever, following the traditional language of the Albright family, means by using the expression "revisionist". Maybe he is just trying to find another word than minimalist, reserving "minimalist" for the apostates from the Albright School who have by now joined the Alt-Noth line concerning ancient Israelite history, the former "minimalists". We may, however, add three more definitions:

- Territorial revisionism, a euphemism for revanchism or irredentism
- Revisionism Theory, another word for Reformism
- The reevaluation of one's experiences with a hindsight bias.

Another definition, again from Wikipedia (https://en.wikipedia.org/wiki/Historical_revisionism):

> In historiography, the term identifies the re-interpretation of an historical account. It usually involves challenging the orthodox (established, accepted or traditional) views held by professional scholars about an historical event or time-span or phenomenon, introducing contrary evidence, or reinterpreting the motivations and decisions of the people involved. The revision of the historical record can reflect new discoveries of fact, evidence, and interpretation, which then results in revised history. In dramatic cases, revisionism involves a reversal of older moral judgments.

However, in the way it is used in combination with minimalism it has more to do with "historical negationism" which can be described in this way:

> In attempting to revise the past, illegitimate historical revisionism may use techniques inadmissible in proper historical discourse, such as presenting known forged documents as genuine, inventing ingenious but

implausible reasons for distrusting genuine documents, attributing conclusions to books and sources that report the opposite, manipulating statistical series to support the given point of view, and deliberately mistranslating texts.

(https://en.wikipedia.org/wiki/Historical_negationism).

In its most perverse form it can be found as the background of "Holocaust denial".

Taking into account the many facets of the concept of "revisionism", there seems to be a lot of reasons for Dever to choose this concept to describe the essence of biblical minimalism.

In 1996, during the excavations at Tel Yizreel in Galilee, I was invited to give a lecture about recent developments in biblical studies to the members of the kibbutz which housed the expedition. The kibbutz was reckoned a liberal and secular one. I presented the early story of ancient Israel in all its minimalistic glory. The audience was unaffected. Abraham had to go and so also Moses and they didn't care. But when I took away the David of the Bible, the kibbutzniks were seemingly disturbed. To non-religious Jews like the kibbutzniks the myths of Israel's origins did not represent historical truth. It was to them not an essential problem. However, when David became the subject it was different. The Biblical David is very much the eponymous hero of the secular society of modern Israel.[23]

The historicity of the biblical image of David has a meaning far beyond its place within the books of Samuel and Kings. Thus he is a major figure of the religious tradition in all three Abrahamic (Ibrahimic) religions. As a colleague once warned me: Don't think you will be popular among Muslims for removing David from history! In Islam David – or Dawud – is a major figure in the Quran, carrying the titles of both prophet (*nabī*) and messenger (*rasūl*). Moreover he is also God's deputy (*khalīfa*); in sum indispensable for Islamic ideas about the fate of the world. In Christianity he is placed at the head in the genealogy of Jesus' forefathers in Matthew 1, and a whole

---

[23] This squares well with the observation that modern Zionism arose as an endeavour to combine traditional Orthodox Jewish doctrine with the position of Christian Zionism transformed into the new view on biblical history which developed first and foremost within Protestant biblical studies of the late 18th century. See on this Goldman 2009 and Sand 2009. It also explains the rejection of modern Zionism and its state of Israel among Orthodox Jews who migrated to Israel before the establishment of the state and for that reason had no part in the intellectual development in Europe of modern historical science. Reading Silberman 1982 makes this very clear in the reluctant if not hostile reaction to the beginning of archaeological explorations in Palestine in the last part of the 19th century.

Christian mythology grew up around King David and his relation to Bethlehem, forcing poor Mary and Joseph to travel all the way from Nazareth to Bethlehem in the middle of the winter in order that Jesus could be born there. In Judaism, David was allotted a no less important role as the Messiah who was expected to re-establish the lost greatness of Israel. In modern reformed Judaism this is perhaps not the most important concern; since antiquity the idea of re-establishing the kingdom of David has not been very successful. The catastrophes of the two Jewish rebellions against the Romans in 65–70 CE and 132–134 CE must have convinced the Rabbis that radical Messianism was perhaps not the way to go if Judaism was to have a future. Messianic literature, as part of the Jewish collection of holy books, was purged from their collections and the Book of Daniel was relegated from its position among the prophets and placed among the Writings.[24] However, with the establishment of the modern semi-secular state of Israel, David became the symbol of the state, and the image of his great kingdom or empire a model for that modern society. The claim of modern Israel to be the rightful heir to the land of Palestine rests, so-to-speak, on the reality of the ancient kingdom of David. Removing David from history would, in many people's eyes, be the same as denying the Jewish people of our own time the right to possess this strip of land. The link from this assumption to the claim that such a removal of David expresses anti-Semitism is close at hand, and has been used constantly against biblical scholars who have expressed serious doubts about the historicity of this ancient king and about his mighty kingdom.[25]

We have, therefore, seen biblical scholars claiming to be in the middle between two extreme fronts; on one side the minimalists and on the other the maximalists, looking for a place for themselves by arguing that although

---

[24] Several differences between the arrangements of the Septuagint and the Hebrew Bible may originate in the Rabbis settlement with Messianism. When we look among the paracanonical literature, the Old Testament Apocrypha and Pseudepigraphs, we find much literature relevant to this subject of the messiah who shall come and make Israel great again, but certainly also in the Septuagint, where Messianism and apocalyptic play a far greater role than allotted to the theme in the canonical Hebrew books. The place of Daniel among the *Ketuvim* instead of among the prophets – thus in the Septuaginta – is another sign of rabbinic censoring.

[25] E.g., Halpern 1999. Instructive of how this kind of defamation works: Thompson 2001 (https://bibleinterp.arizona.edu/articles/view-copenhagen-israel-and-history-palestine). Especially one quotation from Magen Broshi in *Jerusalem Post* from 24 December 1999 is surrealistic, however characteristic: "Is it possible he does not believe in anything? Apparently there is a certain book that he does take seriously. A mutual acquaintance told me that Thompson confided in him that he is a staunch believer in The Protocols of the Elders of Zion" (quote found in Thompson 2001, also quoted in Masalha 2007, 258).

the biblical notion of the great king of Jerusalem and his mighty empire has little basis in history, the figure of David is nonetheless historical, emulating the saying of the German scholar Bernd Jørg Diebner: "You cannot prove it – but it is a fact" (Diebner 1984b). David was probably not the great king respected among other Near Eastern potentates in his own time as described in the Old Testament; if he is a historical figure, he was probably no more than a renowned local ruler whose memory lived on in two manifestations: first, the patronage state of Jerusalem in the Iron Age was probably ruled by a "Davidic" dynasty, the *Bet David*, and second, the memory of this society created the myth of the great king of the past.[26] The only problem for this assertion is that we only have one source, the Old Testament itself. All other references, except perhaps for one, are dependent on the image of David created by biblical historiographers. Such extra-biblical references are not independent testimonies. The exception may be the fragment of an inscription found at Tel Dan in Upper Galilee in 1993 – an additional fragment was found in 1994 – mentioning a king (?) of *Bytdwd*, most likely the "house of David", the patronage name of Judea comparable to the patronage name of Israel found in an Assyrian inscription, the *Bīt Ḫumriya*, "the House of Omri", probably also the Omri mentioned in the Mesha inscription.[27] The inscription poses various problems about interpretation and authenticity which will be discussed in the following chapter. It might be taken as evidence – which it has certainly been – of the historicity of the figure of David, but it does not restore the position of David as the great ruler of an empire in the southwestern Levant in the 10th century BCE. At best it attests to the fact that the expression *Bytdwd* functioned as the eponymous name of a political unit, at a time being personified in the same way as the name of Rome was personified by the name of its founder, Romulus – according to Roman tradition in 753 BCE, or the Kingdom of Denmark, which is named after its apical hero King Dan (Denmark [in Danish *Danmark*] supposed to mean "Dan's field").[28]

---

[26] Scholars never get tired of writing about David. Among more recent contributions to the huge pile of books about this ancient figure, I may mention Halpern 2001, Finkelstein and Silberman 2006, Van Seters 2009, Blenkinsopp 2013, Pioske 2015, and also the very interesting and different perspective in Leonard-Fleckman 2016, a work which is applying in a very clear fashion the source-critical approach of Gustav Droysen, looking for *Überreste* in the legendary legends about David.

[27] On the discovery and early publication of the Tel Dan inscription, Biran and Naveh 1993 and 1995.

[28] Principal source Livy, *Ab Urbe Condita*, ch. 4–6, but plenty of other classical authors include references to him. The principal source to King Dan is Saxo Grammaticus, *Gestae Danorum*, end of twelfth century, although a couple of other Nordic texts from the Middle Age refer to him, the *Chronicon Lethrense* ('Lejrekrøniken'), also from the twelfth century

As mentioned earlier, the two competing sites of the modern debate about the historicity of the biblical imagining of Israel are named as, on one side, the "maximalists," and on the other, the "minimalists". These terms were not invented but represent a continuation of the former polarization between the school of Albright and his German adversaries, Albrecht Alt and Martin Noth. Thus they did not originate in connection with the well-published discussion of minimalism at the SBL National Meeting in New Orleans in 1996 published by the late Hershel Shanks in his *Biblical Archaeology Review* (Shanks 1997).[29] More likely the two terms reflect a much older distinction between critical scholars and evangelical fundamentalists, maybe even pre-dating the use of the term among Albright's followers. By accepting the label of maximalists, many members of the academy probably believe that they will be accepted by the evangelical maximalists – or true fundamentalists – as one of their own. When we analyze the reception, they were only partly successful. It is perhaps what lies behind the characterization of the debate between representatives from the minimalist and the maximalist camps in New Orleans in 1996, by Mark W. Chavalas and Edwin C. Hostetter: "Also the conversation ... where N. P. Lemche, T. L. Thompson, W. Dever, and P. Kyle McCarter Jr. expound their minimalistic views".[30] In the light of a truly maximum conservative reader there was no difference between those scholars, who saw themselves as maximalists although at the same time critical scholars, and the scholars which they dubbed minimalists. To the conservative evangelicals both parties were simply minimalists because neither party would accept an uncritical reading of biblical historiography. In the opinion of both Dever and Thompson, no sun stood still in the Valley of Ayalon! It also shows us that the self-acclaimed maximalists do not stand in opposition to the minimalists alone. As a matter of fact, they have occupied the middle position between the true maximalists and the minimalists but their choice of the label "maximalists" may give a hint of their background.

---

and Snorri Sturluson's *Heimskringla* from the first part of the thirteenth century. As is to be expected the discussions about the historicity of these figures from the dark past are very similar to the one about the historicity of King Arthur, evidently testimonies to the almost total obsession with historicity in our own time, something which often prevents the interested laity from appreciating what is really handed down, important testimonies of the lively creativity of ancient authors and story tellers.

[29] It was not the editor of the *Biblical Archaeology Review* Hershel Shanks who invented these terms but he certainly gave them a new content. It has often been the tactic of shrewd journalists like Shanks to play off opposite positions using such catchwords. Perhaps he simply understood the importance of the issue to the lay reader, his principal readership.

[30] The quotation from Chavalas and Hostetter can be found in in Baker and Arnold 1999, 80n.

Terminology is a tricky thing. In the following the terms "fundamentalism" and "fundamentalist" will sometimes be used, in spite of the objections from the maximalist evangelicals who prefer the term "evangelical". However, "evangelical" is a misnomer for "conservative" because the conservative evangelicals in this way reserve the term for themselves, ignoring that at least the Lutheran denomination, without necessarily subscribing to fundamentalism, is "evangelical". A student of mine from the evangelical Lutheran School of Theology in Aarhus, Denmark[31] chose, in connection with a seminar on James Barr, Luther for his thesis, thinking that he was on secure evangelical ground. However, he came back two weeks later rather disturbed: "Luther is not a fundamentalist"! Probably nobody will call this writer a conservative because he is a member of the Evangelical-Lutheran Church of Denmark. Only a fraction – perhaps five percent – of its membership is "evangelical" in the sense that they are also fundamentalists. The choice of terminology used here is, however, forced upon us because a group of North American scholars who have placed themselves in the "middle" of scholarship have usurped the term "maximalists". I will use the term "maximalist evangelical" meaning the same as fundamentalist, about a person who believes in the inerrancy of the Bible without critical reservations.

And another note on terminology: The very words "maximalist" and "minimalist" are highly prejudicial. The maximum is normally considered a better option than the minimum. Somebody got the maximum out of his or her efforts; another person failed and only achieved a minimum of what was planned. This has little to do with biblical studies *per se* but is nevertheless believed to provide the maximalists with a kind of legitimacy which is not automatically allotted to the minimalists. As indicated above, "maximalists" is of course used as a way to bridge the difference between fundamentalists and semi-critical scholars left in the middle. It is a kind of false pretention of being something which the representatives of maximalism are certainly not: maximalist evangelicals. We will later see how the terminology squares with the content of maximalist attacks on minimalism.

Such differences became unclear probably first and foremost because of the objections raised by scholars like William G. Dever and Gary Rendsburg, who have simply borrowed the language which they use against their opponents from what James Barr always described as the mission-hall tract. At least William G. Dever has never tried to conceal his background in the mission house, his father being a preacher representing maximal conservatism

---

[31] In Danish "Menighedsfakultetet" situated in Aarhus very close to the state university of Aarhus with its school of religion and theology.

(most recently in Dever 2020). Barr had no problems diagnosing the origins of the language and tactics used, he himself coming from a similar background in a Presbyterian community in Scotland.[32] Also it is not difficult to point to the origins of the language used, which goes back to William Foxwell Albright, the renowned founder of the so-called "Baltimore school" which also produced Dever himself.[33] Like Dever, Albright was not a maximalist evangelical Christian *per se* but a scholar who had a background in such an evangelical milieu; born in Chile, where his father was a missionary. Below we will see that language is not the only thing Albright's "sons and grandsons" have inherited from their father.[34] The history, aim and strategies of the Albright School have been described by a number of authors including Burke O. Long, who offended the members of the school by analyzing Albright and his students from a postmodern angle (Long 1997), Thomas W. Davis (2004), and especially Brooke Sherrard who includes a harsh critique of the politics and discourse of the Albrighteans and who has a special paragraph on William G. Dever, exposing his interests in present day Zionism (Sherrard 2011, 181–7).

The similarity of language and of the form of argumentation shared by fundamentalists and maximalists as it is manifest in the contributions by Dever and Rendsburg and their colleagues has blurred the difference between these scholars and the maximalist evangelicals – we may ask: incidentally or intentionally? The Albright family's technique of exposing its adversaries has been almost identical to that of the true evangelicals or maximalists, which has resulted in problems separating them. It has been the politics of fundamentalists as well as maximalists to recruit the support of the general audience, which includes many professional teachers of the Old Testament from colleges and elsewhere, a factor not to be under-appreciated especially in a North American environment with its heavy political overtones. In

---

[32] Which is the spiritual background of Barr's settlement with fundamentalism: Barr 1977 and 1984.
[33] "Schools" in biblical scholarship: There have probably been too many "schools" in biblical scholarship, such as the "Uppsala School" starred by Ivan Engnell, "die göttinger Schule", initiated by Rudof Smend, the "Myth and Ritual School" which was mainly British, and now also the "Copenhagen School", perhaps a sign of how slavishly too many biblical scholars are following the "great" professors of their trade in a peculiar version of the patronage system. The Baltimore School was perhaps a little different because of its political undertones aiming to trash other directions within biblical studies and at the same time supporting the new state of modern Israel.
[34] It seems to be the accepted terminology within the "school" to speak of "sons", such as G. Ernest Wright and John Bright, maybe also Frank M. Cross and David N. Freedman, and "grandsons" like William G. Dever.

continental Europe it has hardly had any serious importance at all, but the European lack of understanding of the North American scene – theatre, if we use the normal American war terminology – had consequences, such as when James Barr, towards the end of his professional career, realized that although he had joined the chorus of critics of the minimalists, such maximalists as he supported, among them Iain Provan, were in fact fundamentalists. The language had obscured the difference, as had also the subjects – not least the endless talk about ideology and philosophy.[35]

Barr's writings about fundamentalism were indeed always merciless. It is not necessary to repeat his arguments in detail here. After all, his main work on the subject appeared more than forty years ago (Barr 1977). In this connection his chapter on conservative biblical scholarship is of interest not because of its details, which now belong to the past, but because of the general exposure of the "technique" of the conservative discourse, which basically always seems to recommend the most conservative solutions (Barr 1977, 130–59). He also repeatedly accused the conservative evangelicals of cheating, pretending to be critical which they are not. As he wrote back in 1977, he regrets the intrusion of conservative scholarship into the critical academic world, a tendency that has not stopped since then; rather it has grown considerably. In sum, by pretending to be critical, they hope to lure the novice in the field into their camp. Jens Bruun Kofoed's recent study on historical methodology is an important example of this trend, so much more inviting because of its carefully presented argument and its lack of desultory language about opponents (Kofoed 2005).[36]

Apart from the general accusation of the critical scholars of not respecting the Bible, i.e., for not taking it verbatim as the truth, the conservative evangelicals' preferred line of attack on critical scholarship circulates around subjects such as philosophy – called "prepositions" – especially evolutionary thinking and of course Hegelianism, named after the German philosopher

---

[35] James Barr (1924–2006) never did much within the field of biblical history, a subject which seemingly did not interest him very much. However, among his last publications we find *History and Ideology in the Old Testament. Biblical Studies at the End of a Millennium* (Barr 2000), which was planned to be a settlement with recent trends in biblical studies, especially postmodernism as he saw it represented by the Scottish scholar Robert P. Carroll. The book failed to make much impression, mostly because its target, Carroll, happened to die just a couple of weeks before its publication much to the regret of James Barr. Barr, however, quotes critics of the minimalist position – especially Iain Provan – with a good deal of approval, but at the end he had sniffed out the background of the criticism: fundamentalism. More on this in Lemche 2000. As far as Iain Provan is concerned I basically refer to his critique of Philip R. Davies and Thomas L. Thompson in Provan 1995 and 2002.

[36] For an answer and discussion cf. Lemche 2011a, and the answer by Kofoed 2011.

Georg Wilhelm Friedrich Hegel (1770–1831), which is for the fundamentalist just a bad word as Barr puts it (Barr 1977, 148).[37] The scholars of the nineteenth century who became the masterminds behind the development of critical scholarship, especially Wilhelm Martin Leberecht de Wette,[38] Abraham Kuenen,[39] and Julius Wellhausen have been rejected as being uncritical disciples of Hegel, which at least when it comes to Wellhausen was never the case (cf. below). It was also hardly the case of de Wette who was in direct personal opposition to Hegel at the university of Berlin. The conservative critics claim that these scholars, who were the fathers of the critical study of Israel's history and of the historical–critical source criticism of biblical books had no idea of the world outside the Old Testament, or so it is argued, and therefore they created a monster moving around in the void: historical–critical scholarship.[40]

Two details are glossed over. While it is correct that historical–critical methodology found its form in the context of the German universities of the nineteenth century, it was not all-dominating. It continuously had to fight for its existence. If we turn to de Wette at the beginning of the nineteenth century, he was forced out of his position at the University of Berlin after his ill-advised letter of consolation to the mother of Karl Ludwig Sand, who was executed after having murdered the poet August Friedrich Ferdinand von Kotzebue. A few years after his dismissal de Wette was substituted by Ernst Wilhelm Hengstenberg, by today's standards a one hundred percent fundamentalist. For his part Wellhausen studied under a conservative although well-known and respected teacher, Georg Heinrich August Ewald.[41]

---

[37] In my previous discussion of this habit, I add that to the conservative evangelicals philosophy is another "bad" word, and even "Wellhausen" is a bad word (Lemche 2005).

[38] De Wette (1780–1849). His perhaps best-known work is Beiträge zur Einleitung in das Alte Testament (de Wette 1806–1807). On de Wette, see Smend 1989, 38–52.

[39] 1828–1891. Kuenen is part of the triumvirate of Karl Heinrich Graf (1815–1869), Abraham Kuenen (1828–1891), and Julius Wellhausen (1844–1918), who are normally considered the fathers of higher criticism.

[40] Obviously, those who maintain such a position against historical–critical scholarship have little idea of what was going on in the world of German universities at the beginning of the nineteenth century. It was the result of studies by a series of German historian like Leopold von Ranke and Gustav Droysen, but the first fruit was the history of ancient Rome by Barthold Georg Niebuhr (1776–1831), the son of the Explorer Carsten Niebuhr, who in 1811 and 1812 published his *Römische Geschichte* (Niebuhr 1811–1812). Accessible electronically: http://www.deutschestextarchiv.de/book/show/niebuhr_roemische01_1811 and http://www.deutschestextarchiv.de/book/show/niebuhr_roemische02_1812.

[41] Georg Heinrich August Ewald (1803–1875), the epitome of a German scholar at his best always engaged in the affairs of his country and sometimes suffered because of his activities. Thus he was a member of the "Göttinger Sieben", a group of seven professors

Wellhausen, who will always be at the centre of conservative criticism, was well-versed in aspects of the world outside of the Old Testament. He began his academic career as professor of the Old Testament in Greifswald, but left and later became professor of Semitic philology in successively Halle, Marburg and Göttingen. He published a whole series of important studies about pre-Islamic Arab culture and early Islam.[42] His "window to the ancient world" was definitely open, although it was not primarily Babylon or Egypt which were at the centre of his interest. The assertion that he was dependent on Hegel has been studied and rejected by Rudolf Smend, and by Lothar Perlitt.[43] As far as the assertion that Wellhausen did not show interest in the Ancient Near East, we probably have to remind our conservative readers that the first place where a decipherment of Cuneiform was announced was at his *alma mater*, the University in Göttingen, where Georg Friedrich Grotefend, in 1837, presented his work on the cuneiform writing: *Erste Nachricht von seiner Entzifferung der Keilschrift* (Grotefend 1972 [1802]).[44] The historical–critical school of Old Testament studies did not originate within a vacuum with no space or no window open to oriental studies. It was, as a matter of fact, the opposite situation when German universities of the nineteenth and early twentieth centuries became some of the most important centres of Near Eastern studies in the world. It is for a reason that the very trend of Panbabylonism, stressing Mesopotamian influence on the literature of the Old Testament, originated in Germany where it was represented by a series of brilliant German scholars: Hugo Winckler, Fritz Hommel, Eduard Stucken, Alfred Jeremias, Friedrich Delitzsch, Peter Jensen, and Carl Bezold. The conservative accusation against the early critical scholars that they lived in a closed ivory tower without any interest in the outside *ancient* world is simply untrue but typical of the mission-house tract going after the man and ignoring the issue under discussion. In the language of today we should call

---

from Gottingen – including also the Grimm brothers who were in opposition to the King of Saxony and sacked for that reason. Later he was member of the German parliament from 1869, and a vehement opponent of the Prussian military politics. Towards the end of his life he was sentenced to prison for three weeks for opposing the Prussian chancellor Otto von Bismarck.

[42] Perhaps the best known: Wellhausen 1887 and 1902.

[43] Cf. Smend 1989, 99–113, and especially on Wellhausen and Hegel: Perlitt 1965. It was far from Hegel who inspired Wellhausen; on the contrary, the lines to Johann Gottfried Herder (1744–1803) are much stronger.

[44] Other works of Grotefend relative to his studying of cuneiform includes *Neue Beiträge zur Erläuterung der persepolitanischen Keilschrift nebst einem Anhange über die Vollkommenheit der ersten Art derselben bei der ersten Secularfeier der Georgia Augusta in Göttingen Hannover* (Hannover: Im Verlage der Hahn'schen Hofbuchhandlung, 1837).

it "fake news".⁴⁵ We will return to this below as it has been one of the main objections of the conservatives that the minimalists are also hiding behind a closed window to the world.

Finally, to illustrate the never-ending fight between conservatism and critical scholarship, Wellhausen's heirs did not follow him to his logical conclusion. I have discussed this phenomenon in a couple of articles from the late 1980s in which I show that his successors simply "tamed" him and – although they never admitted it – published much more conservative versions of Wellhausen's theories (cf. Lemche 1987 and 1988). And of course Wellhausen was not the only scholar in his time to experience such defamations. A well-known example from the history of British critical biblical scholarship is the fate of W. Robertson Smith, who among other things, translated Wellhausen's *Prolegomena* into English.⁴⁶ From my own country the case of Frants Buhl (1850–1932) belongs in the same category. He never became professor of the Old Testament in Copenhagen but had to go into exile at Leipzig. When he returned to Copenhagen, it was as professor of Semitic Philology.⁴⁷

It is absolutely true that today's conservative evangelical scholars are trying to break out of the scholarly isolation and into the world of critical scholarship. Barr's diagnosis was correct and the tendency has only become even stronger since he wrote his works on fundamentalism. Here we are not talking about the old warhorses in the guild like Kenneth A. Kitchen, who simply denounces all things critical when it comes to the Bible, but not when it has to do with his own principal field, Egyptology.⁴⁸ We are first and foremost

---

⁴⁵ On the debate following Panbabylonism cf. Larsen 1995.

⁴⁶ Wellhausen 1886, first published as Geschichte Israels, I, 1878, ET: Wellhausen 1883, with a preface by W. Robertson Smith.

⁴⁷ In spite of his extensive authorship on biblical literature including major commentaries on Isaiah and Psalms, Buhl is best known from his penultimate edition of Gesenius' Hebrew dictionary: *Wilhelm Gesenius' Hebräisches und Aramäisches Handwörterbuch über das Alte Testament* (1915), the principal help in the study of the Hebrew Old Testament for generations of European theological students. Buhl's best known student was Johannes Pedersen (1883–1977), the author of *Israel, Its Life and Culture*, I–II (Pedersen 1926–1947). Pedersen's best know student was Eduard Nielsen (1923–2017), who was my teacher.

⁴⁸ Cf. Kitchen 1966, a work which Barr described in this way: "... there is perhaps not a single book among the conservative evangelical works read in the research for this study that so fully breathes the spirit of total fundamentalism as does Kitchen's work" (Barr 1977, 131). This attitude has not changed over the years. If anything, Kitchen's hatred of critical biblical scholarship only grew worse as time went by, something which is evident if we include Kitchen 2003. Kitchen's best known "contribution" to scholarship is undoubtedly his maxim that "absence of evidence is not evidence of absence", which is simply logical nonsense, because it is exactly what it is: absence of evidence is evidence

focusing on contributions by a group of scholars who all seem to have some kind of relations to the conservative evangelical institution Regent College in Vancouver, V. Philip Long, Iain Provan, and Tremper Longman III,[49] and the reason is that their polemics against minimalism (and biblical studies in general) may present the background for the attacks on minimalism that make them more understandable, both as far as it concerns content and form.

But let us return to the accusation against the minimalists. In Gary Rendburg's characterization of the minimalists they are, apart from being revisionist:

1 Nihilists.
2 They are driven by Marxism and leftist politics.
3 They are apostates from Christianity.
4 They are residue from the 1960s and 1970s questioning authority in every aspect of their lives.
5 They have no expertise in the larger world of ancient Near Eastern studies.
6 They have no experience in dealing with an archive of ancient Near Eastern texts such as those of Ebla, Mari, Nuzi, Amarna, and Ugarit.
7 They never excavated an Israelite or any other archaeological site.

"Nihilism" opens this series of allegations. It is a freighted and favoured expression of contempt used by Albright and his students, going back to the middle of the last century when Albright used "nihilist" to defame a scholar of the status of Martin Noth,[50] much to Noth's chagrin. For some reason it does not seem that Albright dared to bring this expression into circulation in his relations to Noth's teacher, Albrecht Alt, perhaps because he had received Alt's study "The God of the Fathers" very positively.[51] Albright and his students' approach to archaeology was that it should be used to verify biblical claims. Because of his denial of the historicity of Israel's early history

---

of absence (until evidence is eventually found). On this "phenomena", cf. Whitelam 2012: Bileam's ass can speak. This is exceptional: Is it the only ass that could speak? Absence of evidence is not evidence of absence: There must be other asses that can speak; we just haven't found them yet.

[49] V. Philip Long was professor at Regent College from 2000 to 2019. Iain Provan has been professor in the same place since 1997, and Tremper Longman III has acted as a guest lecturer there.

[50] On Albright, Nihilism, and Noth, cf. below. Dever invented the expression "new nihilists", or so he says, cf. Dever 2001, 23 n1 referring to Dever 1995, 81–80.

[51] Alt 1929; ET: Alt 1989b. Cf. on Albright's changing attitudes to Alt, Long 1997, 53–5.

and especially the historicity of the patriarchs, Noth was considered a nihilist. Noth considered part of the traditions about early Israel to have its home within the context of the amphictyony in the Period of the Judges. Therefore, these traditions from Israel's past had a rather doubtful historical content.[52] It is normally glossed over that Noth's view of the historicity of the patriarchs has been almost totally adopted by later generations of Albrighteans, including perhaps most expressively, by William G. Dever.

Then we have the accusation of the minimalists being driven by Marxism and leftist politics, which is an accusation without any documentation – and besides, why is this important? In the scholarly world it is about scholarly excellence and not about some McCarthy-like show-down with Marxism. Rendsburg's remark on this is totally improper. Moreover, is it true? It is difficult to trace the inner world of those normally associated with minimalism – one prominent figure, Philip R. Davies, is no more among us and I have no idea about Philip Davies' political standing, although it was certainly not to the right – but as far as I remember, I myself never voted for any party to the left of the centrist social democrats, in Scandinavian countries normally the ruling party. But to some North Americans this probably counts as Marxism. The only scholar with an expressed Marxist tendency is probably Norman K. Gottwald, who has never been afraid of acknowledging his link to Marxist philosophy – which is something different from but certainly related to political Marxism – but Gottwald is certainly not a minimalist. The reason for the accusation that the minimalists are Marxist left-wing outsiders should probably be understood in the light of the polarization of present day North American society; it has very little to do with the European academic scene, and it ought to have nothing to do with the North American academic scene either.

As if this is not enough, the minimalists are also called apostates (though this expression is not used), i.e., former Christians who have now ended up in post-religious secular circles. The reasons for this accusation must be sought in the very different milieus of Rendsburg and his minimalist opponents. The British members of the inner-circle of minimalists, Philip R. Davies and Keith W. Whitelam, both taught at biblical departments, Davies in Sheffield and Whitelam first at Stirling University in Scotland, and later in Sheffield. Thomas Thompson and this writer taught for most of their academic careers at the Faculty of Theology at the University of Copenhagen, one a catholic, the second a protestant. Basically, the Copenhagen faculty is Lutheran in theological orientation and the majority of its students end up as ministers

---

[52] Cf. Noth 1950, 105–30: "Die Traditionen des sakralen Zwölfstämmebundes".

of the Danish Lutheran-Evangelical Church, but today the department includes other studies, such as Africa and Islam. The only required standard is academic excellence. There are no demands as far as the professors' personal religious observations are concerned. I doubt that many North American theological establishments display such a degree of theological openness.

But what then about the characterization of the minimalists as residue from the 1960s and 1970s? Persons who have rejected any form of authority in their life? Again, I doubt that this characterization is valid for the two British members of the minimalist group, but when it comes to the two Copenhageners it is definitely false. It is probably correct when Thomas Thompson says that a member of his Irish family was hanged by the British more than a hundred and fifty years ago; not an uncommon fate for many Irishmen at that time, but Thompson has, for the last twenty five years, lived in an exclusive quarter outside of Copenhagen under the strict command of his wife, Ingrid Hjelm, herself a principal scholar in Samari(t)an studies, who would never allow such excesses, whereas this writer may also admit that although he was definitely studying in Copenhagen in 1968 (chairing the theological students council in that fateful year), his career does not point to a leftist orientation. Besides his career as an academic teacher, he also had an active military career for more than thirty years; most of the time in the Danish Home Guard, ending his active service as a captain at a military district and chairing the national council of this organization. Today he is a leading freemason (Knight and Commander ranking with the North American 32nd or 33rd degree) in the official order of Denmark which is part of the "Swedish Rite", i.e. Christian oriented freemasonry. It is, however, correct that the students' revolt in 1968 included the demand that traditional ideas and sentiments must be able to defend themselves. Without doubt the most important contribution. Nothing should survive only because of "old age". There was, for these reasons, an openness to all sorts of new ideas and proposals, but the demand was still that such ideas and positions should be able "to speak for themselves"; that is, prove their value in an open debate. It is probably correct to say that this attitude to the environment is still the prevailing one. It is part of an ever changing European intellectual milieu, and I gladly confess that I belong to this European tradition of openness to new impulses, which has so far prevented Europe from ending up as a parody of its own former intellectual greatness.

But after these confessions it is nice to return to something concrete: Our supposed lack of experience in the greater Oriental world, and lack of experience working with archives. But is the accusation true? Again I have very little idea of the status of our two British minimalists, but the backbone of Thomas Thompson's study of the Patriarchs was oriental studies rather than the biblical texts.⁵³ It was especially the information from the Nuzi archives which directed him to his conclusions about Albright's desperate moving-around of the Patriarchs in order to fit them into an ancient Near Eastern context, no matter which (Thompson 1974, 294–7). When it comes to me, my prize thesis from 1968 was titled *Forudsætningerne for Davids imperium inden for og uden for Israel* (the Preconditions for the Empire of David in and outside of Israel) (Lemche 1968). Most of it (more than three hundred pages) consisted of an analysis of Near Eastern sources including Egyptian and Akkadian ones, as well as documents from the Levant, all read in the original language. The first chapter was published as a book in Danish in 1972 and also included an analysis of the Greek material for the amphictyony, which was published separately in English in 1976.⁵⁴ Any person who goes through my bibliography⁵⁵ will recognize several titles dealing with Near Eastern matters, including the more recent book on the Canaanites, and my section about Syrian history in Jack M. Sasson's *Civilizations of the Ancient Near East* (Lemche 1991a and 1995a). As to my control of the relevant languages, my copy of Allan Gardiner's *Egyptian Grammar* has the accession date of May 1962, Greek and Latin I learned in the gymnasium – the classical line – including intensive courses that lasted for three years reading Greek from Homer to Plato and beyond. Hebrew followed during the first year at the university, which was again followed by courses in Ugaritic, Aramaic, Syriac, Arabic, and Akkadian, and studies of Sumerian and Hittite. I have sometimes boasted of knowing all Semitic languages except Ethiopian. I would love Gary Rendsburg and people in his line to present their familiarity with all of these languages. Many among them would probably break down as soon as we talk about German and French, not to mention Italian, Spanish, Russian – you name it.

And when it comes to the accusation that the minimalists do not know anything about archives, it is a clearly a defamatory statement. Philip Davies was one of the principal allies of Hershel Shanks, the editor of the *Biblical Archaeological Review*, in his fight for the liberation of the Dead Sea texts from the entanglements with the first commission for their publication.⁵⁶

---

⁵³ It is interesting to note the names mentioned in the Preface to Thompson 1974, including the Egyptologist Helmut Brunner and the Orientalist Wolfgang Röllig, both from the University of Tübingen, one of the leading German institutions for oriental studies. Thompson studied for many years in Tübingen under the aegis of Kurt Galling.
⁵⁴ Lemche 1972. The Greek section was published as Lemche 1976. Reprinted in Lemche 2013b, 61–8.
⁵⁵ Until 2005 available in my Festschrift: Müller and Thompson 2005, 421–39. The tally in my current bibliography is close to eight hundred.
⁵⁶ On this "battle" see Hershel Shanks 2010, but also Silberman 1994, esp. 213–45.

Thompson's reliance on the Nuzi archive has already been mentioned, and my interest in, not least, the Amarna Archive (where I have my own transcriptions of most of the texts) is obvious from what I have written through a long life in biblical *and* oriental studies. Anson Rainey accused me of mistranslating the Amarna Akkadian of an Amarna Letter (EA 151) and of basing my interpretation of Canaan in the Amarna Letters on this false translation of the letter. It was a mistake. He deliberately forgot to mention that my interpretation was supported by another letter from the same Syrian potentate with the same wording apart from the word "Canaan" (Rainey 1996, and the response by Lemche 1998a). I will invite Gary Rendsburg to present his credentials as master of ancient Near Eastern studies.

As to archaeology, I can only say that when Thompson accused Dever of removing stones at Gezer, an accusation which Dever understandably reacts very negatively to, it is based on an eyewitness report: Thompson was at the Gezer excavation when it happened.[57] My own experiences in the field are limited, although I participated in the excavations of Tel Yizreel in 1996. This does not mean that I have never been in an excavation before (or since). There are practically very few tells in Palestine I have not visited often in the company of excavators or other archaeologists at each site. Thus, I travelled around with my colleague John Strange for three weeks in the summer of 1975 together with my students. At the end of the day and after exhausting visits to countless excavations, a mumble began in the back of the bus: The next tell is the hotel! John Strange began digging with Yigael Yadin at Hazor back in the late 1950s, and was for several years digging with Kathleen Kenyon in Jerusalem from 1962–1967, somehow in between he also succeeded in digging together with Moshe and Trude Dothan in Ashdod, only to continue as part of the Umm Qes-Gadara excavations in Jordan in the 1970s, and ending as director of the Scandinavian excavations at Tall al-Fukhar in Northern Jordan from 1990 to 1993 and 2002 (Strange 2015). Finally, it must be added, in defence of the non-specialists, that it is the duty of the professional archaeologists to publish their excavations in such a form that others not so well-trained in field work can understand them and use them. Much too little has been published and even less in a satisfying form.

But all things taken together, when we speak about the minimalists we are supposed to meet such a degree of incompetence that it is absurd that the present permits the untrained to operate on an equal par with the trained

---

[57] Cf. Thompson 1996, 31n. Dever of course reacted very violent to this accusation of fiddling with evidence, Dever 2001, 10.

– at least according to Gary Rendsburg. I leave it to the readers to judge for themselves.

But this does not exhaust Rendsburg's denunciations of the minimalists. More items are added to the list.

They are

8 Not Jewish
9 Governed by ideology, not objective scholarship

And finally

10 Driven by anti-Zionism approaching anti-Semitism: Denuding Israel of any ethnic identity.

As to the first point, Rendsburg is absolutely right: It is undeniable that the best known minimalists are not Jews. This is hardly a crime, and it is difficult to understand the implications of this fact, except if Rendsburg would argue that it is impossible to write about the history of ancient Israel if you are not a Jew, something that would have consequences for innumerable scholars, from Heinrich Ewald to Axel Knauf, who have written such histories. Something has to follow, and it comes with the added accusation that the minimalists are not Zionists, which is also true, but does that automatically make them anti-Semites? As far as I know, Zionism is not Judaism, but a relatively modern *political* development within Judaism originating in Central Europe before the First World War. As I remember from my first stay in Jerusalem in 1974, there was an inscription painted on the wall in Mea Shearim, the Orthodox quarter: Judaism and Zionism are two very different things. Orthodox Judaism has never embraced Zionism. Therefore, if the minimalists are anti-Semites, the anti-Zionist inhabitants of Mea Shearim are probably also anti-Semites which tells us how ridiculous Rendsburg's accusation really is. The second part, that the minimalists are stripping Israel of any ethnic identity, is different in character, and very imprecise: What Israel and what ethnicity? Are we talking about modern Israel or ancient Israel?[58] The answers might not be the same in both cases. This has to do with a long and sometimes bitter debate between social anthropologists divided between so-called "primordialists"

---

[58] The reader just has to remember the already mentioned distinction made by Philip R. Davies (Davies 1992), between "historical Israel", the Israel of the Iron Age in Palestine, "Biblical Israel", which is the Israel found in biblical literature, and "ancient Israel", the Israel of modern scholars. Cf. above p. 6.

and "essentialists" about how to define ethnicity. I will return to it later; the assertion made by Rendsburg has to do with the understanding of ethnicity in his support base. It is definitely not up-to-date.

Then we have the assertion that the minimalists are driven by ideology; they are, as Dever calls them, "ideologues". It is an issue that is far more complicated than it appears in such a short indictment of the minimalists – but nevertheless it is very often repeated. But already at this point it has to be said that it is an assertion which, like a boomerang, strikes the face of the person who formulated the accusation. Ideology is such a slippery concept and carries in this context more than one meaning.

In combination with other series of indictments against the minimalists, William G. Dever often praises himself for having converted biblical archaeology into Syro-Palestinian archaeology, which is a preposterous title, as Dever has never dug in Syria proper (Dever 1985). Ironically it fits very well with the name given to the territory between the present Israeli-Syrian ceasefire line and the Egyptian border as *Syro-Palestine* presented by Herodotus.[59] This is, however, perhaps not what Dever intended by using the label "Syro-Palestinian archaeology".[60] Because of ideological (political) reasons he could not call it "Palestinian archaeology", something I guess the Palestinian authorities of today are grateful for, making it possible to describe the archaeology in the occupied territories as "Palestinian archaeology" such as the Italian-Palestinian excavations at Tell Sultan/Jericho,[61] and the Dutch-Palestinian establishment of an archaeological park at Tell Balata/Shechem.[62] The renaming of the discipline has to do with Dever's rejection of biblical archaeology

---

[59] Herodotus and Palestine: Cf. the discussion with evidence in Lemche 1997, 131–2.

[60] It is doubtful if Dever's renaming of biblical archaeology has really struck home. Popular introductions still use "biblical archaeology", probably because this label sells better. Cf. thus Cline 2009. To confuse matters Cline considers biblical archaeology as a "subset of the larger field of Syro-Palestinian archaeology" – hardly what Dever intends by changing the name of the subject (Cline 2009, 1). Cline's introduction displays several of the bad habits of the Albright family, including the concept of "nihilism" in his paragraph on minimalism (Cline 2009, 59–68). He, however, illustrates his standing in his "Further Readings" at the end of his introduction where he recommends studies on the Exodus (as a historical event) by James K. Hoffmeier, but also Kenneth Kitchen's 100% conservative-evangelical discussion (Kitchen 2003). A final note: Contrary to what Dever would have us believe, he did not invent the title "Syro-Palestinian Archaeology". Back in 1938, no less a figure than Albright used the term (Albright 1938).

[61] The Italian-Palestinian Jericho excavations took place between 1997 and 2017. The directors are Lorenzo Nigro of the University of Rome, and various Palestinian archaeologist, the best known Hamdan Taha. Preliminary publications: Nigro 2005, Nigro and Taha 2006; Nigro 2010.

[62] On this park cf. Taha and van der Kooij 2020, and Taha and van der Kooij 2014.

as a tool to confirm the historicity of events found in biblical texts, which the Albright school has been (in)famous for, and especially Dever's archaeological mentor George E. Wright.[63] As defined by Dever, Syro-Palestinian archaeology is seen as a non-religious exercise working with objective facts on the ground and useful for historical reconstructions (see Dever 1993). This is not surprising because Dever's career brings him much closer to Rendsburg's defamation of the minimalists than anything else – Dever admits to having left his evangelical roots by becoming a secularist and by leaving Christianity for Judaism.

Nevertheless, according to Dever the minimalists have no pertinent texts, no history, no religion/theology, no ethnic groups to work with, no theory of culture, no idea of literary production, and no idea of archaeology.

It's interesting to see how Dever got there. His monograph, *What Did the Biblical Writers Know and When Did They Know It?* (Dever 2001), may be considered one long diatribe against minimalism, and in language that would lead most "normal" scholars to throw it away in horror, as delicately expressed by a non-minimalist, Rainer Albertz: "Frankly speaking, I am somewhat startled by such personal and emotional polemic in our academic field: I have never encountered anything like this before or after".[64] This book represents Dever's principal settlement with the minimalists, and for that reason it is worth analyzing, if only in part. Albertz's reaction is understandable within a European academic context, but having followed North American political rhetoric not least in recent times may turn you deaf to such language. Dever's, and especially Gary Rendsburg's, diatribe against the minimalists is not a religious, nor a scholarly diatribe; it is a political defamation of their opponents of the sort too often found in non-academic circles in North American society; it should, for that reason, be banned from any learned context of scholars together, and the people who uttered it ostracized.[65]

---

[63] On Albright and archaeology cf. in general Davis 2004.

[64] Rainer Albertz 2018, followed by an answer by Dever (2018). To be honest, diatribes like the ones quoted here by Rendsburg and Dever would in normal academic environments have got the authors ostracized. This would probably have happened in any academic milieu outside of North America. If anything the survival of the authors within the North American academic environment testifies to this environment and has its foundation in a conservative evangelical milieu allowing for such mission hall tracts against the non-believers.

[65] Defamation: Wikipedia's definition: "is the oral or written communication of a false statement about another that unjustly harms their reputation and usually constitutes a *tort* or *crime*". But maybe slander is a better word, cf. this definition: "Defamation is an area of law that provides a civil remedy when someone's words end up causing harm to

Going after the minimalists, Dever's first target is postmodernism, accusing the minimalists of having a postmodern agenda. Dever doesn't like postmodernism or deconstructionism.[66] The agenda of postmodernism and deconstructionism is to destroy history, as he understands it. It is not that he is particularly well-informed about it but he simply does not like it because it is in competition with his own position, according to him a clearly positivistic one. He is also convinced that the minimalists are entangled in this postmodern fad, as he calls it, which has turned them into ideologues, working for a postmodern agenda. This means that the minimalists argue that since all biblical texts come from the Hellenistic period they are perforce "unhistorical" and cannot be used for reconstructing the history of biblical or ancient Israel.[67] They also argue that biblical texts should be liberated from historical consideration; biblical stories are mainly a witness about themselves. Postmodernism is accordingly an "anti historic" movement, claiming that histories of ancient Israel should be substituted with histories of Palestine.[68]

---

your reputation or your livelihood. Libel is a written or published defamatory statement, while slander is defamation that is spoken by the defendant". (https://www.google.com/search?sxsrf=ALeKk00wwgEXaMBqFGq3HMnovfMBog8E6g:1611825327734&q=libel+defamation&sa=X&ved=2ahUKEwj2sOWgpb7uAhX5isMKHSacCK0Q1QIoBnoECBkQBw&biw=1920&bih=970).

[66] Dever has evidently little idea what deconstructionism is all about, misreading deconstruction as destruction. I have only once in Dever's output (Dever 2017, 49) seen a reference to Jacques Derrida (1930–2004), the principal French philosopher connected to the idea of deconstruction. Derrida is easily available in English: Derrida 1978. The best rendering of "deconstructionism" I have seen is "analysis"; to deconstruct a text means to analyze it, but Dever has of course never analyzed a biblical text.

[67] This allegation must rely on Dever's own ideas about texts as historical sources. First the allegation is not correct: Not all minimalists opt for a Hellenistic date of biblical historiography. Philip R. Davies looked for a home for it in the Persian Period, John Van Seters – maybe not a minimalist strictly speaking, but at least in the eyes of Frank Cross and his students a "revisionist" (Van Seters 2018, *passim*) – even earlier in the Exilic Period. Second a late date does not exclude that a source includes historical information. It is well-known that the best version of the life of Alexander the Great is found in Arrian's *Anabasis*. Arrian lived from c. 86/89–c. 146/160 CE, i.e., about four hundred years after Alexander's own time. In this case Arrian mentions that he relies on much older sources, some of them going back to Alexander's own time, but we have only his word for it, although he is supported by other versions of the life of Alexander like Plutarch's (c. 46–c. 120 CE).

[68] It is, of course, an absurd argument. The shift might change from the history of ancient Israel to the history of ancient Palestine, but is this "anti history"? It is still history in a rather traditional sense, but it is most likely not possible to use the history of Palestine as a support to the modern Zionist claim to possess the land of Palestine. Dever's argument is fool-hearted and meaningless, but serves another aim: The accusation that minimalists are anti-Semites. On Dever's pro-Zionistic standing, cf. Sherrard 2011, 181–8.

Altogether these four points show that the minimalists are directed by "ideology, bias, and reams of discourse'" (Dever 2001, 28).

Dever's problem is his fundamental ignorance of what he is talking about. Principally, postmodernism does not imply the negation of everything historical. This is not the agenda of postmodern historians, but postmodernism represents a return to the human factor in perception, and thus places the human observer at the centre of interest. This has been one of the two classical positions in European philosophy since the days of Plato that perception is individual, illustrated by Plato's famous image of the people who, when confined in a cave, can only perceive the real world outside of the cave as shadows on its wall (Plato, *The State*, Book VII). The modern idea of perceiving the world is different and places the material world in front of the individual who understands it through the analysis of the phenomenon in question. These two directions going back to, respectively, Plato and Aristotle, have competed for more than two thousand years. Sometimes, as in medieval scholasticism, Aristotle has the upper hand, while at other times Plato dominates; not least in the form of Neo-Platonism as was the case in late Antiquity and again during the latter part of the Renaissance and the esoteric philosophy that was part of it (see Yates 2001 [1979]).

Plato lost to Kant and his followers in the course of the Enlightenment. Positivism became the gospel of philosophers and scientists beginning at the end of the eighteenth century. However, the pendulum turned again, and the idea of *homo mensura* came back, probably mostly because of doubts about the consequences of positivistic natural science which followed after the nuclear blasts over Hiroshima and Nagasaki in August, 1945. To the post-war generation, positivistic science was apparently not the gate to paradise which the preceding generations had imagined. It was rather a *mirage*, an ideal that blew up (not only metaphorically speaking).

Or did the pendulum really shift? When we think of philosophers like Søren Kierkegaard, Arthur Schopenhauer, and more, or of the breakthroughs in the nineteenth century in literature – not least authors like Dostoevsky, whose novels would have been unthinkable before the nineteenth century – and in psychology, it is perhaps this dualism – even interplay – in European thinking between the stringent observer and the theoretician that has made our culture so intensely diversified and rich. In this way postmodernism, understood as a reaction against a plain and simplistic interpretation, has always been with us. Every author, every artist, was a postmodernist, or they would have been forgotten. Shakespeare never tried to grasp the historical "truth" of anything but instead he presented his version of his "historical" sources, like Hollingshed's chronicle (which itself was definitely not a modern historical textbook). In the same way Raphael's painting *School of Athens*, in spite of portraying historical persons, has very little to do with historical reality , placing Leonardo da Vinci in the middle "playing" Plato while Michelangelo at his right is "playing" Aristotle. The quest for the "truth" in the objective sense is a modern Fata Morgana. This writer rather stands with Pilate: "What is truth?" (John 18: 38).

Dever's attack on postmodernism is so incredibly uninformed that it is hard to imagine that a well-educated person living at the beginning of the twenty-first century should have launched it. Dever is displaying such ignorance of the *history* of European thinking that there must be another reason for it. We will return to that below. But first it is necessary to divert some time to his dominant insistence that the minimalists are ideologues, i.e., driven by – in the eyes of a Biblicist – a negative and distorting ideology.

Ideology

Somehow it is gratuitous to use a word like ideology because nobody knows what it is and, at the same time, everybody knows what it is. Many years ago I participated in a seminar given by Mario Liverani at the Assyriological Institute of the University of Copenhagen. Liverani opened up by admitting that he had studied the concept of ideology for many years and he still had no clue as to what it is. Then three local students from anthropology and elsewhere told him what ideology really is, and it was easy to read Liverani's face: OK, if you say so … and let's get on with it. Ideology has so many facets that saying somebody is governed by ideology does not mean anything. The question must be what kind of ideology is governing, and how we should interpret the concept in connection with one particular person?

First of all, it is clear to everybody in the modern world that nobody escapes being influenced by ideology knowingly or unknowingly. There is no escape. It would be ridiculous to argue against this fact. Ideology in this case means a conglomerate of influences and influencers on a person who have been in contact with other persons, parents, family members, schoolteachers, friends, business partners, high school instructors, professors and the environment in general – you name them/it. But you cannot escape their influence. Even if you were Robinson Crusoe your thinking and acting would be dominated by the fact that you were alone on your island. Combining all these forms of experience means that you are creating a personal understanding of the world, i.e., a personal ideology, which will influence every choice you make in your lifetime. Moreover, such an ideology will never stop developing; it will continually change as new impulses are introduced. To say that somebody is governed by ideology in his or her handling of the Bible is correct, and at the same time nonsense. Everybody is, which makes the whole idea of ideologically driven biblical studies a moot question.

Dever therefore needs to be more specific. Which form of ideology is driving the minimalists? We have already seen the broadside which Gary Rendsburg directed against the minimalists, claiming that they are nihilists, i.e., against everything, leftist Marxists against Christianity, anti-Zionists against the modern state of Israel and in the end anti-Semites. Dever would probably agree with all of this, apart from the last point, at least in public. It can all be boiled down to the claim that the minimalists are anti-culture people, no more, no less than that. But because they are nihilists, and against every kind of authority they also want to destroy the Bible, meaning the historicity of the story of Israel found there, which is of course most relevant to people who almost exclusively sees the "truth" of the Bible as reflected in the history of ancient Israel: The Bible is true if what it relates really happened, and false if it did not. It is a most primitive theology, coming out of the "Biblical Theology movement" of Albright and Wright, where Dever also grew up as a student of Wright.[69]

Dever presents his definition of ideology in this way: "I use ideology here, however, in its proper and neutral meaning, since we all have 'ideologies', or a 'system of ideas', a way of thinking". And he adds: "It should be the content that determines whether a given ideology is good or bad" (Dever 2001, 28). It is difficult to disagree with him at this point. However, in addition he defines ideologues as "those who espouse a particular ideology, often uncritically, to the exclusion of others, and who then become obsessed by visionary ideas" (Dever 2001, 28). And as examples he refers to the usual suspects, Philip R. Davies, Thomas L. Thompson, Keith W. Whitelam, and Niels Peter Lemche, but also Israel Finkelstein (who may have occasionally flirted with minimalism, but who never accepted the title of minimalist).[70]

He summarizes his conclusions in this way:

1 The minimalist approach is hardly innovative, much less "revolutionary"; it is simply another of the fads that so often prevail in our

---

[69] Further on this in Lemche 2008, 351–64.
[70] Dever 2001, 28–44. Finkelstein would normally consider himself to be a centrist. The irony of this claim is that here he will also find his primary opponent from the Hebrew University Amihai Mazar who likewise considers himself to be a centrist – strange bedfellows! Cf. Amihai Mazar 2003, 85–98.

uncertain and cynical times – "New Age pap" that stems largely from a failure of intellectual and theological nerve.
2. It is arrogant and pretentious in its claim to "new knowledge" – not so much "post-Enlightenment" as *anti-Enlightenment*, anti-reason, anti-good sense, and ultimately anti-social despite its Utopian goals. As a supposedly intellectual movement, it is incestuous that it is breeding simple-mindedness.
3. It is ultimately frivolous, parroting slogans and exalting cleverness above sensibility (…). Its deliberately provocative style and other outrageous declarations amount to little more than "offing the establishment". It is so lacking in any attempt at serious engagement that it is tempting to dismiss all this as so much "postmodern piffle".
4. The revisionists' agenda masquerades as "progressive" scholarship. But it is really demagoguery.
5. The minimalist approach in practice does amount to nihilism; this is not name-calling, but simply recognizes that this school has no epistemological foundations, no rational justification for its assertions. … the fact is that nihilism is a "dead-end" … I will go so far as to say that "the revolt against reason", if carried out resolutely opens the way first to intellectual and social anarchy, then to Fascism. Fascist tendencies are already evident in some of the more extreme polemics of the revisionists, particularly in Thompson's diatribes

(Dever 2001, 265–6).

But, then, why does he spend three hundred pages writing about the seemingly worthless minimalists?

Reading this indictment against the minimalists we are reminded of Rendsburg's "critique", down to the last line. That Dever also dares to use libellous accusations of the minimalists as Fascists is extraordinary and really not a scholarly issue; in any other country than the United States of America it would have sent him to court many years ago.[71]

Now it is time to investigate the origins of the language and imagery of these attacks on minimalism. What is the reason, and what is the background? This goes far beyond normal scholarly exchanges, even when they

---

[71] In his time a well-known professor and specialist in Søren Kierkegaard studies at the University of Copenhagen, he never sent anything to be published in a polemical context before his lawyer had seen and approved his writing. In Europe Dever would have had to follow the same wise procedure.

are at their most heated. It is a language and a kind of wild accusation which is most remarkable and definitely says more about the sender than the recipients. Or to say it bluntly: Why do Dever and people on his side hate the minimalists so much? They must feel personally threatened; but why?

Ideology has been the backbone of criticism against the minimalists, as is evident from a famous – in its time – attack on minimalism by Iain W. Provan from 1995, and updated in 2000.[72] It was followed by James Barr, who devoted his last book to the subject of history and ideology (Barr 2000). My original reaction to Provan's first article followed in 2000 (Lemche 2000). It was, as a matter a fact, first of all a response to James Barr. The thrust of Provan's – and Barr's – criticism of the minimalists is that to them ideology came first, and their objective, the writing of the history of ancient Israel second, and neither Provan nor Barr had much faith in the kind of ideology guiding them, especially not the postmodern twist.[73] The postmodern approach to literature is so far removed from the production and reading of literature in ancient time that it represents a serious misrepresentation of the intentions of ancient authors, or so it is maintained. The observation has much which speaks in favour of it. Sometimes when reading a modern literary analysis of an ancient document it is hard to escape the feeling: Did this ancient author really know so much about literary theory? On the other hand, modern critical analysis, long before the arrival of postmodernism, has been able to dig out strategies used by such authors, including their intentionality.

An example: My study of David and his many girlfriends belongs here (Lemche 1978). The outcome of the analysis which dates back to a Danish original from 1974 was that the story of David as told in the books of Samuel was composed in defence of this monarch against accusations of being the murderer of Saul and his sons, and against accusations of having this special hobby of running after other men's wives. It was not necessary to use advanced and sophisticated postmodern technique – I had very little knowledge, if any, of postmodernism at the time of publication – it was enough simply to sort out what the problem was, thereby also laying bare the motives

---

[72] Provan 1995 followed by Provan 2002. This attack was countered in the same issue of the *Journal of Biblical Literature* by Philip R. Davies and Thomas L. Thompson, cf. Davies 1995, and Thompson 1995. Their defense was later on brushed aside by Dever, but also by James Barr, who sums up saying that Provan made the best out of the discussion (Barr 2000, 68-6), while at the same time admitting that Provan so-to-speak harmed his case in his second contribution, casting doubt on his real agenda, cf. also Barr 2000, 81-2.

[73] Barr's position is remarkable because it was his *The Semantics of Biblical Language* (Barr, 1961) which more than anything else opened up for future postmodern analyses of the Bible.

for writing the defence. In principle – we are talking about the early 1970s – I believed in the basic historicity of the narrative about David. Taken together, it was a traditional historical-critical investigation. The criticism of my approach did not come from historical-critical scholars, who generally received it well, but from literary students, especially David Gunn, who thought the analysis naïve and old-fashioned, not taking into account that we are here dealing with a narrative using a number of narrative elements belonging to this genre (Gunn 1978). In light of the development of studies into the period of King David, I would today without hesitation say that Gunn is right, and I will do it not because I have converted to postmodernism but because of developments within historical-critical research which make a postmodern approach to the story of King David highly relevant, since the historical-critical investigations have already shown that this story is literature, and not a historical source allowing for naïve positivistic conclusions relating to events in the tenth century BCE. The point seems immaterial but is really important in this connection.

Truly, Philip R. Davies especially supported a postmodern approach to biblical literature inclusive of the alterations to it caused by analyses of this kind. Whether the same can be said about the other minimalists is not so certain. On the other hand, when James Barr entered the discussion, it was not the members of the usual gang of four who were his primary targets; but the Irish biblical scholar Robert P. Carroll, who in several publications had advocated a postmodernist approach to the analysis of biblical texts, implying also the necessary historical revisions caused by such a different approach.[74] As already mentioned, Barr's principal opponent happened to die less than two weeks before the appearance of his study on history and ideology, making his whole project a bit redundant, something which caused him much regret: *De mortuis nihil sine bene*! However, when it comes to the other minimalists, the issue is not so clear. I am not sure that any of us began as postmodernists; or that we would have, at the beginning of our careers, qualified as such. This will be clearer after the following part of this study where the history of minimalism between 1960 and 1990 will be outlined. At this point I can simply refer to Philip Davies' early Dead Sea Scrolls studies and his dissertation on the Damascus text: Nothing postmodern here, just the classical study of an ancient document (Davies 1983). If we move on to Thomas

---

[74] Carroll 1997. It is said that at one meeting Carroll addressed Abraham Malamat with the question: "Does the word absurd occur in your vocabulary?". Oral tradition, but cf. Grabbe 2002, 174. Malamat was a pleasant but rather conservative Israeli biblical scholar. I had my own *Auseinandersetzung* (fall out) with Malamat (Lemche 1984a), which never prevented the two of us from having a very pleasant personal relationship.

Thompson, it is difficult to see much postmodernism in his famous study of the Patriarchal Narratives; it is absolutely "modern", as was to be expected (Thompson 1974). It was written in Tübingen under the supervision of Kurt Galling (1900–1987), a historical–critical German scholar of the old school who would have reacted strongly if he was accused of being a postmodernist but who also had extensive archaeological experience in Palestine between 1926 and 1938, having studied classical archaeology in Berlin in the years after the First World War, and was also the editor of a remarkable concise handbook of biblical antiquities (Galling 1937). No postmodern "piffle" here. Thompson's comprehensive dissertation takes the reader through the archives from Mari, Nuzi, Egypt, etc. It is as a matter of fact a classical overview of the Ancient Near East as the background of the Patriarchal Narratives. The only place where Thompson develops theological ideas is at the very end in a short paragraph bearing the title "Historical and Christian Faith" (Thompson 1974, 326–30). When it comes to Keith W. Whitelam it would be difficult to find postmodernist motives in his dissertation, published as *The Just King* (Whitelam 1979), and the same verdict applies to his well-known early work on *The Emergence of Early Israel* published together with Robert Coote (who is definitely not a postmodernist) (Coote and Whitelam 1987), a work not even Dever seems to have problems with. As indicated above, the present writer did not originate as a postmodern ideologue. There is very little which I published until the early 1990s which could be considered postmodern, if anything.[75] Even Dever accepts that in the form of his previously expressed interest in my dissertation, *Early Israel* (Lemche 1985), a work he ceased referring to as his ideas emulated mine, e.g., especially in Dever 2017.[76]

Provan's description of the minimalists as postmodernists is simply wrong and the result of his limited readings of the works of these scholars, including almost nothing before 1990. The evaluation of James Pasto that the minimalists are not postmodern but squarely belong within the brotherhood of traditional historical–critical scholars is most likely correct (Pasto 1998). It also squares well with observations in Barr's discussion of minimalism and ideology indicating perhaps a scholar like Dever is probably closer to a postmodern position in very much the same fashion as the conservative evangelical Iain Provan (Barr 2000, 71).

We may wonder at this excessive occupation with ideology in works by Dever and Provan, and it becomes even more marked in the historical

---

[75] As made clear by John Van Seters in his introduction to the collection of my articles: Lemche 2013b, 1–10.
[76] Cf. my reaction in Lemche 2020.

textbook published by Iain Provan, V. Philip Long, and Tremper Longman III, *A Biblical History of Israel* from 2003, where an extraordinarily comprehensive introduction is mostly devoted to the discussion of ideology (Provan, Long, and Longman III 2003, 3–35), and in the already mentioned, in many ways interesting, study by Jens Bruun Kofoed, *Text and History*, where ideology plays a decisive role in the discussion (Kofoed 2005). Intellectually they may all be considered conservative evangelicals; the three authors of the history book all having some kind of relationship to the conservative evangelical institution Regents College in Vancouver, Canada, and the last mentioned to The Free Lutheran School in Copenhagen.[77] At the beginning, Provan succeeded in placating Barr, who did not see through his exposé of ideology which he found quite convincing, but as the discussion in Barr's study goes on it becomes more and more clear that something is not as it seems and that Provan provides ample evidence of his real standpoint as a scholar, among maximalist evangelicals. A close reading of the arguments found in Provan's discussion of minimalism makes it obvious that the criticism of the minimalists for being ideologues includes all critical scholars since the introduction of higher criticism more than one hundred and fifty years ago – because they all, in his and his fellows' view, count as minimalists, i.e. ideologues directed by "bad" philosophy. In this way, the criticism in recent time from conservative evangelicals seemingly directed against the minimalists is simply the traditional one that has been targeting every critical scholar since Graff, Kuenen and Wellhausen.[78] When this is made clear it is also obvious that the word "ideology" in such a conservative evangelical context does not mean "ideology" but "philosophy". In this case it is also clear that we are here confronting the old assertion of the conservative evangelicals that higher criticism was, in its origin, driven by philosophy and especially the philosophy of Hegel, and as we remember from before Hegel and Hegelianism are, in the mouths of the conservative evangelicals, simply "bad words". This was also my conclusion when I wrote about this criticism twenty years ago (Lemche 2000). The conservative evangelicals were using the minimalists, i.e., the members of the Copenhagen School, as straw persons for a general attack on the "ideological",

---

[77] Iain Provan has been professor at Regents College since 1997, and V. Philip Long was professor at the same place between 2000 and 2019. Tremper Longman III is a regular guest lecturer at Genets College, although he was at Westmont Theological Seminary from 1998 to 2017. Jens Bruun Kofoed has since 2014 been professor at the Copenhagen Lutheran School of Theology.

[78] We are reminded of Chavalas and Hostetter 1999 who included a fairly traditional scholar like Kyle McCarter but also Dever among the minimalists (above n. 36).

in reality the philosophical backdrop of critical scholarship in general.[79] Our chief opponent – or at least he has always said so – Dever – was just as much a victim of conservative evangelical defamation as the minimalists. In this light it is understandable that Dever is known to have called himself a minimalist, although I can assure him: No, you are not; there is not a chance of you being a minimalist.[80] It is his self-deception which makes him blind to the status of his own scholarship as grown-out of the Albright school.

The Albright Family

According to William G. Dever and other members of his circle, archaeology is the solution to all problems. This is at least the impression he wants to present in his polemics against the not-so-convinced amateur-archaeologists. Since they have no first-hand experience in field archaeology, they better keep quiet and cede the ground. The clue to understanding ancient Israel's history is not the Bible with its historical narrative; it is archaeology. So, if you have a problem with something presented as a historical event in the Bible, grasp your spade and start digging. Those who cannot see this archaeological light are *nihilists*, the term used above by scholars on Dever's side against the rest, and especially the minimalists.

In this part it is my intention to trace the history of this term and its implications in North American biblical and biblical-archaeological contexts. *Nihilist* is not a word invented by Dever or Rendsburg or their colleagues; it is traditional conservative evangelical language used about anybody with a slightly critical attitude to the Holy Book.

In his lecture at the *IOSOT* meeting in Oxford in 1959, Martin Noth addressed the issue of archaeology and the history of Israel (Noth 1971a, 34–51). It was not that Noth wrote much about archaeology in the technical sense, and he was probably only occasionally engaged in digging in Palestine, and of course for good reasons: After the Second World War German archaeologists were probably not the most favoured guests in this part of the Middle East. Noth, however, was a student of Albrecht Alt, who had the coveted field experience and who moreover for a number of years was the director of the German Protestant Institute of Archaeology in Jerusalem (*Deutsches Evangelisches Institut für Altertumswissenschaft des Heiligen Landes*), a position

---

[79] The conclusion to my study on Conservative scholarship: Lemche 2005.
[80] Dever is according to oral tradition supposed to have said in 2000: "I started writing to refute the minimalists and ended up becoming one of them".

which Martin Noth was to take up towards the end of his life. The institute is definitely engaged in archaeological studies and excavations, although the German title *Altertumswissenschaft* allows for a wider engagement in all things of interest to the knowledge of the Holy Land in ancient times. Among the duties of the director was to lead yearly "Lehrkurse", educational courses including visits to archaeological sites, the results of which were published in the *Palästinajahrbuch des Deutschen evangelischen Instituts für Altertumswissenschaft des heiligen Landes zu Jerusalem* which appeared between 1905 and 1941, and after the war in the *Zeitschrift des Deutschen Palästinavereins*. It was during such an excursion that Noth suddenly died at Shivta in the Negev in May 1968.

Nevertheless, Albright, the "grandfather" if not the godfather of Dever used to characterize Noth as a nihilist, simply because Noth, in his view of the patriarchs, followed the critical German tradition since de Wette (and not only Wellhausen) of seeing the stories about these figures as traditions kept by the early Israelite community in Palestine in the Period of the Judges.[81] Noth's response was to emphasize the value of critical scholarship following the rules of the historical–critical method, and to quote Noth:

> This does not imply that "critical" should be understood as founded on a preconceived fundamental skepticism, but in the meaning of a procedure to "distinguish" between the various objects and phenomena which are the subject of scholarship".[82]

However, in a note in this connection, Noth adds:

> As it is not right to be biased, it is also not right to assume that other persons are biased. After Albright once in connection with a refusal

---

[81] The example given by Noth (1960b, 35n), is "To declare that we are not concerned with so nihilistic an attitude would be easy but would not be judicious, in view of Noth's reputation as a biblical scholar and as a Palestinologist, to say nothing of the plausibility of his reasoning", (Albright 1939). Albright felt provoked to this condemnation of Noth's view on archaeology by Noth's article "Grundsätzliches zur geschichtliche Befunde auf dem Boden Palästinas" (Noth 1938b).

[82] "Die Methode dabei kann nur die sachgemässe historisch-kritische Methode sein, wobei der Begriff 'kritisch' nichts im Sinne irgend einer voreingenommenen grunszätzlichen Skepsis zu verstehen ist, sondern im Sinne einer Arbeitsweise gewissenschaften 'Unterscheidens' der verschiedenen Gegenstände und Erscheinungen, mit denen es die Forschung zu tun hat" (Noth 1960b, 35). This is fundamentally the very essence of historical–critical research since its beginnings more than two hundred years ago not only in biblical studies but in history in general.

of my opinion used the expression "such a nihilistic attitude" (...) it has in many places become a habit to characterize the method used in scholarly studies about early Israel by Albrecht Alt and especially me as "nihilism".[83]

Among scholars who at the time used the expression "nihilism" about the work of their opponents, Noth mentions William R. Stinespring, John Bright and George E. Wright.[84] Noth adds dryly that this is not a proper language to be used in a scholarly exchange. To exemplify John Bright's attitude to Noth's studies let me quote from his *Early Israel in Recent History Writing*: "So we observe that Noth's method leads him to a mistrust of the early traditions of Israel which is little short of nihilism" (Bright 1956, 53–4). Later on Bright brings in Yehezkiel Kaufmann's theories about Joshua's conquest "in healthy contrast to the nihilism of Alt and Noth" (Bright 1956, 64). And still relying on Kaufmann, Bright speaks of "the excessive nihilism of Noth" (Bright 1956, 72). Noth's in many ways classical acceptance of the role of archaeology is finally rejected in this sentence: "Indeed he exhibits a nihilism regarding archaeology that virtually denies it the right to speak to the point at all. And surely this is unsound" (Bright 1956, 87). Stinespring's "contribution" can be found in his review of Bright's *Early Israel in Recent History Writing*, in *The Journal of Biblical literature* and only in connection with Bright's evaluation of Noth's scholarship.[85] Wright's use of nihilistic follows the same line:

This attempt to reconstruct, or rather nihilistically to reduce, the history of early Israel solely by the use of an internal form-critical and

---

[83] "So wenig es gut ist, selbst voreingenommen zu sein, so wenig gut ist es auch, bei anderen eine Voreingenommenheit zu unterstellen. Seitdem W.F. Albright sich einmal in einer Auseinandersetzung mit meiner Auffassung ... des Ausdruck, 'so nihilistic an attitude' bedient hat (...), ist es mancherorts üblich geworden, die Methode der wissenschaftlichen Arbeiten zur Frühgeschichte Israels von A. Alt und vor allem von mir als 'Nihilismus' zu charakterisieren" (Noth 1960b, 35).
[84] Noth in particular points at John Bright, *Early Israel in Recent History Writing: A Study in Method* (Bright 1956, passim).
[85] In his review of John Bright, *Early Israel in Recent History Writing* (Stinespring 1957, 249) quoting Bright, Stinespring concludes: "Curiously enough, Noth, like Kaufmann, gets no help from archeology, in spite of his membership in the Alt School, famous for its archeological work". The result is, according to Bright, "nihilism": "In effect, Kaufmann rejects literary criticism and archeology and ends up with tradition; Noth rejects tradition and archaeology and ends up with nothing. If K. can be called 'gullible', N. would be 'a professional skeptic' (Bright avoids direct application of these terms)".

tradition-history methodology is so artificial and subjective as to be unconvincing

and he adds:

and finally, most curious is Noth's complete refusal to make use of archeological data. He does not do so because the presuppositions of his methodology will not permit him (Wright 1958, 47–8).

We will soon understand why.

The special phenomenon of the "Albright family" has been dealt with extensively in a number of publications, especially in the many eulogies which followed Albright's death in 1971.[86] These are not very interesting in this connection. After all, Dever's note that not much is left of Albright's school characterized the attitude in North America less than twenty years after Albright's death, even by former members of the Albright family.[87] That it is not wrong to talk about an Albright family rather than an Albright School (often also called the Baltimore School) becomes clear when studying a series of critical studies of the phenomenon from the last thirty years among which I will refer to three: First Burke O. Long's study of the tactics of Albright and his students in cementing the position of the ideas of Albright about archaeology and the history of Israel, second Thomas W. Davis' archaeological discussion of biblical archaeology, and finally the dissertation by Brooke Sherrard on the alliance between biblical archaeology and the political phenomenon of modern Zionism (Long 1997, Davis 2004, and Sherrard 2011 and 2016).

Albright's idea about the task of archaeology certainly centred on its ability to confirm the Bible, although not in a fundamentalist way. Whilst he was brought up in an evangelical (i.e. Christian fundamentalist) family, Albright was never himself a fundamentalist sharing the fairly naïve ideas of Christian fundamentalism: As already stated, no sun stood still in Albright's universe!

---

[86] An authoritative example of this kind of hagiography: Leona Glidden Running and David Noel Freedman, *William Foxwell Albright: A Twentieth Century Genius* (Running and Freedman 1975).

[87] Dever 1993, perhaps the most "balanced" (to use the Albright family's slang) of all studies I have read by Dever to this day. He should only have stressed even stronger, that the grandsons of Albright deserted the family home and moved to the house of Alt and Noth, i.e., in their position vis-à-vis subjects like the Patriarchs, the Exodus, and the conquest, they joined up along the lines of Alt and Noth, if they like Dever did not see George E. Mendenhall's proposal of the "Hebrew Conquest" as the new way of explaining these origin traditions.

Still, as a biblical scholar, he belonged within the group of maximalists who will always accept the most conservative interpretations of the Bible and of archaeology's contribution to the interpretation of the Bible. In this way he squared well with Barr's characterization of how conservatism in biblical studies works: it will always agree with the most conservative possibility, and, it can be added, it will cling to the most conservative solution. When I have sometimes likened biblical scholarship to trench warfare, the trench representing, at the moment, the current common opinion about biblical truth as a source for ancient Israelite history, my point was that this obsession with history changed biblical scholarship into a defensive, apologetic enterprise which ended up marginalizing biblical and especially Old Testament studies – something which is very much the case in present day European Protestant faculties of theology[88] – and prevented biblical scholars from being part on an ongoing debate about what theology is really about: The past or the present and the future? The second phase in this process begins when the shelling of the trench makes it uninhabitable, and scholars hiding in it are forced to retreat to the next line of trenches. Then the process of eliminating this second line begins again – and it goes on indefinitely (Lemche 2000, 191).

In the following chapter we will be confronted with a number of illustrations of this procedure. Here our concern is Albright's way of using his expertise to promote his own ideas about archaeology as the most important support of the biblical history of Israel. This attitude to archaeology permeates his well-known *Archaeology of Palestine*, an interesting choice of title seen in the light of the proclamation of the modern state of Israel in 1948 (Albright 1949). Thus the map at the introduction of the book is a map of "Palestine", not of "Israel" and the names presented are primarily the traditional Arab names, not the Hebrew ones as found on modern maps. It is possible that Albright was here simply politically correct, as neither the British former rulers of the mandate of Palestine nor the United States favoured the events of 1947–1950. To publish a study of the archaeology of the Holy Land in 1949

---

[88] The difference between the European and North American "theatre of operations" is very clear: Thus a North American book about Danish theologians (nothing to boast of) had on its front page Kierkegaard and Grundtvig as the representatives of Danish theology in the 19th century. In the twentieth they had Niels Peter Lemche, something my colleagues in systematic theology did not really understand. To most of them Knud E. Løgstrup should have that place. Løgstrup was a systematic theologian, and for that reason not nearly as interesting to biblically oriented North Americans as this writer. However, a recent update of the book sets the record straight, with Løgstrup also included as one of the now two representatives of Danish theology in the twentieth century.

as the archaeology of Israel would probably not have been "correct" in the eyes of the British publisher of his book on archaeology.[89]

However, be that as it may, Albright's interpretation of archaeology in connection with the Israelite conquest of Palestine is a classic example of his "technique", as demonstrated in one of his best-known articles on the Israelite Conquest from 1938 written in opposition to Martin Noth's discussion of the quality of archaeological discoveries vis-à-vis the study of the textual evidence (Albright 1939), perhaps also in his article from the previous year setting a precise date for the Israelite conquest of Lachish (Albright 1938). Noth's presentation of the traditions about the conquest in the Books of Joshua and Judges as mostly representing etiological explanations of certain features in the Palestinian landscape is rejected out of hand – as has been the case among Albright's students ever since (cf. Noth 1938a).

Albright's reaction is quite astonishing:

> If he [Noth] were [!] right, it would be practically hopeless to expect any valid archaeological control of the Israelite accounts of the Conquest. (Albright 1939, 12)[90]

We should therefore expect a detailed criticism of Noth's presentation of archaeological facts, especially of those places discussed by Noth: Hazor, Megiddo, Aj, and Jericho. However, instead of a discussion Albright opens up for a defamation process against his opponent. Thereafter Albright turns to the question of "Gattungsgeschichte", i.e. *Formgeschichte*, the history of forms of literature. Albright seemingly accepts the relevance of this method to New Testament studies – probably not wanting to get into a fight with Martin Dibelius and especially Rudolf Bultmann, the eminent spokespersons for this method (Dibelius 1919; Bultmann 1921) – although he, at the same time, characterizes it as "nihilistic", but also adds:

> It is, therefore, a priori impossible to say whether a given "aetiological" statement is based on authentic tradition or is the result of a

---

[89] For a quite different appraisal of archaeology in biblical scholarship, cf. Albright's contemporary Millar Burrows (1889–1980) (Burrows 1957). For an evaluation cf. Sherrard 2011, 89–109.

[90] As it will become clear from the discussion of the Israelite conquest in the next chapter, Albright was absolutely right because that was exactly what happened when the construction of biblical historiographers of the Israelite conquest of the Holy Land broke down.

combination ad hoc. Only when there is definite external evidence can we be sure of our ground. (Albright 1939, 13)[91]

Following this statement we have an extended discussion of the relation between what we today would call "collective memory" and history which is relevant to the discussion about memory and history, but not very relevant to the discussion of archaeology, because Noth's aim was not to destroy "history" as based on archaeology *and* literary analysis, but to explain how the literary analysis ends up with conclusions which are seemingly different from the results of archaeological investigations.

Altogether it was Albright's contention that archaeology should have the last and decisive word in the study of ancient Israel's history – although one is entitled to ask: How do we know that it is Israel's history if not from the information found in literature, in the books of the Old Testament? The only evidence of a connection between the settlement history of Israel and archaeology is the Merneptah-stele which is also duly discussed by Albright in his rejection of Noth's "nihilism" (Albright 1939, 21–2), but one name in this context is not much of a basis on which to build a palace of hypotheses. On the contrary, the many references to etiologies in Albright's diatribes against Noth and his school function as a major point in the arsenal of arguments used by Albright. Archaeology proves that these allegations of secondary identifications based on etiology have to be rejected in the light of archaeological discoveries. The circularity of Albright's argument has been described in a lively fashion by Mario Liverani (without specifically mentioning Albright): "I would like to observe that the connection between destructions of archaeological strata and a theory of invasion (directly from the biblical text) is a modern use of the old aetiological procedure ... : Modern aetiologies differ from those ancient in nothing: they accept as a given what they should prove, offering as proof of it elements that do not explain the matter but are explained by it." (Liverani 2021, 268)[92]

We will return to more details of this discussion in the next chapter. Here we are tracing the origins of the dismay with opposing opinions in the Albright circle. Noth was decried by Albright as a nihilist. This is not the only instance of this type of language. In another work, *From the Stone Age to Christianity*, Albright returns to the same theme, this time also including

---

[91] Ironically this is also the opinion of the minimalists who have continually asked for external evidence in confirmation of biblical traditions.
[92] On etiologies cf. also Long 1968, and Niesiołowski-Spanò 2011.

Kurt Möhlenbrink among Noth's supporters.[93] The discussion does not contribute anything new to the theme but after having discussed the historicity of traditions about the conquest, Albright changes focus and opens the following paragraph with "As increasingly recognized by competent scholars..." hinting that scholars like Noth who are not following the lead of Albright are incompetent scholars (Albright 1940, 274–5).

Albright attempted to solve the problem thusly: text or archaeology with a proposal to subordinate the biblical text to archaeology although that is not what he explicitly said or wrote. In his writings it is constantly assumed that text and archaeology can only, properly understood, support each other. Basically he is not in favour of critical analyses of biblical texts – although in other fields than history he made several proposals which relied on analyses of such texts as biblical psalms but also hymns from the prophetic literature most often looking for the most ancient possible roots of such texts.[94] Somehow in such studies Albright exchanged archaeology as a counterpart to the biblical texts with literary remains from the ancient Near East used as the lenses through which he read the biblical texts.

Taken together, the conclusion must be that to Albright archaeology is always right, and therefore in historical studies it must have the first and decisive word; the biblical version must be a secondary voice if discord between biblical evidence and archaeological evidence occurs. Well, to Albright it is hardly ever the case that such a disagreement should happen.

The argument is sharpened also in a different way in the work of the principal archaeologist among Albright's students, G. Ernest Wright. The two other important Albrighteans of Wright's generation, Frank Moore Cross (1921–2012) and David Noel Freedman (1922–2008), were primarily engaged not in archaeology but in textual studies, biblical as well as near eastern inscriptions.[95] At the end of their lives, Freedman, more than Cross, accepted

---

[93] Albright 1940. Kurt Möhlenbrink was quite active in the 1930s, but after that nothing is known about his whereabouts. He probably vanished during the Second World War. Klaus Koenen only has 1906 as his year of birth. (Koenen 1998, 39). Nothing about his fate can be found on the internet.

[94] Cf. e.g., his analysis of Ps 68, or his study of the hymn in Habakkuk chapter 3 (Albright 1950–51; 1953 and 1959).

[95] Freedman was especially active in the editing business, a devotion from his early days that not only resulted in the publication of *The Anchor Bible Dictionary I–VI* (Freedman 1992) but also in the magnifique edition of the Aleppo Codex, *The Leningrad Codex: A Facsimile Edition* (Freedman 1998). Cross's academic career was spent at Harvard, publishing relatively little substantial about the biblical text (not disregarding his studies of deuteronomistic literature), but extensively on the Dead Sea Scrolls and Semitic inscriptions in general.

the changing perspectives of Old Testament scholarship. When asked how it could be that he had Niels Peter Lemche write the long entry on the history of early Israel in his *Anchor Bible Dictionary*, instead of the much more conservative Abraham Malamat, who had let him down, Freedman just answered: "Isn't it pretty much reflecting the situation in the field of Old Testament studies today where everything is in a fluid state?"[96]

However, Wright strengthened the importance of archaeology when it is used to confirm the content of biblical historical narrative proclaiming that it is not only a question of historical interest, it is much more; it is decisive for the survival of the Christian religion. As the main spokesperson of a theological school following the doctrine of the "God who acts!" also called "the Biblical Theology Movement", Wright promoted the frequently encountered objection that what is written in the Bible is not true if it hasn't happened as it is written.[97] But he was confident: It really happened; archaeology proves it! The consequence of an approach like this is fatal to theology because it makes the truth of the biblical message dependent on non-biblical facts, in this case archaeology, leaving the text of the Old Testament aside. To Albright and his students this was not a big deal, as they evidently considered their interpretation of archaeology to be the correct one. Archaeology was to them an objective, positivistic discipline, and the results from archaeology therefore objective, and because they saw archaeology to be in agreement with the biblical version of Israel's history, an objective evaluation of the content of the biblical version would result in accepting this version as correct from a historical point of view. Of course, this is a perfect example of what Liverani describes (cf. above) as a circular argument.

Although Dever as the probably most important – at least most vociferous – representative of the next generation of Albrighteans does not follow his teacher G. Ernest Wright to the end and especially has parted with Wright's theological interpretation of the meaning of archaeology, he is still totally obsessed with the idea that archaeology represents objectivism and positivism. It is the whole foundation of his campaign launched against minimalism. Biblical textual studies, where Dever has never worked, is from one end to

---

[96] Oral communications from Freedman and Malamat to this author. The article: "History of Israel (Pre-Monarchic Period)" (Lemche 1992b). The following paragraph on the exodus and conquest was written by William G. Dever, with his preference for biblical archaeology, the one about the monarchy by Leslie J. Hoppe, who doesn't give much for archaeology, and the final about the post-monarchic period by Robert P. Carroll, the declared postmodernist, just to illustrate Freedman's point.

[97] Among Wright's publications on this: Wright 1962, and Wright and Fuller 1965.

the next a subjective discipline led by foreign agendas such as religious and political bias. But is he correct in his evaluation of archaeology?

Absolutely not! After all, he himself abandons the positions of Albright when it comes to the relevance of archaeology for establishing the historical correctness of the version of Israel's emigration into Palestine at the end of the Late Bronze Age as found in the Old Testament. Those archaeological facts, which Albright and after him G. Ernest Wright accepted as "proving" the exactitude of the biblical version of these events, were after all non-facts. Dever gladly explains why this is so in different publications describing his personal moving away from the Albright camp – the "house of Albright" – to the camp of Albrecht Alt and Martin Noth, and even beyond these German scholars. However, at the same time, he does not see how he has made his own standing on archaeology as an objective type of science impossible. He still believes that archaeology *as he sees it* is a positivistic and objective science, but in this case archaeology as interpreted by Albright, or Wright, or Kenyon, or Finkelstein – representing different archaeological schools – to mention just a few, cannot be a positivistic discipline, at least when they are in disagreement with Dever's own position. As it stands, Dever ends up in a hopeless contradictory position where we must ask him: Where do we find archaeological results from excavations which stand by themselves and not as seen through the eyes of archaeologists? If I choose to use his language I would say that he is dishonest. Not being Dever I prefer to say that he is blind to the log in his own eye when he attacks other scholars for having a speck in their eye.

Archaeology is a highly subjective discipline, as probably everyone who was ever part of an excavation will know from personal experience. If we look at probably the most discussed archaeological subject during the last hundred years, ancient Jerusalem, the interpretation of the archaeological findings has changed from time to time and from archaeologist to archaeologist.[98] It is the rule of the day that archaeologists are never in agreement as to what we have of remains from ancient times and how to interpret them. Moreover, there are several archaeological traditions or schools.[99] Dever's post-Albrightean school is certainly not alone in the field. And when it comes to interpretation,

---

[98] A recent but illustrative example is the layout of the discussion of Jerusalem between the Babylonian conquest in 587 BCE, and the early Hellenistic period in Finkelstein 2018, 3–27. Nobody is agreeing about anything.

[99] On one hand the archaeological school of Albright, and on the other the British school of Robert Eric Mortimer Wheeler (1890–1976), John Winther Crowfoot (1873–1959), and especially Dame Kathleen Mary Kenyon (1906–1978) exemplified by excavations at Samaria, Jericho, and Jerusalem, and finally the modern Israeli school exemplified by

Thomas Thompson was, as already mentioned, there in 1967 when Dever made changes to his findings at Gezer, and I remember once at Tell Yizreel in 1996 when one of the chief excavators, John Woodhead of the British School, tried to explain to the participants in the excavation why the four-chamber gate which we had dug out was in fact a six-chamber gate – the only thing we saw was the four-chamber variety. At a lecture in Copenhagen the Dutch archaeologist Margreet Steiner showed an example of how, in her interpretation of a certain feature of her excavations in Jerusalem, Kathleen Kenyon did not follow her own field notes. The interpretation follows the eyes that see![100] But leaving the anecdotal examples, we may mention just a few cases: Jerusalem in the tenth century will be the subject of a more detailed discussion on the part about the United Monarchy in the next chapter. But it is still the best example of changing interpretations of archaeological material. Because it is about Jerusalem it is automatically a highly biased topic because of its religious position in three different religions and its political role in modern Middle Eastern controversy. Kathleen Kenyon challenged in the 1960s Robert A. Macalister's archaeological results from the 1920s, and Yigal Shiloh challenged her results in the 1970s and 1980s, and Eilat Mazar challenged his and Kenyon's results at the beginning of the twenty first century, and everything is challenged by a group of archaeologists from Tel Aviv University constantly in disagreement with their colleagues from the Hebrew University in Jerusalem.[101] There is no end to it.

It is correct to say that Dever is a typical postmodernist in his own distorted view of postmodernism. He accepts his own interpretation as if it is the only possible one, and ignores divergent analyses. His position is definitely one of *homo* (that is: Dever) *mensura*: There is no objective truth; there is only Dever's truth. This position is natural for a person who has never really

---

archaeologists like Amihai Mazar, Israel Finkelstein and David Ussishkin somehow trying to join the extremes of the two other schools.

[100] John Woodhead in daily charge of the excavations at Yizreel really "wanted" to find such a six-chamber gate like those found at Megiddo, Hazor and Gezer, among other places. We might talk about biased interpretation of archaeology, but it is just an illustration of the axiom that you see what you wish to see. The issue of gates reaches a quite hilarious stage, if it is true that Yoseph Garfinkel simply constructed a second gate at Khirbet Qeiyafa to make the place fit to his assumed name of the place as being biblical Shaaraim, "[the City of] Two Gates". The photos published by Israel Finkelstein and Alexander Fantalkin (Finkelstein and Fantalkin 2012, 47 and figs 5–6), and Finkelstein's claim that 90 percent of the gate in question is "reconstruction", speak for themselves.

[101] Macalister dug in Jerusalem from 1923 to 1925, Kenyon from 1961 to 1967, Shiloh from 1978 to 1985, E. Mazar ongoing. I will return to some of the issues of the archaeology of Jerusalem below. Here is a teaser: Steiner 2020. Cf. also Steiner 2014 and 2016).

read much about postmodernism, the "fad" as he styles it, but alas, it is also the case when it comes to the other subjects which he refers to in connection with his settlement with the minimalists such as ethnicity, social anthropology, historical method and more.

Thus he seems to use the Norwegian social anthropologist Fredrik Barth's (1928–2016) definition of ethnicity as the basis of his claim that the minimalists are attacking the very concept of Israelite ethnicity in ancient times, but has he really understood what Barth wrote?[102] I very much doubt it. To me it seems as if Barth simply proposes a concept of ethnicity which is very close to the one put into force in minimalist analysis, especially the concept of constructed identity or ethnicity.[103] Something similar is evident if we move on to Dever's anthropological thinking in combination with his interpretation of archaeology. When it comes to archaeology he praises Ian Hodder (b. 1948) for distancing himself from the system theory dominated archaeology

---

[102] Dever is referring to Fredrik Barth's introduction to *Ethnic Groups and Boundaries* (Barth 1969). He still maintains that ethnicity is revealed in material remains in spite of Barth's warnings against such easy identifications. I have discussed Barth's definition of ethnicity a number of times, thus in Lemche 1998b, 1–21, in a chapter named "Prolegomena: Inventing the Past. Ancient Israel – Ethnicity, Nation, and History as the Mode of Interpreting Ancient Cultures". This theoretical introduction to ethnicity also formed the background for the following discussion of the "ethnicity" of biblical Israel, "Archaeology and Israelite Ethnic Identity" (Lemche 1998b, 65–85). It would be nice if Dever for once showed some knowledge of the discussion of the concept of ethnicity outside the narrow confines of North American biblical studies. I can recommend him the reader edited by John Hutchinson and Anthony D. Smith (Hutchinson and Smith 1996), which is especially important as the two editors represent two very different ideas of the origins of ethnic groups, one of them a primordalist, the second an essentialist. A primordalist is, when simplified, a person who believes in the continuity of the identity of an ethnic group; an essentialist – among them Barth – reckons ethnicity to be a dynamic concept always in the way of being re-constructed. I can also recommend Thomas Hylland Eriksen, *Ethnicity & Nationalism: Anthropological Perspectives* (Eriksen 1993) and Steven Fenton, *Ethnicity* (Fenton 2010). On Barth, cf. Eriksen 2015. And then, if he really wants to be offended by a modern approach he should consult Dermot Anthony Nestor, *Cognitive Perspectives on Israelite Identity* (Nestor 2010). Nestor in his highly technical discussion goes far beyond what can be found in other discussions involving biblical scholars. Maybe it is too technical because we see very few references to his important work.

[103] Along the same lines as the previous note: If only one day Dever would read something about the concept of ethnicity in an antique context. A good start could be McInerney 2014, and then of course the brilliant use of the concept in several studies by Erich S. Gruen, such as Gruen 2018 and 2020, but also the comprehensive volume edited by him: *Cultural Identity in the Ancient World* (Gruen 2011). And when Dever has finished reading Gruen, I can also recommend Doron Mendels' books, such as Mendels 1987, 1992, and 1998.

of Lewis Binford (1931–2011) (Hodder and Hudson 2003 in contrast to Binford 1972). I have had my problems with system theory as previously expounded by several North American social anthropologists and historians as well (Lemche 1985, 216–223, and Lemche 1990). Hodder seems to be much closer to the position of the minimalists than to Dever's idea of archaeology as an objective science.[104] He is truly postmodern and even post-postmodern, to employ modern language, but everything postmodern is at the same time also post-postmodern and soon post-post-postmodern, because it comes after modernity. So far so good; in archaeology Dever sides with the postmodernists, but does he understand that anthropology has also moved on? The system theory of the 1960s and 1970s is hardly relevant anymore. I am not sure that it will still be possible to write a history like Charles Redman's *The Rise of Civilization: From Early Farmers to Urban Society in the Ancient Near East* (Redman 1978); I am not even sure that Charles Redman would write such a book today in light of his other more recent titles. However, the fact is that social anthropology, even in North America, has moved on from positions taken up by outsiders like Dever to something in accordance with the movement within archaeology proper. Dever's tragedy is that he got caught between the two subjects accepting one – social anthropology – for what it was once upon a time in North America and at the same time embracing archaeology for what it is today – in North America.[105] We have to tell Dever that the stew he cooked from these two ingredients, anthropology

---

[104] As a matter of fact, already in the introduction to the first edition of his book, Hodder turns against the idea that archaeology is science, or objective. Post-processual thinking is the opposite of system theory, and in this way much closer to my own ideas about system theory (cf. preceding note) than to anything which Dever claims it to be. The Wikipedia article "Post-Processual Archaeology" (https://en.wikipedia.org/wiki/Post-processual_archaeology#:~:text=Post%2Dprocessual%20archaeology%2C%20which%20is,the%20subjectivity%20of%20archaeological%20interpretations) opens in this fashion: "Post-processual archaeology, which is sometimes alternately referred to as the interpretative archaeologies by its adherents, is a movement in *archaeological theory* that emphasizes the *subjectivity* of archaeological interpretations". We have to ask: Is Dever mocking us?
[105] A major source for the confusion is the different academic arrangement of archaeology and anthropology in North American universities and in European universities. In North America social anthropology is placed in connection (same departments) as archaeology, whereas in Europe social anthropology may as ethnology either be independent, and even a part of faculties of science, or seen in connection with general history. European social anthropology at one side followed structuralism as evidenced by Edmund Leach, e.g., in his *Culture and Communication: The Logic by which Symbols Are Connected. An Introduction to the Use of Structuralist Analysis in Social Anthropology* (Leach 1976) who was himself heavy influenced by Claude Lévi-Strauss, whose semiotic approach is most easily accessible in his *The Savage Mind* (Lévi-Strauss 1989 [1962]).

and archaeology, seems unable to keep its parts together. In many ways his view on, respectively, social anthropology and archaeology, is contradictory. At the end he finds himself caught up in the postmodern "malarkey" where he thinks that he finds his minimalist opponents (Dever 2000).

In many ways Dever represents the dying school of Albright. He embraces many traits borrowed from the Albrighteans including the bad language and furore against dissidents. This is a heritage that can be traced back to the origins of Albright – and of Dever: The mission hall. The language is also decided by the special North American tradition of cancel culture where it is a sin to start a discussion with those who disagree with you.[106] You just indulge in name calling and defamation. The inability to discuss properly with dissidents, which characterizes Dever's literary output, has its background in this "culture". Scholarly discussions are, in segments of North American biblical study, a game following political "rules" rather than representing a *wissenschaftliche* (a scholarly) occupation.[107] If people vote for you and not for your opponent, you have won. It is as far from the European scholarly way of thinking as we can imagine, and the reason for the reactions mentioned here from Martin Noth and Rainer Albertz, reactions which show these scholars' unfamiliarity with the North American university tradition – or at least with its more questionable sides.

Who Won the War?

Not all wars have a clear winner. Sometimes a "hot" war just continues as a "cold" war. Exchanges are rarely as acrimonious as they used to be, but the fronts are still obvious and may exist for many years. This is very much the case in the historical part of Old Testament studies. The battle went on from the beginning of the 1990s, and continued unabashed for about fifteen years. Then it more or less ended without a ceasefire and without any clear winner. Over the next many years it continued as a cold war with disengaged lines between the two fronts of, on one side the maximalists, and on the other the minimalists. In no-man's land the centralists remained more or less in peace, vacillating between the two fronts and trying to create independent room for action of their own. All three parties have been locked in a kind of stalemate

---
[106] On cancel culture, cf. the definition in Wikipedia: "Cancel culture (or call-out culture) is a modern form of ostracism in which someone is thrust out of social or professional circles – either online on social media, in the real world, or both".
[107] As Burke Long aptly presents it, the tactics were laid out already by Albright and his original circle (Long 1997).

where nothing happened. Every party tried to add new arguments to bolster their respective positions but in general it was not in historical studies things happened. This lack of new ideas was not limited to historical studies. Not much happened within other parts of the historical–critical study of the Old Testament such as analyses of the sources of the Pentateuch, or of the Deuteronomistic History. No new ideas presented, no revolutions which were not already in evidence some thirty years ago. I will return to some recent trends in the third and final part of this study, especially the growing Pan-Hellenism which I am definitely guilty of having instigated.

2 The Road to Minimalism

"Ideology" was the magic word in the previous chapter. The concept of ideology and the derived notion of "ideologues" formed the scarlet thread which tied the various negative responses to minimalism together. Because of an anti-religious bias, a perverted form of idealism, the minimalists made their attacks on the history of ancient Israel, denying the biblical version all legitimacy as a source for this history. The basis for such statements can easily be said to rely on ignorance; not an ignorance that has to do with any lack of knowledge about the status quo of biblical studies at the beginning of the third millennium, but of the history of scholarly historical studies which led to the positions of the minimalists – acknowledging what especially Philip R. Davies has explained several times, that the representatives of minimalism do not form a phalanx marching in one and the same direction, but a group of scholars representing a similar approach to historical and biblical studies, though often ending up with different opinions about many details, the most serious being perhaps the general dating of biblical literature to either the Persian (Philip R. Davies, perhaps also Keith Whitelam) or the Hellenistic-Roman Period (Niels Peter Lemche and Thomas L. Thompson) (Davies 2002).

Above I mentioned that the severe lack of insight displayed by Iain Provan in his rejection of minimalism is fatal. Provan, like many of his colleagues, seems to be of the opinion that minimalism started its devastating attack on well-established biblical scholarship around 1990, so to speak out of the blue, because the ideological standings of the minimalists demanded that they reject everything. Now it was not so difficult to unmask the discourse of Provan and his colleagues as being basically conservative-evangelical. Their discourse claims that all critical scholarship is based on (bad) ideology, which is really philosophy as it developed during the Enlightenment and early Romanticism and which paved the way for a critical thinking that did not only produce modern science but also a concept of history which moved the genre of historiography away from earlier collections of fables and myths retold as historical evidence. Anyone with the slightest idea of what happened in European thinking between, say, 1700 and 1850, will recognize the importance of these changes which certainly formed the background of emerging critical studies of the two testaments. It is not just a coincidence that Hermann

Samuel Reimarus (1694–1768) could formulate his critical questions to the Exodus tradition; it was the triumph of logical thinking over the credulity of the past.[1] It was simply a consequence of those methods which paved the way for the scholarly breakthrough during the Enlightenment.

The accusation of false ideology has simply to be more precise. How can it be that this ideology has led biblical scholars in the wrong direction? Since it has become clear that it is the philosophy of Hegel which is intended, we are entitled to ask: Why is this philosophy so dangerous in the context of biblical studies? We all know by heart the essence of it: Thesis plus antithesis form the basis for a synthesis. Everything is moving; nothing is stable. One day a certain idea governs, the next day it has been challenged by a different idea. The day after these two opposing ideas unite – becoming the new consensus – they are themselves challenged by even newer ideas, in an unending sequence of discussions. But what is wrong with this? Simply that Hegelianism, and evolution as Darwin taught us, points in the same way: Πάντα ῥεῖ, *Panta Rei*, as Heraclitus said. The conclusion is that the conservative-evangelical protest against ideology in biblical studies is simply a protest against all modern western philosophy and science which is founded on such notions as those formulated more than two hundred years ago by, among many others, Hegel. We are talking about an anti-intellectual movement; it has nothing to do with what scholars believe or do not believe at the present. Provan's attack on critical scholarship was hidden behind an attack seemingly directed against the minimalists only, but to a true conservative-evangelical all critical scholars are minimalists.

It is worse when critical scholars, or scholars who are supposed to be critical, join forces with the conservative-evangelicals. It could be regarded as treason against their peers who follow historical-critical methods, even if in a postmodern disguise, as if there is a fundamental disagreement here between modernism and postmodernism. The problem is that being a critical scholar signifies that you are forced to be a hundred percent critical. There is no such thing as fifty or eighty percent critical. There are no questions that should not and cannot be asked, and there are no subjects that should not and cannot be taken up. When it comes to some of the great figures in the biblical narrative like Moses or David, no critical investigation can disregard problems which have been raised against the very existence of these figures. It is very much like the debate in New Testament studies about the historicity of Jesus.

---

[1] Reimarus' "commentary" on the plausibility of the Exodus can be found in a fragment published by Gotthold Ephraim Lessing in 1777. Available in an English translation at http://www.gkoehn.com/wp-content/uploads/2015/08/ReimarusThirdFragment1.pdf.

Questions such as "did he really live?" have to be asked – and answered. The answer might well be in the affirmative, or it can be in the negative, but the issue is there and the question has to be asked. For reasons like these the alliance between critical scholars such as those having their home within the Albright family and conservative evangelicals is an unholy one although not a unique phenomenon in biblical studies. As a consequence, those quasi-critical scholars have no home. They are not welcomed among the conservative evangelicals, and critical scholars scorn them.

And one more thing: You don't need to be a minimalist to be a critical scholar. There is no such thing as opinions which are not allowed to be challenged. Everything coming from the pen of the minimalists will sooner or later be revised if not rejected by other critical scholars on the basis of the ever-changing character of the evidence and the interpretation of it. When Sarah Mandell writes that biblical scholars in another hundred years will still be reading minimalists like Thomas Thompson and this writer, she adds that it will not be because they have spoken the last word, but because they changed the direction of biblical studies (Mandell 2012). She might be right. After all, this is actually the status today of scholars like Hermann Gunkel and Sigmund Mowinckel. As already indicated in the introduction, nobody reads Gunkel's commentaries on Genesis or Psalms as the latest news about Genesis or Psalms but they read them because they represent an enormous inspiring approach to biblical texts in comparison to previous (and much later) studies on these books (Gunkel 1917 and 1968). The same can be said about Mowinckel (who, incidentally, was a student of Gunkel). His classic on the Psalms and the Messianic tradition will probably only be read today for what they are really now, very insightful elaborations on biblical texts which may be correct, or they may be a shot in the dark; this is no longer very important. The intellectual level of these studies is, however, something you cannot admire enough whatever your own position is (Mowinckel 2004 and 2005). But both Gunkel and Mowinckel were critical scholars and must be respected for what they were.

In this chapter it is my intention to present a critical overview of "the road to minimalism", which covers the main features of the development in studies devoted to the historical referent in the text of the Old Testament since the last moment of unity which can be dated to c. 1960. When we overview the situation as it presented itself some thirty years later, it is obvious that almost everything had changed. This applies to everything historical but also to the understanding of the development of the religion reflected in biblical writings, and it certainly also includes the study of the biblical texts with an astonishing change in attitude to Scripture as a historical source and to its date of origin. It is my intention in this part to investigate how we came from 1960 to post-1990. The investigation will be partial and definitely partisan. I have no intention of presenting a complete history of research. There are still fields where surprisingly little has happened, such as the poetic literature of the Old Testament, and even the Prophets. In a conversation almost thirty years ago at a conference in Bern, the late Oswald Loretz whispered to me that we are expecting *"eine Götterdämmerung der Prophetenforschung"* (The Twilight of studies in Prophecy). So far we are still expecting it.

The subjects to be discussed below are 1) the idea of an Israelite political tribal society in the Period of the Judges embodied in the theory of an Israelite "Amphictyony" of twelve tribes, 2) the idea that the patriarchal narratives in Genesis reflect a historical age, not to say the acts of historical persons, 3) the debate over the character of the Israelite conquest of the land of the Canaanites, including the tradition of the sojourn in Egypt and the Exodus, and 4) the United Monarchy of David and Solomon and the so-called divided monarchy. Two more subjects, 1) the importance of having been sent into exile, and finally 2) the date of the historical narrative in the Old Testament will be kept for the third and last section of this book. The paragraphs of this chapter reflect the progress of scholarship rather than a historical order, whereas the next chapter is summing up what happened because it is not only about the date of the Historiographic tradition in the Old Testament; it is also so-to-speak the very foundation of any modern reconstruction of the ancient history of the subject in question, Israel as part of a Palestinian region of the Southern Levant.

The Last Moments of scholarly Consensus about the History of Ancient Israel: John Bright and Martin Noth

Around 1960 two major histories of Israel had recently appeared, marking off the ground for debate. In 1950 Martin Noth published the first edition of his *Geschichte Israels* (Noth 1950a), and in 1959 John Bright presented his *A History of Israel* (Bright 1959).[2] These two syntheses of Israel's history became the standard works for the next generation. Very little of interest appeared before J. Maxwell Miller and John H. Hayes published their new history for the North American public in 1986 (Miller and Hayes 1986), which was definitely of a different orientation from that of John Bright's *A History of Israel*;

---

[2] Noth 1950a was translated into English in 1960 (Noth 1960a). Bright 1959 was, to make the score even, translated into German a few years later (Bright 1966).

and Herbert Donner produced his version for the German market in 1984 (Donner 1984), which was mostly an update of Noth's *Geschichte Israels*.[3]

The span of years between Noth's and Bright's histories made it possible for Bright to include several references to Noth, not in the abusive style we were met with in his separate discussion of modern studies of early Israel reviewed in the previous chapter (Bright 1956), but surprisingly with a lot of positive things to say about Noth's studies in tradition history. Thus Bright acknowledged Noth's study of the traditions of the Pentateuch as found in his *Überlieferungsgeschichte des Pentateuch* (Noth 1948. ET Noth 1972) to be of fundamental importance. In his analysis of the Pentateuch, Noth had isolated a series of basic traditions ("Überlieferungselemente"): 1) the theme of the exodus, 2) the theme of the immigration into Palestine, 3) the covenant with the Patriarchs, 4) the wilderness stories, and 5) the theophany at Sinai. These core traditions had developed during the transmission of tradition history by including a number of motifs found in the first book of Moses. These themes had been joined into a coherent narrative including all themes, and finally this narrative had been turned into literature resulting in the different sources of the Pentateuch.

It is evident that Noth's analysis builds on the traditional system of source criticism found in the Graff–Kuenen–Wellhausen source criticism hypothesis, but he changed its course into something which Bright definitely found useful, and we will see that Bright based his analysis of Israel's early history on Noth's model, presenting almost slavishly the same range of themes as the foundation upon which he builds his history (Bright 1959, 61–69).

Turning to Noth, the centre of his construction is the amphictyony, the league of twelve tribes which he supposed to have existed in the Period of the Judges. His history opens, after a prolegomena covering the land of Israel, with Israel's place in the world around 1200 BCE, and a survey of the sources for the history of Israel. By contrast, Bright opened his history almost in a Herodotian way with an overview covering, in a few pages, the history of the ancient Near East from the beginning of the Stone Age to the end of the third millennium BCE (Bright 1959, 7–37).[4] After this prolegomena, Bright

---

[3] Miller's and Hayes' *History*, was preceded by the midway assessment of the progress of critical historical studies in Hayes and Miller 1977.

[4] In his *Histories*, Herodotus opens with a general outlook on a world where the events of the Greco-Persian wars took place, including ethnographic descriptions of ancient Babylon and Egypt, and only after this survey the essential part of his "investigations" (history in Greek does not mean history in our sense but investigation) can begin, the story of Greek and Persia until the fateful defeat of Persia in 480–497 BCE. It is world history in so far as the idea is that it was about two contrasting civilizations that struggled. Basically

immediately turns to the Patriarchs; the overview of many thousands of years of near eastern history is only presented to give life to the scene where the drama of the patriarchal narratives is supposed to have been played out. Only after his discussion of the Patriarchs does Bright turn to the sacral league of twelve tribes which he sees as the place where Israel's religious tradition found its lasting form. In between the patriarchs and the amphictyony, Bright places his discussion of the Exodus and the conquest of Canaan, handling it in very much the same manner as the opening discussion about the Patriarchs.

Noth will know nothing of the kind. His league of twelve tribes comes first, when he presents the conditions for its existence which is placed in the land of Israel, preceded by an emigration from neighbouring areas ending in the consolidation of Israel as a tribal league in the land. The traditions of the Exodus, and of the Patriarchs, as well as the tradition of the covenant concluded at Sinai between Israel and its God have their home in the context of the amphictyony. They are not treated as historical traditions *per se*, i.e., standing alone.

The similarity between the two histories is in many ways astonishing as are also the differences. Bright is convinced that these parts of Israel's traditions that had their home in the sacral league were basically historical, or are reflecting a historical memory. Noth has much less sympathy for the idea of historical kernel traditions although he also reckons with a place for them at the central sanctuary of the amphictyony. It is obvious that two conflicting approaches to understanding the formation and content of traditions are on a collision course. Bright explains it very clearly (Bright 1959, 61-9). His scenery of the Patriarchs' activities provides him with the proof of their existence, although he admits that we have very little precise information about anything. His discussion of the Patriarchs is very close to the characterization of this kind of biblical scholarship by Bernd Jørg Diebner (already quoted above) that although you cannot prove anything, it is a fact – because it has to be a fact (Diebner 1984b). When playing his cards, Bright's "winning" argument is that nothing disproves that the story told in Genesis is true, an argument we normally associate with the position of conservative evangelicals, and not with critical scholarship. It is one of the traditional winning cards used against minimalism, that we should not expect the Bible to tell us lies before we can prove that it is indeed telling lies.[5] Now the argument can be

---

Herodotus' imagining of a contrast between an oriental world and a European one has survived to this day.

[5] This is of course a perverse kind of argument. Why should we think of the Bible as telling us lies? The question is really: What is it really telling us? What kind of information does it provide?

used as a sort of indictment against the scholars belonging to the Albright group, showing where their spiritual home really is.

So far we have reached a partial conclusion: When it comes to the discussion of the Patriarchs, both Noth and Bright consider the stories about them to reflect tradition. The difference is that Bright believed these traditions to refer to historical persons, the Patriarchs and Moses – persons who really existed once upon a time. Noth followed a German tradition that goes back to de Wette (and not primarily Wellhausen) which says that these stories belong to an invented past. It is of importance for the understanding of Noth's position that the line from de Wette to Noth was not an unbroken one. After Wellhausen, most German biblical scholars who wrote explicitly about Israel's earliest tradition would be much less willing to skip the historicity of the stories about this early history than normally assumed today. Histories by Hermann Guthe (1849–1936), Ernst Sellin (1867–1946), and especially Rudolf Kittel (1853–1929) would, so to speak, reinvent the historical past in their endeavours to neutralize the influence of Wellhausen.[6] It is not without reason that Bright, a number of times, refers to Kittel (Kittel 1883) in his chapter on the Patriarchs. Both are very much in line in their respective versions of the early history of Israel and the methods to be followed when discussing this subject.

When we move on from the Patriarchs to the history of Israel in Egypt, of the covenant at Sinai, and the conquest, there are of course a number of differences between Bright and Noth, and some of them are major ones. Bright is true to his origins in accepting most of the biblical narratives as history as it stands whereas Noth believes these stories to have had their home among the members of the amphictyony. It will, however, come as a surprise to some that Noth accepts a historical nucleus behind the present Exodus tradition. The main thing that separates his approach from Bright's has to do with the size of the event and not the event itself, since he argues that it was an event in which only a section of later Israel participated. It was only within the confines of the amphictyony the Exodus tradition in combination with the Sinai tradition developed into the founding legends of all twelve Israelite tribes, because such an organization only arose in Palestine. It was not part of early Israel's pre-Palestinian history.

The position of Noth, who places the historical establishment of Israel as a tribal league in Palestine, has consequences for his understanding of the Israelite conquest of Palestine as well. The question of how Israel arrived in its future land was perhaps the most vexed issue in Old Testament

---

[6] For a more complete overview of the "taming" of Wellhausen, cf. Lemche 2013b, 95–132.

scholarship around 1960 with two seemingly very different positions in a bitter infight. On one hand we had the Albright school's insistence of a violent conquest following the outline of the Book of Joshua as far as possible. Although presented as resting on archaeological evidence it can hardly be described as anything but a paraphrase of the Book of Joshua. On the other hand, the explanation of the conquest among German scholars was quite different as far as the physical character of the conquest was concerned. Noth's and his colleagues' position was generally decided by two studies of Noth's teacher Albrecht Alt, published in 1925 and 1939 respectively.[7] Contrary to the North-American model, Alt's and, following him, Noth's description of the Israelite migration into Palestine did not at first result in a major series of destructions of Canaanite cities. As a matter of fact, there were no such destructions. Violence only followed when a growing Israelite population in the second stage of their settlement in the land began to expand their territories at the expense of the local Canaanite population. This second stage was described in the second of Alt's articles on the settlement, the one never translated, and for that reason ignored by most North-American scholars.[8] Of course it did not help that it appeared in 1939 just as World War II began. When it finally became available to scholars outside of occupied Europe, in 1945, it was, in the minds of post-war scholars, something that already belonged to the past.

Again we have the same picture: American biblical scholars submitting to Albright's choice of a model for the conquest as close as possible to the biblical version, whereas their German colleagues were modifying the biblical version when they argued for the development of the idea of a conquest by force, which began to form already from the very beginning of the Israelite presence in Palestine. However, in spite of a lively discussion that lasted for years, the differences between the two approaches to the origins of Israel were not as fundamental as often assumed. Both scholarly traditions had one basic idea in common: they were in total agreement when it came to Israel's origins outside of Palestine. This was really of fundamental importance and it became clear during the decades following that we had entered into a ceasefire period, established in 1960.

The word which brought the two positions together was "tradition", and especially *oral tradition*. Around 1960 this had become an ever more important concept, building on what biblical scholars of that time believed to be a

---

[7] Alt 1925 and 1939. Only the first was ever translated into English in Alt 1989, 133–70.
[8] Cf. also the layout of these two stages in the Israelite conquest of Palestine in Noth 1950a, 131–51.

characteristic of non-literate societies. The most dedicated advocates of the conviction that oral tradition is able to transmit information of historical value from the past were found in Scandinavia within the "Uppsala school" with Henrik Samuel Nyberg (1889–1974) and Ivan Engnell (1906–1964) as the unofficial leaders. Other notable members of the group were Gösta W. Ahlström (1918–1992) and Eduard Nielsen (1923–2017), the latter from Copenhagen. Another notable representative of this school was Rolf August Carlson (1928–2001) whose main work was a highly interesting tradition-historical study of the David tradition breaking with the usual division of this narrative into two: the accession of David and the story about David's succession. In Carlson's view it was one story about David first blessed by Yahweh, later to end under the curse of Yahweh (Carlson 1964). The idea that oral tradition is a valuable source for knowledge about the past, even the remote past, had its origins in Nyberg's studies of Islamic tradition – only relatively late in his career did he turn to Old Testament studies, where he stood out in opposition to the prevailing German higher criticism of the endless dissection of biblical texts.[9] Engnell presented his methodology in his *Gamla Testamentet: En traditionshistorisk inledning. Första delen* (Engnell 1945).[10] By far the easiest introduction to oral tradition as seen from Uppsala (Copenhagen) was published by Eduard Nielsen, in a work often referred to even seventy years after its first appearance.[11] We will return to the issue of oral tradition later. The debate has hardly been brought to a conclusion, but will have to be seen in light of the presently thriving field of memory studies. This discussion is of no relevance at this point. It is only important here to realize that John Bright refers to the influence of this Scandinavian school with regard to his own idea of the value of oral tradition.

Martin Noth was hardly as impressed by the Scandinavian studies of oral tradition as his North-American counterpart; neither was he a true heir to the type of literary criticism found in traditional German scholarship. Noth definitely supported the idea that Israel's traditions about its prehistory before

---

[9] On H.S. Nyberg, professor in Semitic Philology at Uppsala University from 1931 to 1956, see the extensive article by Christopher Toll, in *Svensk Bibliografisk Lexikon* (Toll 1990–1991). Available at https://sok.riksarkivet.se/sbl/Presentation.aspx?id=8431. In his opposition to German literary criticism he shared views with his Danish colleague Johannes Pedersen, professor in Semitic Philology at the University of Copenhagen from 1922 to 1950, who expressed his doubts in Pedersen 1934. On Pedersen, cf. Lemche 1996b. Nyberg's most important work in this field was Nyberg 1935.

[10] It was never translated, and the second volume only exists in a template version of a never finished manuscript. English speaking readers might find help in Engnell 1969.

[11] Nielsen 1956. Original publication in Danish: Nielsen 1952.

the settlement in Palestine went through an oral stage; still he preferred to keep these traditions as memories from the past and not as proper historical remembrances. It was not because he had no imagination as far as Israel's early history is concerned. I would say, on the contrary, he was probably too keen in creating a history on the basis of his analyses of the biblical information. It is not for nothing that a later generation of German biblical scholars could refer to Alt and Noth and their generation as "die großen Hypothesenmacher" (the great creators of hypotheses). To mention only one example, we might refer to a series of studies which Noth devoted to the early Israelite history in Transjordan (Noth 1971b). The level of information which Noth extracted from his biblical sources is astonishing and far surpasses anything produced by the members of the Albright school. Yet it is all speculation. The truth is that there is no lack of Noth's and for that matter Alt's investment in Israel's early history. The difference between their approach and Albright's and his students' is more or less limited to a different evaluation of what archaeology can be used for. Noth is showing no trace of nihilism as far as the Bible goes; his nihilism is simply that he is not prone to accept Albright's biblical archaeology intended to *prove* the veracity of events mentioned in the Bible's retelling of the first phases in Israel's history. In this way, the only issue for Albright would have been to question Noth's attitude to *Albright's* archaeology but of course this would not make sense to Albright as his archaeology was *the archaeology* of ancient Israel. When it came to the excavation of biblical texts for the purpose of writing history, Noth far surpassed Albright (and his students), who had no clue about what to do with the biblical information but elevated the information in these texts into a different category by linking them slavishly to archaeology – and to repeat myself: to *Albright's* archaeology. In this way the attitude of the Albright clan is preposterous and can more or less be explained by a lack of method when analyzing texts. The only weak point in Noth's approach is: Do we really know as much as he believed he was able to extract from his biblical sources?

The conclusion that there was very little not shared between Bright and Noth and the groups of biblical scholars which they represented in North America and in Europe respectively becomes much more obvious the moment we proceed with their respective histories and turn to the Period of the Judges. Bright's chapter on this period has the title "The constitution and Faith of Early Israel: The Tribal League" (Bright 1959, 128–60; Noth's version bears the name "Israel als Zwölfstämmebund" (Noth 1950a, 54–130). Bright's version is subdivided into paragraphs on 1), the Faith of Early Israel rotating around the interpretation of the covenant and its importance; 2) the Constitution of Early Israel: The Amphictyony and its Institutions, and, 3) The history of the Amphictyony: The "Period of the Judges". In its first part, Noth's version includes overviews of the territory of early Israel and his and Alt's version of the Israelite settlement. The second part deals with the system of the twelve-tribe league and its institutions, and the third part with the traditions of this organization: the Exodus, the Patriarchs, and the Sinai covenant: Taken together we find the same outlook; very little differentiates Bright from Noth.

The same can be said about the period of the Hebrew monarchy. Hardly anything separates Bright's version from the one found in Noth's history. Details may vary (but not often). It is the same story. Even the subdivisions of this period are the same, of course as provided by biblical historiography: First the United Monarchy of David and Solomon followed by the divided monarchy, and finally Israel's fate in the shadow of the great empires of Assyria and Babylonia (Bright 1959, 161–320; Noth 1950a, 152–270). In both cases we may talk about a paraphrase of the version found in the books of Samuel, King's and Chronicles. If anything the two authors only provide a modern version – a hyperstory as Liverani terms it (Liverani 1999); we might even call it "rewritten Bible" – of the biblical text.[12]

The exile and the post-exilic period follow without much difference in outlook between the two biblical historians. Noth spends relatively few pages on the long period between Nebuchadnezzar and Bar-Kochba from 587 BCE to 135 CE (more than seven hundred years), presenting only a sketch of this historical development in little more than eighty pages (Noth 1950a, 322–406). Bright's treatment is longer but Bright cuts off his history of ancient Israel with the Maccabees (Bright 1959, 321–445).

A Paradigm shatters: The League of Twelve Tribes

When a ruling paradigm breaks down, the cracks normally first appear in its weaker parts, in the periphery and not in the centre. This was not the case when the peace in biblical scholarship broke around 1960 and, in the following decades, was substituted by sometimes bitter and unending disputes. The first attacks were directed not against minor matters but at the very heart of the paradigm: The sacral league of twelve tribes at the centre of which the traditions about Israel's origins are supposed to have their home. If the league

---

[12] I will not be too hard on Noth or Bright for indulging in such paraphrases. After all, everyone did in those days. I cannot play innocent either, when I quite consciously did the same in Lemche 1988b, just saying that when it comes to the Period of the Hebrew Kings, just read the version in the Books of Kings.

is shown never to have existed, a huge chain of interrelated problems arise: If not in the Period of the Judges, then when did the notion of the twelve tribes arise? Furthermore, if there was no early sacral league of twelve tribes, where are we then going to look for a home for the traditions about Israel's earliest history? Very few scholars realized the problems involved when the discussion about the amphictyony began, although not all scholars – in this case almost exclusively German – supported the idea of the existence of such a league. One exception was Kurt Galling who as early as 1928 excluded the possibility of an Israelite unity including all twelve Israelite tribes. Never before David did the Judean parts form a unity with the central and north Palestinian tribes (Galling 1928, 70). Another exception was Sigmund Mowinckel, a Norwegian, who based his criticism of the theory on the evidence of the Song of Deborah, which only allows for a confederation of six tribes at the most (Mowinckel 1958).

Martin Noth put forward his hypothesis about the existence of the twelve-tribe league in 1929 following a lead that, according to oral scholarly tradition, goes back to Albrecht Alt, and from Alt back to Heinrich Ewald (Noth 1929). The intention was, as he emphasizes in the introduction, to trace the origins of the concept of the twelve tribes because, as he puts it, everybody speaks about the number twelve as fundamental to the biblical tradition but nobody seems to have been interested in tracing its historical background. Accordingly he entered into the, in his day, popular business of extracting historical information from every bit of text, including references to persons and places found in the books of Joshua and Judges. In light of the later accusations against Noth of being a nihilist, the accusation should probably be turned round against the scholar who accused him of nihilism – read Albright – and he should be presented as a maximalist squeezing the maximum of information out of legendary sources. Noth, as with other biblical scholars of his time, paid little attention to Eduard Meyer's denunciation of this praxis (which, on the other hand did not prevent Meyer from proceeding with speculations of the kind rejected by him) in this quotation:

> Besides, then and now I regard every endeavour to be futile and beyond dispute, which tries to answer these questions or even to translate the Israelite sagas into history according to the very much appreciated fashion. Generally, they deliberately skip – without considering how fantastic the enterprise is – half a millennium and deal with the narratives as suitable historical sources, irrespective of their recent age and after they have brushed them up by rationalizing means. They even

consider these sources to be the imperturbable basis of Israel's nationality and religion.[13]

In this way Noth was able to present a detailed history of the league of twelve tribes, including the changes in the membership of the league, the various places that might have acted as its centre, and the composition of the administration of the league, including as the most important part the place of the judges as the leaders of the league, although this part constituted an elaboration on the original hypothesis (Noth 1950b).[14] However, what made his day was when he drew parallels to leagues in other parts of the Mediterranean world, first and foremost ancient Greece with its various leagues of sacral unions centred around central sanctuaries, the most famous being the Delphic league, or *amphictyony*. The Delphian league thus gave its name to Noth's Israelite league, and also provided the model after which the Israelite league was formed. This was, to Noth, not just a remote analogy, but Noth reconstructed the institutions of the Israelite amphictyony following the set-up of the Greek one.

As already stated, although Noth's amphictyony became extremely popular and assumed a position within Old Testament scholarship which was quite unheard of – it belonged to the part of the curriculum in biblical studies which every student had to pass a test on as to whether or not the professor supported the hypothesis or rejected it – not all of his colleagues endorsed the hypothesis. A few dissident voices were raised. I have already mentioned two, Kurt Galling and Sigmund Mowinckel, but others may be included on the list such as Otto Eißfeldt (1887–1973), Roland de Vaux (1903–1971), Harry Orlinski (1908–1992), Siegfried Herrman (1926–1999), and Georg Fohrer (1915–2002), but although these scholars belonged to the upper cadre of biblical scholars in their own time, their voices were generally ignored.[15] As already mentioned, Sigmund Mowinckel was critical of the hypothesis, though only of the idea that it consisted of twelve tribes. Mowinckel's tribal league had a more limited membership (Mowinckel 1958).

---

[13] Translated from Meyer 1906, 50. Cf. also Engel 1979a, 77–8. Meyer was of course the author of the highly respected *Geschichte des Altertums* I–V (Meyer 1884–1902). My translation of the quotation was used the first time in Lemche 1984, 94.

[14] It should, in this connection, be remembered that Noth distinguished between the so-called minor judges and the war heroes of the Book of Judges, the minor judges only appearing in two lists, Judges 10,1–5 and 11,12, (7) 8–12. Only the minor judges counted as officials of the amphictyony.

[15] For reference: Eissfeldt 1935; de Vaux 1978, cf. above p. 73; Orlinski 1962; Herrmann 1962; Fohrer, 1966.

At the end of the 1960s and the beginning of the 1970s a more concerted criticism appeared, simply because of the weight of the paradigm which in the manner described by Thomas Kuhn became too heavy to be able to sustain itself: It explained everything, but remember that what explains everything explains nothing (cf. Kuhn 2012). It did not contribute to the stability of the hypothesis of the amphictyony when some elements were added to the model which made the theory a much easier target for criticism such as the overwhelming role which covenant theory played (more about this below). Noth's inclusion of the major judges within the context also contributed to its downfall, as it was all too obvious that he had overstretched his evidence.[16] Otto Bächli produced a survey of the discussion that led to the demise of the amphictyony without subscribing to all criticism (Bächli 1977). His main witnesses were this writer and A.D.H. Mayes, whose books on the amphictyony hypothesis appeared respectively in 1972 and 1974.[17] Mayes' work has its origins in a dissertation from Edinburgh from 1969, and mine from a prize thesis from the University of Copenhagen in 1968, but we were not the only critics in the field. It would be more accurate to say that we were only two among many. Two years after the appearance of Mayes' study, C.H.J. de Geus' study of the presuppositions of the amphictyony followed (de Geus 1976). De Geus expanded the discussion to include sociological matters and therefore pointed forward towards the discussion about the character of Israel's settlement which followed during the next years.

In principle it is the same list of topics under discussion which we meet in these three critical studies of the hypothesis about an Israelite amphictyony: a) the lists of twelve tribes, b) the central sanctuary, c) the judges, d) tribal borders, and e) tribal wars. To this list I added a discussion of the Greek "prototype" for the Israelite tribal league, the amphictyony, first and foremost the one in Delphi, which was quite useful and damaging because it became obvious that early Israel could not have borrowed the model from Greece, as the amphictyony hardly came into being before the eighth or seventh century BCE (Lemche 1976).

The similarity between the results presented by all three studies was remarkable: When it came to the tribal lists, it became obvious that it would be problematic to use the different versions of the twelve-tribe list for historical purposes. The role of the tribe of the priests of Levi created problems

---

[16] See also the criticism of the concept of the amphictyonic judges in Richter 1965.
[17] Lemche 1972; Mayes 1974. Mayes also wrote the chapter about "The Period of the Judges and the Rise of the Monarchy" in Hayes and Miller 1977, 285–331. My book represented the first chapter of my thesis from 1968 (Lemche 1968).

especially, because a very long discussion had made it more than doubtful that there once existed a secular tribe of the Levites which later specialized as a priestly tribe.[18] However, the presence of two or three versions of tribal lists in the Pentateuch had been mercilessly exploited to create a history of the development of Israelite tribal society. All of this was put aside. My conclusion, which did not differ very much from that of Mayes and de Geus, was that the differences between the various lists were caused by literary progress and were not the result of historical development. The membership of the original list changed as the narrative of the story of the Israelite society progressed and it became necessary to revise the list in order to exclude members no longer having a part to play in the story, and to add new members when necessary.

In all three studies the question of the central sanctuary got the lion's share of the discussion. In order to establish an amphictyony, one has to decide which sanctuary should play the role of the centre of the league, and here the competition between a series of candidates seemingly makes it unlikely that there was, in premonarchic Israel, ever a single place that was accepted by all members of the league as *their* holy place. Shechem seems to be the best but not the exclusive candidate. Several other places had been proposed such as Shilo, Bethel, Hebron, and Beersheba and more. Furthermore, when we move on to the status of the judge as the leader of the amphictyony a general doubt arises because no judge is ever said to have led all of the amphictyonic tribes against their enemies. We don't know much, if anything, about the minor judges, but it was my evaluation that the difference between the major and minor judges was mainly a literary one: The major judges had stories told about their activities, the minor judges had none. Moreover, the stories told about wars in the Period of the Judges involved the same array of enemies as Israel fought against after having become a state: Canaanites, Philistines, Moabites, and more. My conclusion was – or it moved towards – the realization that the history of the time of the judges was hardly based on historical records; it was a story which was manipulated to suit much later needs and realities and should be understood as such. It would not take a long time before the judges changed status from being historical persons to become ancient heroes of the kind found almost everywhere in narratives about people's past, whether in the Ancient Near East, Greece, or Middle and North European folklore in the way proposed by Hector Munro Chadwick more than a hundred years ago (Chadwick 1912).[19]

---

[18] A major contribution to this discussion was Cody 1969.

[19] The concept of an early heroic age preceding normal human history goes back to Hesiod (eight to seventh centuries BCE), who in his *Theogony* and especially *Works and Days*,

At the end of the day, the hypothesis about the existence of an Israelite amphictyony broke down not because of a "minimalistic" attitude from the scholars who opposed the idea but simply on the basis of a regular historical-critical approach to the subject. The theory collapsed because it could not be sustained in the light of the evidence found in biblical literature about the Period of the Judges. I made my final statement about the discussion of the tribal league in an article from 1983, and a couple of years later Georg Fohrer summed up the *status quaestionis* at the *IOSOT* meeting in Jerusalem in 1986 with the remark: "Dem ist nicht hinzufügen" (no reason to add more).[20]

Two questions remained, one a theological – or mainly theological – issue, the second a historical – or rather historic-traditional – issue. All issues and sub-issues had to do with the changing situation when it was no more possible to find a home for the traditions about early Israel in the heart of the amphictyony at the central sanctuary because such a centre had never existed. We will return to one of the major questions shortly, the place of the traditions of the Patriarchs involving at the same time their historicity. Another major issue which demanded a wider discussion had to do with the origins of the Israelites, because even before the demise of the hypothesis of the amphictyony new proposals to understand the historical development that led to ancient Israel were on the table. However, perhaps the most important issue was the very idea of the twelve tribes of Israel. It had, so-to-speak, lost its *Sitz im Leben* in the moment a consensus established itself that there never was an amphictyony of the kind designed by Noth and for that matter Bright, and this happened within an amazingly short period. If this concept of Israel's twelve tribes had any *historical* setting, it must have been at a time where Israel's different parts were united in an organization which embraced all of them. If this development did not belong to the pre-state period, it must have been after the formation of the Israelite state under David. Accordingly, it became mandatory that it was during this short span of years when David's, and after him his son Solomon's, kingdom existed that this idea of an ancient united Israel in the pre-state period came into being, invented in order to glue the dispersed membership of this state together. After Solomon, the kingdom broke down and the southern tribes were separated from the northern ones making a pan-Israelite ideology redundant.

---

includes such a period in his overview over the five stages of early human history. For a full-blown literary application of the concept we may turn to Livy (first century BCE) in his description of early Roman history. Moving back in time, we may include Gilgamesh among such heroes, as well as the Ugaritic heroes of Dan'il and Kirta. The phenomenon is ubiquitous.

[20] Lemche 1984b. For Fohrer's appraisal, cf. Fohrer 1988.

In this way the story about early Israel before the monarchy had changed status. The narrative was no longer about something that had existed once upon a time. On the contrary, what could be deduced from the stories about life in Palestine said to be inhabited by the tribes of Israel showed a political system harassed by external as well as internal enemies. There was no evidence that all of the Israelite tribes ever acted in unison. The only case could have been the coalition against Hazor which is the subject of Judges 4 and in a poetic form also Judges 5, in the "Song of Deborah", but not even on this occasion did all tribes of Israel show up; maybe the conflict only involved the Galilean tribes.[21] The story in Judges is about a kind of "winner takes all", and the conclusion to the story about the misdeed in Gibeah: "There was no king in Israel; everyone did what he found best", is in no way in conflict with the rest of the Book of Judges; it rather functions as the motto for everything described about this part of Israel's history.[22]

The realization that there never was an early Israelite unity which embraced all or most of the Israelite tribes has other consequences. Some of them should be a consolation to scholars who have had problems with elements of the earliest history, especially the Exodus from Egypt, and the migrations in the desert including the covenant at Sinai. Above I referred to Reimarus' two-hundred-and-fifty-year-old criticism of the exodus tradition, claiming it to be impossible to align this event as described in the Old Testament with anything historically possible. His famous argument was that with the number of Israelites leaving Egypt – about six hundred thousand men plus their families, probably three million persons in all (with an average family size of about five persons) – the last Israelites would not have left Egypt before the first were already in the Land of Canaan, the distance between Palestine and Egypt taken into consideration (in praxis not much more than 150 miles).[23] The changing perspective on how Israelite unity came

---

[21] The song of Deborah has traditionally been considered perhaps the oldest piece of literature in the Old Testament often dated to the Period of the Judges – today to the pre monarchical period. As such it is often considered contemporary with the events of the song, although as Giovanni Garbini argues, it is a kind of dating that would put the *Iliad* in c. 1184 BCE and the *Song of Roland* 778 CE, cf. Garbini 1978. Garbini dates the song to the eleventh to tenth century BCE and is highly skeptical as to its relevance as a historical source.

[22] As to Judges 19–21, I am inclined to refer to my old discussion in Lemche 1972, 94–9, discussing the various tradition-historical and historical problems relating to these chapters. The most original analysis of the chapters is without doubt Liverani 1979, a kind of preparation for his later analyses of biblical historiography in his *Oltre la Bibbia* 2003.

[23] The author of the story had no idea about the problem of moving large numbers of people. When Napoleon attacked Russia in 1812, it took him more than a week to move his

about – not before the settlement in Canaan – makes it unnecessary or rather redundant even to consider the possibility of a large scale emigration out of Egypt. If scholars still wish to keep to the notion of such an exodus, they can follow the proposal of several scholars of previous generations who argued that not all of Israel was in Egypt; as a matter of fact there only was an "exodus-group" which, under the command of Moses, escaped from Egypt and met its God, Yahweh, somewhere on the Peninsula at a place called Sinai, either in the north at Kadesh Barnea or in the south at Mt. Sinai.[24] It had been a problem to many scholars (and to be honest it still is) that no Egyptian source relates anything like an exodus of a major group. After all, an escape of a population group counting millions would hardly go unnoticed even by partisan Egyptian chroniclers.[25] Small-scale migrations between the desert (Sinai, Libya, and more places) and the sown land (Egypt) happened all the time, but Egyptian tradition only knew of one major migration out of Egypt, the Hyksos who, however, did not escape from Egypt but were thrown out of Egypt c. 1550 BCE, at least according to the Egyptian tradition.[26]

---

army of c. 600,000 men across the border even though he started from several different bases. As everywhere in the Old Testament when great numbers come up, there is absolutely no sense displayed of the physical realities. Of course this is no better in classical sources, e.g., when Herodotus calculates the size of Xerxes army which attacked Greece as being as big as 2,500,000 soldiers (*Histories VII*, 186). Armchair generals are in abundance among civilian historians who never care about logistics (and probably have no idea what it is about).

[24] The present article about the Exodus in Wikipedia provides an up-to-date and extensive analysis of the Exodus legend, describing the current three opinions among biblical scholars which range from a total dismissal of the Exodus tradition as historical via the mediate position mentioned here that only a minor group was involved to the maximalist view that everything told here is historical. The bibliography presented is also most convincing. https://en.wikipedia.org/wiki/The_Exodus (16 March 2021).

[25] An "easy reader" to the problem of the Exodus can be found in Frerichs and Lesko 1997. The general consensus which also includes William G. Dever, is that such an Exodus never happened, although the presence of a small Moses-group is deemed possible. See also Dever 2003, 7–22 for a more detailed analysis of the question.

[26] This is not the place to take up the vexed problem of the Hyksos, especially not because so much new evidence has been extracted from excavations in the Delta of the Nile over the last generation or two. It is thus clear that the post-Hyksos Egyptian testimonies are highly tendentious and do not reflect the real status of the Hyksos. Most likely the biblical historiographers took as their departure the version of the expulsion of the Hyksos from Egypt from Manetho (third century BCE) or from a similar source (Manetho was certainly not the first to tell the story about the expulsion of the Hyksos), and linked this version to the story of the Exodus in a similar way to how Josephus handled the tradition (*Contra Apion*, I, 127–150). In this way the Hellenized Egyptian version of the "Exodus" belongs to the same period as the *Exagōgē* of Ezekiel the Tragedian, who wrote his play on

Another consequence of the lack of unity between Israelite tribes before the settlement is the redundancy of the conquest theory of scholars who believed in a violent and bloody Israelite conquest of the future homeland. The view of the immigration entertained by most – noticeably by Albright and his students – becomes impossible the moment we have to postpone any idea of a unified Israel to a period coming after the time of the judges. I shall return to the discussion about the conquest shortly, but it simply makes no sense to imagine a unified bloodthirsty Israel conquering Canaanite cities, butchering their inhabitants, and celebrating their victory at Shechem as it is related in the Book of Joshua chapter 24, after which everybody left "for his tent", and starting fighting his Israelite neighbours incessantly until the appearance of the Israelite kingdom.

The remaining theological issue has to do with covenant theology which dominates large parts of the narratives in the Pentateuch, but certainly also has a role to play in other parts of biblical literature. The old paradigm of Albright demanded that the biblical story about the meeting between Moses and Yahweh at Sinai and later between Israel led by Moses and Yahweh in the same place was essentially true in the historical meaning.[27] According to this view the Yahweh religion became the spiritual foundation of the future Israelite society that not only conquered the Promised Land but also established mono-Yahwism as the only permitted form of religion within its border. This remained the backbone of the self-perception of the Israelites right down to the Babylonian exile and beyond. Covenant theology had for a long time been a dominant issue and its theological implications had been enormous as everybody who grew up in its shadow without doubt remembers.[28] And it is certainly a dominant feature in Old Testament Scripture, in the historical literature from Genesis to 2 Kings, and among the prophets. The question was simply: How old is this idea of a covenant of the kind found in the Old Testament? If it could be linked to an event like the revelation at Sinai as an integral part of it, it would lose its historical home because other analyses had demonstrated that such traditions belong to an imagined past by a much later

---

the Exodus in Alexandria most likely in the third century BCE. The fragments of Ezekiel's tragedy are translated by R.G. Robertson in Charlesworth 1985, 803–20. As to Hyksos as migrants from Asia in Egyptian wall paintings, see the painting of the group of immigrants (traders?) from Asia led by the Hyksos Abisha in Khnumhotep II's grave from Beni Hassan from c. 1900 BCE. (https://en.wikipedia.org/wiki/Khnumhotep_II#/media/File:Procession_of_the_Aamu,_Tomb_of_Khnumhotep_II_(composite).jpg)).

[27] As expounded by Albright 1940, 249–72.

[28] Thus the theme of covenant totally dominated the major theology of the Old Testament by Walther Eichrodt (Eichrodt 1962–64).

Israelite society.²⁹ As a matter of fact, it was this exclusivity of the covenant religion of ancient Israel which became suspect, not least because of the debate about the date of biblical historiography which broke out in earnest at the end of the 1960s (more about this below). And then we are counting on the huge progress in our knowledge of the common religion in Palestine in the Iron Age which makes the biblical imagery of Israelite religion suspect if not impossible.³⁰

The fate of George E. Mendenhall's attempt to find external examples of the covenant theology among Hittite vassal treaties of the Late Bronze Age illustrates this point. Mendenhall, himself a member of the Albright school, proposed in 1954 in total accordance with the Albright approach to see these Hittite treatises as parallels to the Sinai covenant (Mendenhall 1964). In Mendenhall's view, the Hittite treaties between the king of Ḫatti and his vassals in Asia Minor and in Syria were not only contemporary with the supposed time of the Sinai covenant, but also exhibited the same forms and structure. It was for this reason likely that the Sinai covenant followed the muster found in a system of treaties peculiar to the time when Israel according to the Albright school came into being and found a lasting expression of its religion.³¹

---

²⁹ Gerhard von Rad saw this problem already in von Rad 1938. The Sinai tradition is not part of the so-called *little historical credo* as found in Deuteronomy 26: 5–9, according to von Rad and following him Leonhard Rost (Rost 1956) the earliest expression of Israel's faith.

³⁰ Cf. Lemche 1991b, arguing that any study of the religion of Israel must follow the lines of the reconstruction of its history, or the religion would miss its *Sitz im Leben*. Since then a comprehensive number of studies have appeared presenting a quite different view of Israelite religion from the one found in older studies, including the minutes of the conference in Bern in 1993 in Dietrich and Klopfenstein 1994. Also Albertz 1992, should be seen in this light (with my reservations *in mente* as expressed in Lemche 1998b, 145–48). Albertz and Schmitt 2012, should definitely also be included here, as also the discussion about Yahweh's Asherah, a classic example of how a couple of inscriptions have forced a revision on accepted ideas of the religion of Israel. Cf. on Asherah Olyan 1988; Wiggins 1993; Binger 1997; Merlo 1998; Dever 2005. For an edition and commentary of these texts cf. Renz 1995: Ḥirbet el-Qom No. 1, pp. 202–11; Kuntillet Ajrud, Pithos 1–2, pp. 59–64.

³¹ It is, however, surprising that Mendenhall, in his article, never cites the treaties directly from either their Akkadian or Hittite originals, easily available in his time. The treaties in Akkadian were published (Akkadian text and translation) by Ernst Friedrich Weidner (Weidner 1923), and the treaties in the Hittite language by Johannes Friedrich (Friedrich 1926–1930). Mendenhall had no problem with German and thus quotes Korošec 1931, for its time an excellent analysis of the texts. Today the treaties are easily found in an English translation: Beckman 1999.

Over the next couple of decades the concept of covenant became a kind of "catch word" in Old Testament studies. Everything was about covenant. Thus the Book of Deuteronomy was simply formed according to the pattern of the treaties or displayed several features in common with the Assyrian treaties.[32] Then scholars realized that the Hittite parallels introduced by Mendenhall were in no way exclusive. Assyrian treaties from Neo-Assyrian times provide just as relevant if not more relevant parallels to the Israelite covenant.[33] The exclusivity of the Hittite treaties had vanished. The final blow to Mendenhall's proposal was delivered by Lothar Perlitt, who in 1969 closed the discussion by pointing out that the Israelite concept was more of a Deuteronomic invention than having ancient roots (Perlitt 1969). Since then not many biblical scholars have spoken about the covenant except within the framework of biblical theology. As a historical phenomenon the old Israelite covenant has been a dead issue for almost fifty years.

Summing up so far

Only conservative evangelicals would today subscribe to the version of early Israel presented by biblical historiography. It has been shown how impossible it is to keep the narratives about Israel's sojourn in Egypt, of the Exodus, of the covenant at Sinai, and of the conquest as historical remembrances. All of these are invented stories of a later time. German biblical scholars promoting tradition history had already, a long time before it was realized among North American scholars, pointed to the fact that such traditions belong to the realm of memory, which in a substantial part of biblical scholarship in the twentieth century was believed to have had its home in the religious centre of the tribal league, the amphictyony, in the Period of the Judges. The amphictyony was not itself a part of the memory; it was an institution with a historical base, a real fact belonging to Israel's early existence in Palestine. However, the Old Testament did not say anything conclusive about its existence. As a matter of fact the Old Testament did not say anything at all about such an institution. For this reason the process of breaking down the theory of such a tribal league was not opposed by conservative evangelical scholars or by the members of the Albright school. To the conservative evangelicals, it was

---

[32] Cf. especially, McCarthy 1963, and on the Assyrian reminiscences in the Book of Deuteronomy, Weinfeld 1972.

[33] The Assyrian treaties are easily accessible in transliteration and translation thanks to Simo Parpola and Kazuko Watanabe (Parpola and Watanabe 1988). Cf. also Richard Jude Thompson 2013.

unproblematic simply because the hypothesis of the amphictyony belonged to the scholarly world; it was not part of the biblical picture of early Israel. These scholars began to understand, too late, the consequences of the disappearance of the amphictyony from history and only then did they react strongly against the consequences. It was too late because other scholars had already drawn the carpet away under the very ideas which they consider decisive for the faith of ancient Israel and consequently for every later tradition, whether Jewish, or Christian. But was this caused by nihilism? Certainly not; it was very much a consequence of traditional historical-critical scholarship which by analyzing the biblical text had to give up a much beloved concept of Israelite unity that had become the bearer of the peak points in Israelite earliest history. When scholars of the period removed the amphictyony from history, none of us had any idea about the consequences. That was soon to change.

The Patriarchs

If we remember John Bright's attitude to the historical problem of the Patriarchs, it was probably the best example of Diebner's description of biblical scholarship already quoted a couple of times, that although we know nothing, it is a fact – because it is a fact. Bright travelled around in the world of the ancient Near East in the second millennium BCE, as he understood it, to find a place for the Patriarchs. His problem was not that he didn't find any place for them, but that he found far too many places where they would fit in. Reading his chapter on the patriarchs we can easily understand his bewilderment. He had to stay with the traditions about Abraham, Isaac, and Jacob, because his background (Albright) demanded it, but he was definitely not feeling good about it. Bright was, in many ways, a regular historian, and it is very unlikely that he should not have understood the problems involved when it came to the historicity of Israel's apical ancestors. However, even in the posthumous fourth edition of his history, he seems mostly ready to repeat what he wrote as early as the first edition (Bright 2000, 67–104).[34] The editor of the fourth edition, William P. Brown, presents a different view on Bright's history: It is

---

[34] The lack of development in Bright's *A History*, was already duly noted and censured in Gösta W. Ahlström's review of the second edition (Ahlström 1975). In his preface to the fourth edition of Bright's *A History*, William P. Brown presents the changes that occurred from the first to the third edition (the last revision, the fourth edition was published after Bright's death) but also stresses the continuity. In the appendix, Brown presents a sweeping view of the developments in the idea of Israelite history since the third edition, which more or less nullifies the position of the very book which he had introduced in the preface.

not at all a history in the usual sense of the word; it is a theological history, a kind of restatement of the theological meaning of what the Old Testament has to tell its readers. Brown might very well be right, and if this is the case we should not consider Bright's *A History* a history of Israel as such, but a history of Israel's faith as related by the Old Testament. In this way the real competitor to Bright's history is not Noth's *Geschichte* but Gerhard von Rad's *Theologie des Alten Testaments* which appeared almost simultaneously with Bright's history (von Rad 1957–60).[35] The main concept of von Rad's theology is *Heilsgeschichte*, "salvation history", the story of how God saved his people, although as argued by Franz Hesse the history of Israel is more of a *Unheilsgeschichte*, a history with a bad end (Hesse 1971).[36]

It has often been stressed that Bright distanced himself from Noth's tradition-historical approach to the history of Israel, and this is seemingly true; but as shown above it was probably only paying lip-service to his "father" the great Albright. In practice he followed Noth almost to the end, and the only real difference was that Bright accepted as history what Noth considered tradition. On the other hand, reviewing Albright's approach to the study of the Patriarchs, Albright is following exactly the same "methodology" as Bright, exemplified in his *From the Stone Age to Christianity*, where he spent about two hundred pages before arriving at the entrance to the Kingdom of God, ancient Israel.[37] The Patriarchs first turn up several pages later, and then in very much the same manner as in Bright's history, introduced by another overview of the ancient Near East. Sometime this emphasis on the ancient Near East, before getting to the subject, becomes almost parodic, as in one of Albright's more famous articles about Abraham as a donkey-merchant at the beginning of the second millennium BCE (Albright 1961). This article opens with an extended and very technical discussion of the archaeology of the Negev and Sinai, dating from the beginning of the second millennium, followed by a pretty long review of donkey-caravans and -trade in the same period, moving from Anatolia via Elam in Iran to Egypt to, where exactly? Finally he presents his thesis of Abraham as a caravaneer. The argumentation is hopelessly naïve and circular; it is as if Albright was simply afraid of tackling the biblical evidence and tried to talk it away by this long series of more or less immaterial facts, seemingly aiming at the obscuring of history with

---

[35] ET: von Rad 1975. We should, in this connection, not forget the role of the covenant as the ruling concept in Walther Eichrodt (1962–4; ET: Eichrodt 1961).

[36] On this perspective cf. Lemche 2008, 347–48. My point in dealing with Old Testament "theologies" of the twentieth century is that they were not real *theologies* but tradition history, if not *Ideengeschichte*, Cf. Lemche 2008, pp. 255–392.

[37] Albright 1940, 200: "When Israel was a Child".

facts, trying to overwhelm his readers with all kinds of information whether relevant or irrelevant and hoping that they will give up trying to make sense of all the material which he has presented to them and just accept what Albright is telling them.

Bright following the lead of his master and focused on the second millennium BCE. His timeframe was the period of the great archaeological discoveries from Mari on the Euphrates and Nuzi close to the Tigris. The Mari excavations, which began after the discovery of ancient Mari at Tell Hariri in 1933, close to the present Syrian–Iraqi border, had unearthed a large archive of more than twenty thousand cuneiform tablets mostly if not exclusively of the royal administration of the state dating from the eighteenth century BCE.[38] The Nuzi tablets, more than five thousand in number, were a couple of hundred years later and mostly of a different kind, being in large part private legal texts of various kinds and not necessarily from a public source.[39]

The texts from Mari was used as *prima facie* evidence of the image of the Patriarchs as pastoralists, whereas the Nuzi archive was searched for information about family habits among the Patriarchs, which they were supposed to share with the inhabitants of Nuzi. Furthermore, the Mari letters were scanned for information about the history of the Amorites, in the Bible a people belonging to the predecessors of Israel in Palestine. The presence of the Canaanites and Amorites in the Old Testament were, for many years, understood to illustrate historical conflict between the original inhabitants – the Canaanites – and the newly arrived immigrants – the Amorites.[40] Bright, like Albright, belonged among those who viewed the Amorite migration from "the desert" to Palestine as a "proof" of the existence of the Patriarchs and their migration from Upper Mesopotamia as reflected in the movement of Amorite herdsmen towards the West, to Syria and Palestine.

Both Bright and Albright found evidence in Nuzi – not far removed from the Mesopotamian home of the Patriarchs in Harran in northern Mesopotamia – of the lifestyle of the Patriarchs, and Albright devoted much energy to

---

[38] So far more than three thousand texts have been published, in cuneiform, and translations. A convenient translation of almost thirteen hundred of these texts (basically the edition *Archives royales de Mari*), is available in Durand 1998–2002. In English the best selection is Heimpel 2003. Studies on the civilization of Mari: Margueron 2014.

[39] No similarly easy-to-find and comprehensive publication of the Nuzi archives exists. Rather a bewildering arrangement of volumes have appeared in very different contexts. See, however, now the publication of many of the relevant texts in this connection (transliteration and translation) by Maynard Paul Maidman (Maidman 2010). For an overview of the Nuzi civilization and an evaluation of the status of publications see Maidman 1995.

[40] Symptomatically as presented by Kenyon 1966.

finding analogues between Nuzi domestic slave contracts and biblical passages such as the "adoption" of Mesheq from Damascus, although the whole sequence where this Mesheq is found (Gen. 15:2) is entirely enigmatic.[41] With these and other similar observations they found the Patriarchs securely placed sometime in the second millennium, and preferably in the Middle Bronze Age in the first half of the millennium.

Albright, however, moved away from this position when he, late in his career, chose to introduce the phenomenon of the *ḫabīru* as a serious parallel to the Patriarchs, or rather he saw Abraham as a *ḫabīru* and pretended that *ḫabīru* should be translated as "donkey-man. Donkey driver, huckster, caravanner" (Albright 1963, 5).[42] The manner in which the argumentation develops is revealing. Albright opens with a description of southern Palestine at the beginning of the second millennium BCE, and continues to the settlements in the hill land which are described as thinly spread out, and finally he takes notice of missing references in the patriarchal narratives to the coastal plain of Palestine. Then focus changes to Egypt as the power which controlled the southwestern Levant with a general reference to excavations at Gezer, Megiddo, Byblos, Qatna and Ugarit. Next in the argument is the relative free trade in this period illustrated by the Beni Hassan wall painting mentioned above, and finally he gets to the *ḫabīru* as tradesmen. In this connection it has to be added that not one point in his argumentation can stand closer scrutiny. The worst part is probably that he needs an empty central Palestine in order to settle Abraham and his family here, while he, in the same moment, requires Egyptian hegemony to secure *ḫabīru* donkey caravanners to travel freely in all of the Ancient Near East. These two parts don't go together: On one hand he operates with an empty area without much settlement, on the other with an Egyptian control, which makes travels possible. Travelling would be between centres, mostly built-up ones. If Albright wants Abraham to be a tradesman, he also needs places where Abraham can trade. We may say that

---

[41] רַגְעִילָא קַשְׁמַד אוּה לְתִיב קֶעַמ־רָבוּ. Litt. "Eliezer Damascus he (is) my house and the son of Mesheq". Whatever translation that is offered to us, in it will be more speculation about the meaning of the text than a "neutral" translation. The text is basically untranslatable. For a discussion, Pitard 1987, 9n in connection with a general debate on the name of Damascus. True to his ability to "think outside of the box" the late Giovanni Garbini has some very interesting proposals for the interpretation linking Gen 15:2 with Hellenistic-Roman information, "Abraham and Damascus", in Garbini 2003a, 22-36. Garbini sees in this enigmatic passage a residue also found in other Hellenistic Jewish writings connecting Abraham physically to Damascus.

[42] The technical background for this is the article from 1961 on "Abram the Hebrew" (Albright 1961).

the archaeological explorations in Palestine and Syria had not yet provided enough evidence either to verify or to falsify Albright's case. It is still a problem not solved. Worse, of course is his interpretation of the *ḫabīru*. In this case the issue of the *ḫabīru* had (almost) been solved and the results published in 1954 in a volume edited by Jean Bottéro with a summing-up which is anonymous but nevertheless attributed to no less than Benno Landsberger (1890–1968), one of the foremost if not the foremost Assyriologists of the mid twentieth century (Bottéro 1954).

The *ḫabīru* were not donkey tradesmen. They were refugees. They didn't represent any ethnic unit, not even a sociological unit. Moreover, they appear in documents from all over the Ancient Near East in the second millennium BCE, and from all periods of this millennium. If an Israelite was a *ḫabīru*, it was not because of his ethnic affiliation but because he had fled from his own society and found refuge in another.[43] Albright found support for his thesis in the way Abraham is described in the story of his battle against the four great kings in Gen. 14:13, as "Abram the Hebrew" living at Mamre close to Hebron. Albright supported his interpretation by representing the fairy tale of Genesis 14 as very old. However, most scholars before and since he published his idea about Abraham the Hebrew donkey caravanner consider it to be quite recent.[44] Summing up: this example of Albright's scholarship shows how irresponsibly he could use material from the Ancient Near East to help his case if he deemed it necessary. We therefore have to ask: How about the other building blocks in his, and for that matter Bright's, defence of the historicity of the Patriarchs? Do we find the same kind of manipulation of evidence there?

It is one of the ironies of history that almost simultaneously two decisive studies appeared absolutely independently of each other and both challenging Albright's and Bright's view of the Patriarchs, the one by Thomas L. Thompson (Thompson 1974), the second by John Van Seters (Van Seters 1975). The approach of the two scholars was on the one hand very similar, and on the other very dissimilar. Thompson, who wrote his book in Tübingen, Germany, partly under the supervision of Kurt Galling, concentrated on the evidence from the Ancient Near East, and included discussion of two major issues: first the Amorites and second the evidence from the Nuzi texts. In between he made short process of Albright's caravanning Abraham, and of Albright's fabulations about the historicity of the events of Genesis 14, and Abraham's

---

[43] On the *ḫabīru*, cf. Lemche 1992a, 95 and 106–112. For a penetrating article from the time when Albright published his "research", cf. Liverani 1965.

[44] It is probably worth noting that on Genesis 14 and history a very useful discussion can be found in Thompson 1974, 187–95. John Emerton published a convenient survey of opinions about this chapter, in Emerton 1971.

battle against the four great kings. Van Seters opened with a section on the evidence from the Ancient Near East, less detailed than Thompson's but including most of the same issues and reaching similar results. However, Van Seters' second part opened up following his lifelong settlement with the classic documentary hypothesis, not by denying its value but by changing its basic content in a fundamental way. We will return to the issue of dating biblical texts in the next chapter.

In essence Albright, and following him Bright, proposed to link the migrations of Abraham to the movements of the Amorites at the end of the third millennium BCE and in the first part of the second millennium BCE. It seems to be a reasonable assumption that if Abraham was a historical person and moved around as an example of a nomadic lifestyle, he could have been a part of this movement – if he was a historical person and if there was such a migration of Amorites. The problem is that there was hardly anything like an Amorite migration with its direction towards the west; Amorite, or in Akkadian *Amurru*, means "westerner", meaning simply a person coming from the west and travelling towards the east and the south-east. Thus Amorites did not migrate from Ur in Chaldea, they migrated to Ur which was not in Chaldea before, at the earliest, the beginning of the first millennium BCE and arrived pretty early here as shown many years ago by Giorgio Buccellati (Buccellati 1966).[45] Principally, when we are talking about "Amorites", we are first and foremost indicating persons speaking North-West Semitic dialects in contrast to East Semitic (Akkadian) or South Semitic (Arabic and various old Arabic dialects) speaking populations. Furthermore, such Amorite speaking persons were present in Syria and Palestine long before they turned up in Mesopotamia where they, around 2000 BCE, founded a number of city-states, being ruled by West-Semitic speaking dynasties, the best known being Hammurabi's dynasty in Babylon, which was in charge in central Mesopotamia in the Old Babylonian period (roughly 1894–1595 BCE). These city-states immediately began a never-ending series of fights for control between them, a process that gradually molding the area into one or two major political structures. This was the case when Hammurabi (c. 1810–1750 BCE) put an end to the Kingdom of Mari, his former ally.

---

[45] The problem of anachronisms of which the patriarchal narratives abound, is another matter. The old explanation was that such anachronisms owed their presence to "updates" of the patriarchal narratives at a later date. This explanation is sometimes found repeated even in recent literature, but generally it is accepted that such "anachronisms" are not "updates" from a later stage of text editing; it dates the text, meaning that if Abraham travelled from Ur when the Chaldeans ruled the city, then there were Chaldeans around when the story of his travels was put into writing.

Thompson's analysis of the material about the Amorites involves historical issues as well as linguistic ones. The linguistic material concerning Palestine in the "patriarchal age" is analyzed, as are the relations between Egypt and the West Semitic speaking people, and the nomadic character of the so-called Intermediate Bronze Age, or EB IV/MB I is discussed. In short, every single angle used to analyze the Amorite question by scholars of the Ancient Near East is taken into consideration, and the lack of any basis for a theory of Abraham as belonging to an Amorite movement of people at that time made clear. It is an analysis executed by a person well acquainted with the study of the ancient Near East; it is, or was in its time, a state-of-the-art discussion putting together a puzzle of issues which we normally talk about when we refer to the Amorites. Thompson's conclusions, in relation to the issue of the Amorites, were very much the same as found in Van Seters' (similar but more simplified) discussion, and were devastating for any support of a historical Patriarchal Age in the first part of the second millennium BCE. Of course much more is known today about the question of the Amorites, but scholars of the Ancient Near East have continued in the track where we were also to find Thompson.[46]

The comprehensive study which follows of the texts from Nuzi, in which Albright wanted to find parallels to the life and customs of the Patriarchs, is more directly linked to family matters in the Abraham story in the Old Testament. The Nuzi texts are first and foremost considerably more recent and do not belong to the so-called "period of the Amorites" – they are separated by some two or three hundred years. Thompson finds the emphasis on the Nuzi evidence groundless. The Nuzi examples are not exclusive and the same can be said about the examples of the family life of the Patriarchs. Patriarchal customs are similar to customs found in other parts of the Old Testament, and the same can be said about the Nuzi examples; they are not exclusive for the time and place in which the customs mentioned belonged. Moreover, when Albright introduced the Nuzi evidence into the discussion, he did not tell his readership that Nuzi civilization was not Amorite, not even a Semitic speaking society: It was basically Hurritic, sharing a non-Semitic language spoken by Hurrians, whose presence in Northern Syria and Upper Mesopotamia in the second millennium BCE expanded as far west as Alalaḫ and Ugarit and

---

[46] For an overview, Whiting 1995, and Liverani 2014, 175–81. For a recent study showing the complexity of the issue, cf. Burke 2020.

whose presence is reflected in the biblical mentions of the Horites.[47] In his overview of Nuzi civilization, Maynard Paul Maidman simply writes:

> Much has been written (some of it surprisingly recently) on the close resemblance of Nuzi to the society of Israel's patriarchs as described in the book of Genesis. There is no meaningful resemblance. Much has also been written about Israelite origins in a Nuzi-like milieu. There are no such origins. As is increasingly acknowledged, all such "scholarly" writings are worthless for students of Nuzi and Israel alike (Maidman 1995, 947).

Tempted to once more use Georg Fohrer's comment on this writers' final article on the amphictyony in the Period of the Judges (see above), I would add: There is no more to say.

There is no reason to say more about the status of patriarchal studies, although both Thompson's and Van Seters' volumes were followed by a review of the oriental and biblical evidence by William G. Dever (Dever 1977). Dever, who at the time of writing knew both Thompson's and Van Seters' contributions, simply tried to present a rationalistic paraphrase of his honored "grandfather" William Foxwell Albright, and is just as much at odds with Near Eastern studies as was his revered mentor. Dever simply ended up defending what cannot be defended.

In or outside of Palestine: Israel's Origins

During the 1986 IOSOT meeting in Jerusalem I was invited to the home of the Nestor of Israeli biblical scholarship, the former vice chancellor of the Hebrew University, Benjamin Mazar. It turned out that Benjamin Mazar wanted to discuss George E. Mendenhall's ideas of the origin of the Israelites, and his question was: Did Mendenhall sacrifice the history of early Israel in order to rescue its religion? It was a long and enjoyable afternoon because the two of us ended up agreeing on the basic issues: George E. Mendenhall (1916–2016), who grew up within the Albright family, definitely broke with the historical part of Albright's – and Bright's – reconstruction of Israelite

---

[47] In general on the Hurrians, cf. Gernot 1982. Otherwise the main reference is to the series *Studies on the Civilization and Culture of Nuzi and the Hurrians*. On Alalaḫ and the Hurrians, cf. the comprehensive study by Eva von Dassow, *State and Society in the Late Bronze Age: Alalaḫ under the Mitanni Empire* (von Dassow 2008).

origins while, on the other hand, he supported the idea of Yahwism as formulated in the covenant – remember Mendenhall's idea of the similarity between the Sinai covenant and Hittite vassal treaties – dictated to the few members of the Moses group who escaped from Egypt. Basically, early Israel came into being as a revolutionary movement founded on the revolutionary message of early covenantal Yahwism, a movement that arose among dissatisfied impoverished Canaanites living in a highly stratified but dysfunctional system of feudal-like city-states. In short, the earliest Israelites did not arrive in Palestine from neighbouring countries, they were refugees within their own country; they were *ḫabīru*. True to his former habit of publishing his most important contributions in a semi-popular forum, his far-reaching thesis on Israelite origins was published in 1962 in *The Biblical Archaeologist*, a journal founded by George E. Wright (Mendenhall 1962). As already mentioned, these *ḫabīru* were foreigners wherever they appeared in ancient documents; definitely a problem for societies that at the end of the Bronze Age around 1200 BCE had been known for many hundreds of years but not believed to have peaked before the end of the Late Bronze Age, when Bronze Age civilization became more and more stressed because of an environmental crisis caused by draught as well as a plague which is best known from Hittite documents because its most prominent victim was the Hittite warrior king Šuppiluliumaš I (reigned c. 1350–1322 BCE [48]). The pre-condition for relating the problem of the *ḫabīru* to the origins of the Israelites is the identification of the two terms, on one side *ḫabīru* and on the other *Hebrew*.

From a philological point of view, this equation is rather unproblematic and today disputed by very few.[49] From an historical perspective, it is a problem that Hebrew in the Old Testament is an ethnic term, if not a national one, whereas *ḫabīru* is a sociological term without any primary ethnic meaning, although it is obvious that the way *Hebrew* is used in the Old Testament the term somehow carries both meanings; the sociological as well as the ethnic

---

[48] Using the data in Bryce 2005, xv.
[49] Akkadian *ḫ* used as a transliteration of Hebrew ע. The Cuneiform writing originating among the Sumerians has problems transliterating Semitic laryngals. The b/p equation is common. The equation is disputed by Anson F. Rainey, e.g., in Rainey 2008, 51–55. Rainey's distancing of himself from the equation is definitely to do with his view of Israelite origins which seems rather close to that of Albright and/or Alt. They were Sutu nomads (same article). He didn't have the same problems when *ḫabīru* was understood as an ethnic term which had been usual among the early members of the Albright family. Cf. thus Speiser 1931–2. It has to be added that Speiser later revised his view on the *ḫabīru*, cf. Speiser 1964, 102–3.

one.⁵⁰ Whenever "Hebrew" is used in the Old Testament it is not about normal Israelites living their daily life in their villages, it is about Israelites in special circumstances, such as living as refugees in Egypt (the story of Joseph and Israel in Egypt in Genesis and Exodus) or as brigands in their own land (Books of Samuel). The social meaning of the term is still preserved although all persons considered "Hebrews" in the Old Testament are at the same time Israelites.⁵¹

As mentioned above, the *ḫabīru* appear everywhere in the Ancient Near East for most of the second millennium BCE, and in the most various connections. They are not easily classified as belonging only to one stratum of society, being represented by unskilled labourers, and mercenaries, but also a future king lived among them, Idrimi of Alalaḫ (late fifteenth century BCE), who, in his own inscription, tells about his seven-year-long stay among the *ḫabīru* (Smith 1949). The Amarna Letters from Syria and Palestine from the mid–late fourteenth century BCE contribute in this connection most important references to the *ḫabīru* and provides the textual material for Mendenhall's hypothesis of a Hebrew revolution as the background of Israel's emergence in Palestine.⁵² In several texts from Palestine and Syria the *ḫabīru*, often written SA.GAZ^(meš) or simply GAZ^(meš) – SA.GAZ being a pseudo-Sumerogram for Akkadian *šagāšu* "murderer" – appear as an unruly element; "enemies of Pharaoh" in the words of the local rulers of the small cities of Palestine and Syria.

Now Mendenhall went further and identified these unruly elements with the ancestors of Israel, and understood the many references to their activities as evidence of a reaction against Canaanite rulers of the country which in the late fourteenth century BCE was still spontaneous and not guided by mutual agreements between the *ḫabīru*, although sometimes it seemed that local politicians made good use of their presence in their internecine fights against neighbours. Not every *ḫabīru* was a *ḫabīru*. Sometimes the word was

---

⁵⁰ Cf. Lemche 1979, and independently Na'aman 1986.

⁵¹ This also applies to the mentioning of the Hebrew slave in Exod 21:1–6, although this is based on the context. Cf. Lemche 1975.

⁵² These letters were "discovered" in the bazaar of Cairo in c. 1887 after being found by Egyptian local treasure hunters in the ruins of the capital of Pharaoh Akhenaten (1353–1336 BCE), and represents the foreign correspondence of this Pharaoh and his father Amenhotep III (1391–1353 BCE). The cuneiform editions of these texts are, to put it mildly, complicated, the main parts of the letters being divided between three museums, in Cairo, London and Berlin, plus more letters scattered around in other museums over the world. The standard edition of the transliterations and translations is Knudtzon 1907/1915. A recent complete edition was provided by Anson F. Rainey, with the help of Zipora Cochavi-Rainey and William Schnidewind: Rainey 2015. Complete Translations: Knudtzon 1907/1915, Moran 1992, and Liverani 1998–1999.

used simply in a derogatory fashion about any person who might be considered (by his colleagues) an opponent to Egyptian rule.[53] However, a hundred years later, they found their spiritual guidance in the Moses group which arrived from Egypt and Sinai and had a new message to preach to the believers, the faith in Yahweh, and inspired by this new faith they simply "conquered" Canaan, took over control from the corrupt local rulers and their by now weakened Egyptian overlords.

Mendenhall's new proposal was so "revolutionary" that it was, for several years, hardly noticed. Thus in his well-informed and respected survey of the problem of Israel's settlement, Manfred Weippert still concentrated on the usual suspects, Albright and Alt (Noth). He included the first serious discussion of Mendenhall's alternative hypothesis but dismissed it as unlikely (M. Weippert 1967). This was soon to change, and for good reasons.

Mendenhall's proposal was in many ways beguiling. If we for a moment accept it, it would seem to explain most of the issues created by a seeming variety of contrasting data, including the biblical versions of an Israel that left Egypt *en masse* and concluded its covenant with a new God, Yahweh, the one who saved the Israelites from the oppression of Pharaoh and promised them a new land of their own. But it was also this Yahweh who sent condemned Israel away to wander in the desert for forty years before the Israelites could invade and conquer their future land in a huge campaign which also involved mass murder of the previous inhabitants. Finally, all Israelites met at Shechem to reconfirm their covenant with their God. This is also very much the same story told by Mendenhall. Israel – now a tiny group – fled Egypt, led by Moses, encountered this God Yahweh at the holy Mountain and proceeded to the Holy Land. They didn't need to conquer this land, it was enough that they brought with them the message from Yahweh about a new social reality dominated by egalitarian ideals and freed from the oppression of the Canaanite petty kings of the country. The new religion united the rebellious but dispersed *ḫabīru* bands roaming the countryside and turned these groups into a considerable force which was soon able to purge the country of unjust Canaanite lords.

Benjamin Mazar was absolutely correct; Mendenhall really threw the history out and only kept a vestige of the biblical version by reducing its scale to almost nothing. On the other side Mendenhall kept the religious aspect, promoting Yahwism to become the very religious force which shaped the future of the population in the land of Israel. It should, however, have been

---

[53] On this understanding of the *ḫabīru* in the Amarna Letters cf. further Mendenhall 1973, but also Liverani 1979.

expected that Mendenhall would be met by protests among his own kinfolk, the members of the Albright family; but that did not happen, at least not in any conspicuous way. This was just another confirmation of the fact that for this group of scholars religion was far more important than actual history. This is a fact that may still explain the opposition to minimalism among Albright's heirs, because minimalism is not only about factual history but also involves religion; the religion of ancient Israel should not be separated from the secular history of this society (cf. above n. 30). And if I might offer a personal memory in this connection: When I gave my key-note lecture on Israelite religion at the IOSOT meeting in Leuven in 1989, one member of the audience jumped up and simply started shouting in a fashion totally unintelligible. The next morning the same person, a very well-known and respected professor, approached me and apologized: I had said something that should not be said and his head just blew up, or so he told me. It was a very honest confession, and understandable because this really is a problem to many if not most theologians and religious people. The minimalists are simply saying things that should not be said, and from their theological perspective these critics are correct; it illustrates very well the problem of confessional theology in the academy where it is inevitable that basic religious – Christian as well as Jewish – dogmas will always be challenged, or should be challenged, as Hector Avalos has correctly described the issue (Avalos 2007). Mendenhall never challenged any religious beliefs; he rather reinforced them and for that reason he was harmless, or was considered to be harmless among his peers.[54]

The semi-popular character of Mendenhall's article on the Hebrew conquest prevented it from being properly documented. The documentation followed several years later when he, in 1973, published his *The Tenth Generation* (Mendenhall 1973). Here it becomes obvious that Mendenhall, in his 1962 article, was building on social anthropological models, especially those formulated by Elman R. Service (1915–1996) involving four stages of human political development: band, tribe, chiefdom, and finally state.[55] Service was professor at the same university as Mendenhall back around 1960 when Mendenhall developed his view on Hebrew origins, and Mendenhall got his inspiration from Service, opening up not only for the reintroduction of social anthropology in biblical studies, a sorely neglected field in his day,

---

[54] This observation is remarkable because we cannot say that Mendenhall did not formulate his criticism of, e.g., Albright, in a most pointed way. Cf. Mendenhall 1973, 5n: "there is no pre-Mosaic social unity of which Israel is the socioreligious continuation", as a response to Albright's world of the Patriarchs.

[55] As explained in Service 1962. For a critique of Service, cf. Renfrew and Bahn 2020, 176–9.

but also for the related *cultural evolutionism* which became dominant in this period especially in North American sociology, history and archaeology. The basic idea was that human social and political evolution is predictable and that models can be established for how it develops. Cultural evolutionism does not, however, include a model for religious developments and, at the end, this was the undoing of Mendenhall's theories which had been attached rather randomly to a specific social model.

The fate of Mendenhall's thesis was to be reformulated in a study accepting most of its sociological foundation but skipping its religious content published in 1979 by Norman K. Gottwald (Gottwald 1979). It could also be said that sociology came back to biblical studies with a vengeance in the shape of Gottwald and his more than nine-hundred-page long *The Tribes of Yahweh*.[56] Leaving Mendenhall's religious part out, Gottwald presented an up-to-date study of early Israel based on an extensive application of social anthropological theory as it was at the time of publishing. It has often been said concerning Gottwald that his study had a definitive touch of Marxist philosophy,[57] which is absolutely true but as I said earlier this is not really a problem if it

---

[56] Occasionally biblical scholars have invoked social anthropology as part of their argumentation but it was never done in a systematic way. Gottwald very pointedly opens his huge thesis with a paragraph called "the scandal of sociological method" (Gottwald 1979, 5–7), and a scandal it was. In the from a methodological point of view a very conservative world of ancient Near Eastern studies to which Old Testament studies belong, such a thing as a methodological update that also included insights from the behavioural sciences was a thing unheard of. We may say that the reconstructions of ancient society almost never involved modern studies of, say, nomadic societies of the Middle East, although ethnographic information were to be collected from works by explorers (none of whom were primarily social anthropologists or trained as such) like Charles M. Doughty (Doughty 1888)), Alois Musil (especially Musil 1928), and Max Freiherr von Oppenheim (von Oppenheim 1939–1968). A work like Antonin Causse's *Du groupe éthnique à la communauté religieuse : La problème de la religion d'Israël* (Causse 1937) was ignored. Happily, probably many will say, Causse (1877–1947) published in French! On Causse, cf. the study by Kimbroug 1978. Mario Liverani published back in 1966 an article deploring the sad stage of oriental scholarship as seen from a modern methodological angle (Liverani 1966). Cf. also his "Introduzione" to Liverani 1969. Because of their preoccupation with ancient language creating a feeling of superiority bordering on arrogance, specialists in the Ancient Near East have little time for, or interest in, being updated with recent developments within neighbouring disciplines such as sociology. The attitude is simply: If you can read a text, you can also understand it. We have for close to two thousand years seen how it works in biblical studies: It does not work at all.

[57] Of course Dever would not miss such an opportunity, cf. Dever 2003, 53: "A committed Marxist with a long history of both liberal Christian theological involvement and social activism".

is used for what it is, a philosophy entailing a consistent methodological approach to its subject.

Mendenhall's reaction to Gottwald's thesis which, indeed, supported his own thesis of a revolutionary early Israel based on egalitarian ideology was extraordinary in a very special way (Mendenhall 1983). Mendenhall simply unleashed an attack on Gottwald that was unprecedented and considered bizarre at the time. It is, however, the case that Mendenhall's reaction is perfectly understandable. Mendenhall discussed the origins of Israel as a theological issue. Gottwald did not; his approach was sociological including Mendenhall's specific angle. In Mendenhall's view, Gottwald simply presented a materialistic distortion of his own approach, which from Mendenhall's perspective is absolutely correct. Religion can be a very strange bedfellow!

Initially, Gottwald's "revision" of the Mendenhall hypothesis was well received, even by this writer,[58] but problems emerged when I realized that Gottwald's anthropology was "arm-chair" anthropology. An extensive study of the Middle Eastern social set-up made it clear that theory was a far shot from practice. These societies did not follow the rules of Gottwald's game. As a matter of fact, his approach involved too many stereotypes about how a premodern society functions. Gottwald's sociological model had to be rewritten, and that in a serious way.

Working with social anthropology is not very different from working with archaeology. In archaeology we have a series of textbooks from Albright to Wright and via Kathleen Kenyon to Ammon Ben Tor and Amihai Mazar and many more.[59] But as Dever maintains, you must at least once in your life have participated in an excavation to really understand what is going on. The only alternative is to rely on precise primary excavation reports, although such reports often lag behind and are delayed almost indefinitely. In anthropology the best thing is to participate in anthropological field work, visit a social group and study it "from the inside". The alternative, if this is not possible, is not to read general books about social anthropology, although there are plenty of worthy ones, but to study the primary reports from anthropologists who work among other peoples.

This is not enough though, because in order to utilize this material it has to be systematized. Every field report is a building block, and the way to make

---

[58] Cf. Lemche 1982. The dean of the Theological Faculty at the University at the time – himself a Marxist theologian – was very pleased when he read this article and was very disappointed when I, in Lemche 1985 tore Gottwald's reconstruction apart.

[59] Some of these has already mentioned, but a (very) short list: Albright 1949, Wright 1957, Kenyon 1965/1979; Ben-Tor 1992, A. Mazar 1990. Ironically far the most comprehensive survey is in German: H. Weippert 1988.

use of these blocks is to work with case studies. It is not good enough just to collect randomly from a series of such reports; they must be selected with a purpose. In my *Early Israel* I used this approach to social anthropology (Lemche 1985). I was helped by a Danish social anthropologist, Klaus Ferdinand (1926–2005), who had done most of his field work among nomads in Qatar and Afghanistan.[60] When he read the first draft, he just said "arm-chair sociology", but as the first opponent to my dissertation he was very satisfied with the final outcome which represented a total rewriting of the anthropological part of the thesis. Using this approach meant that the chapter on nomadism was based on five case studies, the *al-Murrah* from Rub'al-Khali (Saudi-Arabia), the *Basseri* from Fars (Iran), the *Baḫtiyari* from Zagros (Iran), the *Yörük* (southeast Turkey), and the bedouins of the Negev.[61]

When dealing with traditional Middle Eastern society, investigators normally talk about a tripartite society, divided between nomads, villagers (farmers), and city dwellers. Consequently, the next section was devoted to the villagers and people living in cities, involving case studies of three villages, *Tel Toqaan* (Syria), *Al-Munsif* (Lebanon), and *Kufr el-Ma* (Jordan), and two traditional cities, *Al-Karak* (Jordan), and *Kerman* (Iran).[62]

The conclusions were, shall we say, extraordinary. Many stereotypes about traditional Middle Eastern society are simply wrong, and that includes studies of ancient social groups as well as more recent ones. The image we get from case studies like the ones mentioned – many more could have been included and are included in my study of *Early Israel* – is simply that our ideas about the oriental society have been distorted not only in the sense of an Edward Said (Said 1979), but from a fundamental social anthropological angle, and the conclusions are relevant for the Near East from ancient times to almost the present, say from Jean-Robert Kupper to Victor H. Matthews and Michael Rowton to present day anthropologists.[63] The qualificative "almost" has to do with a series of developments since the end of the Second World War representing modern, mostly western influences such as the emergence of a city-based middle class.

---

[60] His work among the Bedouins of Qatar is documented in Ferdinand 1993, and his work in Afghanistan is documented in Ferdinand 2006.
[61] Lemche 1985, 95–163, based on respectively Cole 1975, Barth 1964, Ehmann 1975, Bates 1973, and Marx 1967.
[62] Lemche 1985, 164–84, based on Sweet 1960, Gulick 1955, Antoun 1972, Gubser 1973, and English 1966.
[63] Kupper 1957, Matthews 1978; Rowton, in a series of articles on "dimorphic society", including Rowton 1973a, 1973b, 1974, and 1976.

First of all, Near Eastern society is not dimorphic, split between nomads and farmers. The nomads do not live in a dimorphic society at odds with – and in competition for – resources with farmers and city dwellers; they are, so to speak, themselves part of the resources. Far from living in a dimorphic society as claimed by Rowton, they are living in a "encapsulated" society meaning that they are surrounded by other occupational groups where they live.[64] They live in and among farming societies, often controlled by the city authorities. Their economy is dependent on markets primarily in cities. They are not self-sufficient but will have to acquire everything apart from meat from other sectors.

Second, there is no such a thing as *the* nomad. There are scores of different types of nomads. To make a distinction between, say, full-nomads meaning camel nomads and semi-nomads, so-called sheep-nomads, is a distinction decided by the choice of strategy based on the available resources, i.e. on the environment, and there are all kinds of subdivisions and interrelated groups.

Third, in a certain region there is no necessary ethnic distinction between nomads and farmers, or for that matter city-dwellers. A population with a common ethnic identity may embrace every different form of occupation.

Finally, Near Eastern society is not tripartite with boundaries between the different occupations; it is a *continuum* of social forms, a polymorphous society including, on the same scale, everything from so-called full nomads at one end, people who never come into contact with city-dwellers, never enter a city's gates, to fully settled city-dwellers at the other end who, for their part, never leave the gates of their city; never move "into the desert", a place full of demons.[65]

However, the revisions to the classic misinterpretation of Near Eastern society went further. In a cultural line from mobility to immobility, expressed as the longing of the nomads for a settled life in peace, nomadism was invariably understood by European observers as always on the brink of settlement whenever and as soon as it was possible. *Sehnsucht nach den Kulturland* (the zeal for the cultured land) as it would be described in German, a yearning for the comfort of settled life, was the ideology believed to have provoked repeated nomadic incursions into the land dominated by villages and cities.

---

[64] The concept of the encapsulated life of the nomads was formulated by Fredrik Barth (Barth 1973).

[65] I had this personal experience of superstition back in 1975 with two Arab bus drivers from Jerusalem who were scared to death when then had to take my party down into the desert of Sinai. They were convinced that they would never survive their visit to this evil place. On the road back from Sinai they almost got the whole party killed by their insane driving to get away from these desolated places of the desert.

An important example of this *Sehnsucht* was found in the description of the nomads in the Mari letters in the many references to the way the administration handled the various problems of the Benjaminites,[66] although it mostly had to do with the migrations of the Benjaminites passing through the territory of the state of Mari and not with the possible settlement of the Benjaminites. If anything, these documents tell us that a dynasty – the royalty of Mari – itself of Amorite origins, was engaged in controlling other Amorites moving around in their territory. In this way the problem of the Benjaminites at Mari was not their attempt to become settled, about which we hear nothing, but about control: The state seeks to remain in control of nomads roaming around in its territory.

Furthermore, nothing in the anthropological material indicates that the final aim of the nomads is to settle in villages to become farmers. On the contrary, the opposite seems to be the case: Nomads try to stay nomadic, nomadism offering them a better life with many more economic possibilities than settled life as peasants, limited to the ground which they till and totally at the mercy of the officials of the state where they live. The very backbone of traditional ideas of Israelite migrations into the cultivated land is simply a modern myth. If we look at the sedentarization process in the Middle East it is actually always the consequence of the activities of the authorities who, from their bases in cities, encourage or compel nomads within their territory to settle down, if for no other reason because this is a way to control herdsmen and to force them to pay taxes.

Therefore the sedentarization of nomads will normally be a process associated with the presence of strong central powers. It is not likely to happen in a territory which is not under the control of a central power. The classic example which I presented in *Early Israel* was the nomadization of the Middle East after its conquest by the Turkish in the sixteenth century CE. As a consequence of Turkish mismanagement – the Topkapi in Istanbul was simply uninterested in investing much effort in the control of this huge territory – the local Arabs changed strategy and became nomads – up to seventy five percent – as life in villages became intolerable because of official interference in local life which also entailed the impoverishment of the peasants by moneylenders living in cities such as Aleppo, Damascus, or Jerusalem.[67] During the last phase of Turkish occupation of the area, in the fifty years immediately before

---

[66] Often written DUMU.MEŠ *jaminu*, but the writing *banujaminu* has been attested. On the Benjaminites at Mari, cf. Lemche 1994.

[67] Topkapi – the palace of the Sultan in Constantinople (meaning "the cannon gate") – was for hundreds of years the centre of Turkish administration. Their politics in the occupied Arab territories can be followed through the centuries following the Turkish conquest, as

World War I, the Turkish authorities changed tactics and involved themselves in the well-being of the people who lived in their provinces, and the result certainly showed up before long with a marked decrease in the percentage of the population who were nomads.[68]

Returning to the settlement of the Israelites in Palestine – or, from now on, perhaps better to say the *alleged* settlement of Israel – the revised view on the relations between nomads and settled people have several consequences. In a Near Eastern context, first and foremost, the old idea of a massive invasion of foreigners, in this case the Israelites, is meaningless. However, the competing idea about a massive nomadic settlement makes no more sense. Nomads do not settle voluntarily. They settle because of pressure from other parties that make it impossible or increasingly difficult to remain nomads.[69] If we have a massive reappearance of settled life in unfortified villages in the mountains of Palestine as stressed by, among others, Israel Finkelstein, it would have been caused by political circumstances that forced non-settled people, nomads and others, to settle.[70] It would have been a political force that was strong enough to guarantee the good life of the settlers. Otherwise the project would have been doomed from the beginning.

The inhabitants in such new settlements would, for the most part, have been local people who changed their strategy for economic survival, induced to this change by other factors. They would normally not be foreigners, people from far away with no connection to the place where they now settled. In his study of the settlements of the Israelites, Finkelstein is imagining a settlement process which involved nomads living in an area to the east of the Late

---

most documents have been preserved. The standard work, when I wrote *Early Israel* was Hütteroth 1978. Focussing on Palestine, Ma'oz 1975.

[68] Turkish defeats and setbacks in Europe, especially in connection with the Russian-Turkish war of 1877-8 forced upon the Turkish government the need to revise its economic politics in the Middle East after losing most of its economic assets in Europe. One of the means was the establishment of a state sponsored agricultural bank which removed the negative influence of local money-lenders and usurers.

[69] Although a qualification has to be introduced: This is the general rule which does not prevent different sedentarization processes at other times and places. On sedentarization see Lemche 1985, 136–47. Here also the variables which may account for more settlements are mentioned: Nomads become too poor (without livestock) and are for this reason forced to seek employment in other sectors of the society just to survive, or they become too "heavy", meaning too rich in livestock (in the Middle East, flocks of more than one hundred thousand sheep are known), so they settle down and form a kind of city nobility while their herds are taken care of by hired herdsmen.

[70] Referring to the development of a village culture in the highlands at the beginning of the Early Iron Age, cf. Finkelstein 1988.

Bronze Age cities in the central mountains of Palestine, and he was doing so still in 1988 when he spoke about Israelites without making the ethnic classification very clear. When Dever opposes Israel Finkelstein's view on the sedentarization process, and points in a different direction, he is basing his discussion on totally false premises, his primordial view on ethnicity, postulating that the settlement had to do with the self-identification among the settlers understood to be a special group which came into being before the settlement. In this way he tries to rescue at least a tiny part of the old paradigm nursed by the members of the Albright school. Dever has on occasion called the inhabitants in these new settlements proto-Israelites.[71] This is gratuitous, as we have no idea what they called themselves, nor of any allegiance to other powers who might have guaranteed their survival. The central force behind the settlements could have been the Egyptians whose sway over the country did not end with the Amarna Period. On the contrary, it continued and was strengthened during the Ramesside Period in the thirteenth century BCE, and continued into the twelfth century BCE, several years after Pharaoh Merneptah postulated that he had destroyed Israel forever – whatever Israel meant at that time. Another possibility is the "forgotten kingdom", a political formation with Shechem as its likely centre with roots going back to at least Lab'aya, the local regent in the Amarna Period (Finkelstein 2013). The consolidation of a major local power in this period would certainly have created possibilities for the resurrection of settled life within its territory.[72]

The frustrating part to a nihilist, if we can use this improper term again, is the appearance of "Israel" in Merneptah's famous inscription. Few ancient inscriptions have attracted so much attention as this one, with opinions ranging from considering it a proof of the presence of biblical Israel to being a literary text of little interest for the historian. The last position is probably the least productive one, because it does not explain the origins of Israel in this

---

[71] Thus in Dever 2003. The answer is, well, they might have been but 1) what evidence do we have when we have no inscriptions relating to any ethnic identification, and 2) Dever's assertion has only one basis: The idea of Israelite ethnicity as presented by the Bible, i.e. he turns the discussion about the origins of this population (nomadic/sedentary, from inside Palestine/outside Palestine) on its head in a logical potpourri which leaves his readership in the dark. Because we do not really know what "Israel" meant in the Early Iron Age, we reintroduce the idea of Israel taken from the Old Testament being perhaps between five hundred and a thousand years later, and use this later or secondary documentation (in the historical context of the Iron Age) to explain ethnic identities of the late second millennium BCE. This is of course madness.

[72] For the discussion until 1979, cf. Engel 1979b. My own discussion of the inscription can be found in Lemche 1998b, 35–8. For a quite a different view, see Hjelm and Thompson 2002.

place. We have never heard of it before, so why is it here? There was no Israel in the time of Lab'aya – or at least nobody refers to its existence – but two hundred years later we find it mentioned in Merneptah's inscription. Perhaps it was also new to the Egyptian scribe and for that reason included.[73] Also, the geographical location of this Israel is disputed, although this writer has, from an early point of his involvement in the question, used the inscription's topological information to point at a location in the centre of the mountains to the north of Jerusalem as the most likely place. A location around Shechem would not create problems.

Of course we don't know; it is only a proposal but it creates a possible new scenario for the establishment of an entity called Israel in the Highlands of Samaria reaching back to the Late Bronze Age. At least the relations between Israel in one form or the other and Shechem with its holy mountain of Gerizim seem assured. If anything, this relationship grew stronger over time, even into the Hellenistic Period; so strong, indeed, that Israelites living in other places in the Greek-Hellenistic world used their connection to the sanctuary on Gerizim as the core of their self-identification.[74] This forgotten kingdom may have been the "Israel" said by Merneptah to have been destroyed. It probably had little to do with biblical Israel apart from the name, and the traditions about the almost eternal conflict between this Israel and especially Jerusalem reflected in biblical tradition may refer to much later circumstances such as the conflict between Samarians and Judeans in early Hellenistic era, which led to the Hasmonean destruction of the temple at Gerizim and the ostracizing of the Samarians. But there might have been a tradition of such an enmity between Jerusalem and Shechem before this time, as it was already present in the letters from Palestine found among the Amarna letters referring to the activities of Lab'aya of Shechem and Abdi-Ḫeba of Jerusalem, a situation which influenced the life in other parts of Palestine in the Amarna Age to such a degree that one of the petty rulers could write to Pharaoh:

---

[73] Israel in the Merneptah stele is written with the gentilic for a people, which is quite different from that of a city or a state. It is correct, as is often argued, that the Egyptian scribes in the late New Kingdom were known to be sloppy in their use of such designations, but the question is: Why absolutely here? The scribe behind the inscription did not really know what he was writing about, so he played safe and choose the gentilic sign.

[74] On these Israelites who wrote in Greek, cf. Lemche 2012b. The inscriptions were published by Pierre Bruneau, "'Les Israelites de Delos' e la Juiverie Delienne" (Bruneau 1982). Few biblical scholars have noted their importance, apart from – I am tempted to say of course – Giovanni Garbini (Garbini 2008, 205).

"Moreover, Lab'ayu, who used to take our towns, is dead, but now [an]other Lab'ayu is 'Abdi-Ḫeba, and he seizes our towns".[75]

The classical positions to the question of Israel's origins in or outside of Palestine have been shown to rely on a false understanding of the social anthropological possibilities, and especially on a totally mistaken identification of the problems of the nomads. As it has been often noted there is no cultural discontinuity between Palestine in the Late Bronze Age and Palestine in the Early Iron Age. Basically, the kind of society which we encounter when bronze turns into iron is the same.[76] This opens up the way for a discussion of the final issue in this connection: the kind of society found in traditional Palestinian society in the Bronze Age *and* in the Iron Age.

The traditional way of understanding Israelite society is to see it as a tribal society, and it is absolutely true that tribal affiliation had some importance for the self-identification of the members of a tribe, but was it really the decisive political factor or just an overlaid ideological claim which hid the real socioeconomic factors governing the kind of society found in Palestine in the second and first millennia? The tribe was one of the most discussed subjects among social anthropologists a generation ago but it is probably still the majority opinion that it is also the most problematic issue around. What is a tribe? That's the question. In my review of the discussion in *Early Israel* it was evident that biblical scholars did not have a clue as to the meaning of tribe but relied on all kinds of stereotypes whose roots are lost somewhere in the hidden past of popular ideas about the life and customs of so-called primitive societies, a term no longer in use.[77] My conclusion to this discussion in *Early Israel* was that the tribe is the maximum social organization in stateless societies and as such provides not only identity but also a kind of protection to its members. There are no limits to the size of a tribe; some are very small, like those found among the Negev Bedouins counting a few hundred people, some enormous like the Tiv of Eastern Africa whose membership approaches a million people. Tribalism has little to do with social structure, and on the local level the much more important social group is the *lineage*, the family group – a term which was practically never used among biblical scholars pretending to discuss the social structure of ancient Israel.[78] In short, the

---

[75] EA 280:30–35. Translation from Moran 1992. From Šuwardata of Qeltu to Pharaoh.
[76] As I made it clear in Lemche 1996.
[77] Cf. from the time when the subject of tribes was most discussed, Morton Fried 1975. With a special emphasis on the Middle East, Lemche 1985, 202–44.
[78] On the importance of the concept of the lineage in a discussion of ancient Israelite family structures cf. Lemche 1985, 245–73. Sad to say, not much has changed. Biblical scholars still speak of "clan" where they should have spoken of lineages. If anything, clan is a much

concept of the tribes of Israel in traditional biblical scholarship was no more than a romantic stereotype with little basis in real societies. The concept was the result of the previously governing tradition within European humanistic scholarship of "speculation", a tradition which has its roots among the ancient Greeks who spurned the idea of actually testing the results of philosophical speculation by confronting it with evidence from the real world. The famous example of Plato also helped ancient thinkers not to commit the same mistake as he, who in order to see his ideas from *The State* put into practice in Sicily, followed an invitation in 366 BCE by Dionysos II, the tyrant of Syracuse. After a short time the project was shut down and Plato on the verge of being sold as a slave.[79] As a consequence of a similar attitude, the speculations of the German sociologist Max Weber (1864–1920) enjoyed enormous popularity and are still discussed, even though Weber never sought any first-hand knowledge of the issues which he was discussing. This follows a tradition in Germany going back at least to Immanuel Kant who wrote a highly regarded (in its time) study of religion also including foreign religions without ever leaving his home town of Königsberg (Kant 1793).

Leaving the stereotypes aside, the really important part of the social structure was – and still is in traditional Mediterranean society – patronage, also called the dominating Mediterranean family system: Tribes and lineages may exist, but it is the system of patron–client loyalties that binds the society together, united by its two components; those "who have" with those "who have not", the well-to-do and the powerless part of the population. I have described the functions of and the ideology behind such a society in a number of publications and have also shown how the ideology turns up in biblical literature as well,[80] and the subject has been taken up and expanded considerably by Emanuel Pfoh in an ever-growing series of publications.[81]

Approaching the conclusion to this paragraph it has become increasingly notable that the biblical story of Israel's origins has become more and more irrelevant, except as an example of how people not in the habit of critical thinking, and without the necessary educational tools, handle myth and legends

---

used and badly defined concept which may not really be present in the Middle East. It has been implanted on Middle Eastern societies from other places, of course especially from Scotland where the "clan" originates. Probably European observers confuse the Middle Eastern patronage-system with a Scottish clan-system. On patronage, Pfoh 2016, 123-67.

[79] The primary source to these adventures of Plato is his own seventh letter. The discussion goes on about whether or not he really wrote this letter, but it is the common opinion that the content of the letter is factual.

[80] Lemche 1995b, 1995c, 1996a, 1999 and 2013a, 158–68.

[81] But see first and foremost Pfoh 2009a and 2016.

when they, as in this case, were compiled by ancient authors who themselves had not learned to think historically-critically in any way comparable to modern historians – that was to take another two thousand years before we or the few among us were taught to think logically and evaluate our sources in a critical sense. History was to the ancient nothing except *cultural memory*, and memory is not history. The demands of cultural memory are different from those of proper historical reconstructions of the past; nobody asks the same kind of questions of memory as of an historical essay.[82]

One question remains: Where should we look for the home of this memory? In 1960 the home for the traditions about Israel's early past was considered to be the twelve-tribe league. It has now vanished into the blue and has been replaced by quite a different story that doesn't have time and space for the version narrated by the biblical authors. It has taken a lot of time for biblical scholarship at large to realize the consequences of the demise of the presumed place for the twelve-tribe ideology that bound all of Israel together in a primordial unit. The ideology was still present in the biblical stories about early Israel, but where should we now look for it? The natural choice for most biblical scholars was to look to the time of David and Solomon, when two kings out of Jerusalem ruled over all of Israel's twelve tribes, a time normally set in the tenth century BCE. However, this choice was destined to become a trap which ended up propelling the whole narrative about Israel as found in the Old Testament into the realm of myths and legends.

David and His Kingdom

Above, I described the triumphant publication in 1993 in the *Israel Exploration Journal* of the first mention of David in an ancient text not part of biblical literature in the form of an inscription found that year during excavations at Tel Dan in northern Israel (Biran and Naveh 1993). Two years later, two more fragments of the same inscription were published in the same place (Biran and Naveh 1995). The language of the inscription was Aramaic, perhaps a pidgin-type of Aramaic as claimed by Frederick H. Cryer in an article which challenged the already then canonical dating of the inscription to the ninth

---

[82] On this Lemche 2012a. On the factor of forgetting the study by Harald Weinrich, *Kunst und Kritik des Vergessens* (Weinrich 2005) is mandatory, and on the relationship between history and memory I may refer to Cubitt 2007, and the studies found in Climo and Cattell (2002). Further recommendations: le Goff (1992), Hutton 1993, Ricœur 2004), and Tumblety 2013. I cannot expend much space here on this issue but plan to publish a special study on cultural memory with the working title: *Cultural Memory is not a Paper Tiger*.

century BCE on the basis of a meticulous paleographic investigation of the form of the script used on the inscription (Cryer 1994). According to Cryer, the inscription should rather date to the eighth century BCE than the ninth century BCE. Otherwise, the inscription was linguistically without serious problems, a phenomenon Cryer noted as exceptional since no other inscription of the time and of a similar size and complexity has ever presented itself in a similarly unproblematic way; somehow they all have at least one phenomenon which has to be discussed among specialists for years. The Tel Dan inscription knows of no such problems; it is totally translatable.[83]

The reception in those days was almost universally positive, if not simply overwhelmingly positive. The only exception was the Italian specialist in Northwest Semitic languages Giovanni Garbini (1931–2017), who simply rejected the inscription as a rude falsification.[84] Apart from a few linguistic arguments, Garbini based his rejection of the inscription on its similarity in content to, especially, the Mesha stele; it is as if you lifted the text of Tel Dan Fragment A and placed it over a similarly sized section of the Mesha inscription, an astonishing amount of identical phrases and issues appear.[85]

The main battle over the inscription's authenticity was, however, not fought over linguistic details; it was quite different and had to do with physical peculiarities. It is often maintained that the minimalists had to reject this inscription as genuine simply because it represented a blow to their very minimalism which rejected the historicity of King David.[86] Those waving such opinions are unaware of two things: First of all, the Tel Dan inscription is not a proof of the existence of King David, only at best of a house of David. This is hardly a distressing surprise to the minimalists, because it is exactly what is to be expected, because there is no dearth in the Old Testament as far as references to this "house of David" go. The title "the House of David" makes David as historical as "the House of Windsor" makes Windsor a historical person, as

---

[83] Although this is in need of clarification: The inscription is easy reading; still discussions exist about, among other things, the issue of consecutive forms in Aramaic. For a proper discussion of the language including such linguistic matters, cf. Athas 2003, and Hagelia 2006.

[84] "Una grossolana falzificatione", Garbini 2008, 18n. See the analysis in Garbini 1994. See also Garbini 2006, 119, where he simply declines to include the inscription in his chapter on Aramaic inscriptions "perché falsa". Garbini's book on epigraphy is a must read for those who have tried to smear the reputation of a great scholar. If anything, he was more than well-acquainted with North-West Semitic philology and inscriptions from this world. Cf. already Garbini 1960 and the follow-up Garbini 1988a.

[85] Cf. also Lemche 2003c, 46–67.

[86] Of course Dever had to join the party. Cf. Dever 2001, 29–30.

it has been put.[87] The second thing is that the minimalists – or not all of them – did not consider the inscription a fake from the very day of its publication. On the contrary, we were just as thrilled by this new discovery as everybody else. Frederick Cryer wrote serious articles about it and its epigraphy, which would only make sense if he considered it as genuine; and the same can be said about this writer, although my first contribution to the discussion is probably not known because it was in German.[88]

The change in attitude came late, in 1995, when Frederick Cryer returned to Copenhagen from a visit to Jerusalem where he had been at the Israel Museum with Russell Gmirkin. Gmirkin had taken a couple of perhaps not quite legal photos of the inscription. Cryer brought them back to Copenhagen for a seminar and just handed them over to me with the question: Can you see it? And it was easy to see: in the almost non-existent first line the vertical line in the "m" did, at the edge of the inscription fragment, suddenly turn to the right (it was supposed to continue in an angle to the left) – down the broken side. This means that if this is really so, the text on the slab has been engraved on it after the slab had been "produced", which again means that it must logically be a fake inscription and not an ancient one. Gmirkin later published his photos in *The Scandinavian Journal of the Old Testament*, but the quality of the photos here are insufficient to give a decisive impression (Gmirkin 2002). In a PowerPoint lecture held in Amman in 2001, I presented some additional pictures from available material on the net as well as a number of slides illustrating other anomalies (Lemche 2003c).[89] Still, I had to conclude that the evidence was inconclusive. George Athas discusses Gmirkin's evidence but dismisses it as "scratches", which they of course definitely are (Athas 2003, 35-9): Nobody ever said that the slippage was intentional. Finally – and it is really an ironic coincidence (?) – the problems are very clearly exposed in an unusually clear photo of the inscription by Zev Radogan printed on the

---

[87] The first reference to this analogy I have seen was in a commentary to an article by Philip R. Davies (Davies 2012) on the list *Bible and Interpretation* by Jason Silverman (20/6/2012): "The House of Windsor is quite apropos to the issue of the House of David – it certainly proves that the Kingdom of Judah was founded by King David, just as the dynasty name proves the British Crown was founded by King Windsor..." (https://bibleinterp.arizona.edu/articles/dav368018), If any reader should be in doubt, "House of Windsor" is a family name accepted by the British royal family during the First World War, when the family's old German name, Battenberg, had become a bit embarrassing. Battenberg was kept within the royal family in an anglicized form as Mountbatten.
[88] Apart from the article already mentioned, Cryer 1995a, 1995b and 1996, Lemche 1995d.
[89] The edition in Arabic has some better quality photos (partly in colour): Lemche 2003d.

cover of a book by Megan Bishop Moore and Brad E. Kelle, *Biblical History and Israel's Past* (Moore and Kelle 2011).

Such problems are never discussed. It is obvious that the inscription has been accepted in modern Israel as a kind of magna carta for the relations between the modern state and ancient Israel, a holy text, even more holy than the Hebrew Bible and as such beyond discussion – including any discussion about the meaning of the "house of David" part of the inscription. It is noted that the writing: *bytdwd* is unusual. Otherwise, words in this inscription are separated with a marker, a dot. Accordingly, we should expect *bytdwd* written as *byt . dwd*, in two words. No such marker is found here. If it is an ancient inscription we have no way of knowing the reason for this omission; perhaps a slip from the side of the engraver, but then we should ask: Why exactly here? Was it intended to catch the eye of the reader? It is simply too much of a coincidence?[90] In the early part of the discussion this led to a series of alternative proposals to understand the meaning of the *bytdwd*, including proposals that it was the name of some locality in the vicinity of Dan, a sanctuary or the like.[91] As the interpretation of the inscription assumed canonical importance, such divergent opinions were simply dismissed without further discussion. The peculiar writing *bytdwd* received, after Cryer's intervention, no more attention, although it is exceptional to find the word *bayit* "house, temple, family, dynasty" written in early Aramaic as *byt*.[92] Normally the -*y*- is left out. We should have expected in normal writing *bt . dwd* or maybe simply *bt . dd*, and the discussion should have started from this point.

One more issue has to be addressed before we can leave this inscription behind: the combination of the two (three) fragments into one text. It is no more seen as problematic, but it was when the combination was first made. The fragments (A and B_{1-2}) do no align. This is obvious if we try to do so as I did in my Amman-lecture (Lemche 2003c, 53). But do we have a join where they meet? The authorities of the Israel Museum definitely think so. I only have the opinion of a leading Israeli archaeologist of my own generation who was able to inspect the fragments before they were joined, and his response was: There are no joins. George Athas made an ingenious reconstruction of the inscription based on the angle of the chisel used to cut out the inscription

---

[90] As I learned from an artist: If you wish your painting to be seen, put in something which is not natural, such as the smoke from the chimney going in another direction than the flag blown by the wind.

[91] E.g., Davies 1994, 23–24, Knauf, de Pury and Römer 1994.

[92] Readers may consult the entry on byt_2 in Hoftijzer and Jongeling 1995, 156–63. The writing *byt* is Phoenician and was one of the reasons Cryer dubbed the language of the Tel Dan Inscriptions "pidgin-Aramaic".

on the slab, and it turned out that the angle is different on fragment A and fragments B_{1-2} (Athas 2003, 191). Comparing the angles of the letters of the inscription he placed fragment B_{1-2} further down than fragment A, bursting, in this way, the usual interpretation of the inscription as a victory stele of Hazael of Damascus. Of course in the light of the ongoing canonization of the inscription his challenge was never taken up and the usual but most likely impossible interpretation remains in force.[93]

As already said, the discovery of the stele was celebrated because it represented the oldest appearance of the name of David outside of the Bible. But why was this so important? We have known for a long time that the royal house of the Kingdom of Judah called itself "the house of David". The problem was not David as a historical person or, more believable, as the apical ancestor of a ruling family somewhere in the southern end of the central highlands of Palestine. David may refer to a historical person or it may not. How important is this really?

We are now moving past the 1990 limit which I set for this survey of the changes in the general view on the history of Palestine in ancient times. The discussion at the end of the 1980s and the early 1990s was, however, absolutely decisive and had consequences for biblical studies from which it still suffers. The biblical story about King David, which includes most of the second Book of Samuel and only reaches its end at the beginning of the First Book of Kings, belongs to some of the most beloved narratives from the past in Western civilization. For the first time an ancient text from the Ancient Near East presents a "living being" to our eyes. The biblical David is a person with many sides, positive as well as negative. Everybody knows how he killed the Philistine giant Goliath, and everybody has heard of Bathsheba, who was to become his destiny. We will never come across anything like this again before we are safely seated among the Greek classics, and even here

---

[93] A question not taken up here is the one of the circumstances of the finding of the fragments. There was some confusion about the exact place where it was found, but definitely not as part of a wall of fortification. Fragment A was extracted from below a wall somehow sticking out in the open where it was discovered by the Israeli archaeologist Gila Cook. The first photos of the inscription in *Israel Exploration Journal* 43 (p. 82) did not show it *in situ* but moved from its original placed out to the plaza in front of it and standing up. The confusion became total when *The Biblical Archaeology Review* (March/April 1994, p. 38) published a photo of the inscription *in situ* (*sic*!) but inverted. The conditions surrounding the discovery of the two other fragments are not much different. As to the joining of the fragments, Hagelia presents an overview of the interpretations of the stele (until c. 2005) (Hagelia 2006, 13–50). A recent view separating fragments A and B can be found in Knauf and Guillaume 2016, 94, repeated in Knauf and Niemann 2021, 208, where Knauf admits to be the originator of this separation in his "histories".

such plastically described figures like David, Joab, and Bathsheba first show up in Greek drama of the fifth century BCE.[94] As a matter of fact, the two narratives about David, the story of his ascension to the throne, and the other about the succession to the throne after him were, two generations ago, considered more or less eyewitness reports, recording what had really happened when Israel became a United Monarchy, melded together by a young David, only to fall apart again after the death of his son King Solomon.[95] The beginning of western civilization was simply tuned to begin with King David, and it was normal to date the beginning of his reign to 1000 BCE (sometimes with a qualification: c. 1000 BCE). Less would not be good enough.

His kingdom is described by the biblical stories as an empire embracing almost all of the southwestern Levant, all of Palestine, including both the north and the south, and the cities on the plain – apart from the five Philistine cities and the city of Gezer which was still Egyptian territory, although Gezer is situated only some thirty kilometres from Jerusalem, his splendid capital. East of the Jordan River, he ruled over Ammon, Moab, and Edom to the south and all the land of Gilead to Hermon. He conquered the Arameans from Damascus and pushed the borders of his rule to the banks of the Euphrates. His northern border was closing in on Hamath in Syria.[96]

Of course this was too good to be true, except for the conservative maximalists. Historians began to question the historicity of what was related about David and his son Solomon. They could hardly find space for such a regional empire in the tenth century BCE, and they especially found it strange that no ancient source outside the Old Testament mentions either of the two Israelite kings. The normal counter-argument was always that the tenth century BCE was a dark period in so far as very little inscriptional material has survived from this century. This is of course the usual loophole employed by biblical maximalists to counter critical questions, the "logic" being the same as behind Kitchen's anti-critical argument that absence of evidence is not evidence of absence (see above). In the way the argument is used, it is almost an argument in favour of the very existence of this empire. But in the perverted logic of conservative biblical historiography this makes sense. We cannot prove

---

[94] Dissenters may think of the Homeric epic (post 800 BCE), and not without reason. However, although the plot of *The Iliad* centres on the motive of love (Paris – Helena, Achilles – Briseis), the motive is not dominant as, e.g., in Euripides *Medea* (431 BCE).
[95] The major study of the story of young David is still Grønbæk 1971. On the succession story, see Rost 1926. For a study in English, see Whybray 1968.
[96] Cf. the stories of David's wars and conquests in the Old Testament, 2 Samuel 8; 10; 12:26–31.

that a Davidic empire ever existed, but it is a fact that it did, and the argument is that you cannot disprove its existence.

The criticism of the idea of a Davidic empire in the tenth century BCE did not originate among the minimalists; it is present also in many mainstream histories, or it used to be part of them. However, if we follow the development of Jan Alberto Soggin's (1926–2010) version of Israel's history, he had already presented a conventional review of David's and Solomon's time in Hayes and Miller's *Israelite and Judaean History* from 1977, beginning with a solid discussion of the sources, all in the Old Testament itself (Soggin 1977). Then he continues with a paraphrase of what is really only the deuteronomistic version of David's reign in 2 Samuel and 1 Kings: "David's rise to power over Judah and Israel", "the Davidic empire", civil and military administration under David", "political tensions within the Davidic empire", and "religious developments under David". The same can be said about his chapter on Solomon; it is nothing but a paraphrase. Soggin, who had studied under Noth (his published dissertation is dedicated to Noth; cf. Soggin 1967), went on to write an, in its time, popular history of Israel, *A History of Israel: From the Beginnings to the Bar Kochba Revolt. AD 135* (Soggin 1984). Still a paraphrase, but only from the time of David and Solomon onwards, his history included a remarkable new thing: Soggin followed the input of his master, Martin Noth, and considered the stories about the Patriarchs, Egypt and the Exodus, of the conquest and about the judges as traditions belonging to a time when Israel was united and all twelve tribes were together, but to Soggin this was not in the Period of the Judges; this period had changed status in Soggin's version. The place and time when the traditions of early Israel were collected into one narrative was the time of David and Solomon. Soggin simply bowed to reality: The central idea on which biblical historiography relies is the existence of an Israel in which all twelve tribes are united could only have arisen when this was an actual fact. We need to have this twelve-tribe Israel as a historical fact before we can begin to develop ideas about its early history. However, as he proceeded with his historical studies more changes followed. The second edition of his history had changed its title in a remarkable way: *An Introduction to the History of Israel and Judah* (Soggin 1993). Gone was the assuredness with which he had earlier approached his subject. Now he was no more able to write *a history of Israel*; it was only an introduction to such a history. Looking through his references to modern scholars it is obvious that he had learned enormously from two of his Italian colleagues, Mario Liverani and perhaps even more from Giovanni Garbini, and from the last mentioned perhaps his study of David's empire (Garbini 1988b, 21–32). We find the same development in the view of David when we move from the first to the second edition of J. Maxwell Miller and John H. Hayes' *A History of Ancient Israel and Judah* (Miller and Hayes 2006). In the first edition everything is pretty normal but, in the second, doubts have begun sneaking in, leading to a short paragraph: "The Biblical David and the Historical David" (Miller and Hayes 2006, 159–60). The biblical David is not the historical David, which is an argument I have been propagating for years.[97]

Things began to move swiftly when a serious discussion arose among archaeologists about the status of Jerusalem in the tenth century BCE, presumably the time when the city was supposed to have been the centre of a mighty empire. Jerusalem has always been a kind of *enfant terrible* among archaeologists. In spite of being the most excavated place in the world, as it is said (Rome will probably protest), confusion appears everywhere. One of the recurring reasons for confusion is the lack of congruence between the written records and the archaeological "facts on the ground". The first time we confront such a problem is in the Late Bronze Age, when Pharaoh's *ḫazānu* in Urusalim, ÌR-Ḫeba, sent a series of messages to Pharaoh which have been preserved among the Amarna letters (EA 285–290).[98] So far nothing indicates that Jerusalem was a city in the Late Bronze Age (cf. Steiner 2001, 39–41). Still, the name is there.

We have a similar situation when we, in the papyri from Elephantine in Egypt, dating from the fifth century BCE, find a correspondence between the Jehudian inhabitants of Yeb – the local name for the Island – dealing with problems after a local group had destroyed their temple, and the *kahana rabba* in Jerusalem (Cowley 2005, no. 31:18). The title "high priest" and the

---

[97] I have to confess that the development of ideas in Soggin's and Miller and Hayes' histories is not very different from my own changes in perspective. In Lemche 1984c, 124–5 (ET Lemche 1988b) my attitude to the monarchy of David and Solomon was quite conventional. Later I was often asked to revise this book but rejected such proposals, as it would, in practice, involve a total rewriting. In the reprint in the *Cornerstones Series* (Lemche 2015c) I simply added a new introduction identifying the "hot spots".

[98] *Ḫazānu* is the title used by the Egyptians of their local representative who in their own eyes considered them "kings". They were not, but their position was probably very much the same as the later Arab *mukhtar*, a local leader, sandwiched between his Egyptian master and local people. Urusalim: in Amarna Akkadian URUù-ru-sa-lim. ÌR-Ḫeba: The second element is a name of a Hurrian goddess. The rendering of the first part, written with the Sumerogram ÌR meaning "slave" is debatable, but nowadays scholars mostly settle with West-semitic *'abd* "slave", although this is far from certain. It is very possible that ÌR-Ḫeba was one among relatively many members of the *ḫazānu* group who carried non-Semitic – often Indo-Aryan– names like Šuwardata from Qiltu or Biryawaza from Damascus, a fact that should perhaps make people speculate a little more about what ethnicity looked like in Palestine in the Late Bronze Age (and beyond?).

name of Jerusalem make it likely that this high priest named Johanan was head of a temple which must have existed in Jerusalem when the letter was written, in 408 BCE. But what about Jerusalem at that time? Here we will soon see when we return to the city of David how the archaeological departments at Tel Aviv University and the Hebrew University in Jerusalem are at odds, when archaeologists from Tel Aviv tell us that there hardly was a Jerusalem – perhaps a minor settlement or village on the spot – before we approach the Hellenistic Period, in defiance of claims from their colleagues in Jerusalem.[99] However, if we follow the opinion of these archaeologists, there was no city – perhaps a small village or hamlet – in Jerusalem when the letter was sent from Yeb to Jerusalem in 408 BCE, but there was still a temple and a priesthood. Diana Edelman proposed major building activity, including the building of the new temple in Jerusalem during the reign of Artaxerxes I (465–424 BCE) (Edelman 2005). We may add: Probably not as extensive as imagined by Edelman, but then perhaps a minor sanctuary, a "temple". Perhaps the religious tradition was always much stronger at Al-Quds, "the holy place" as the Arabs call the city, than the secular importance of the city, as it has remained to this day.

When we turn to Jerusalem in the tenth century BCE, the alleged time of the mighty kings of Israel, David and Solomon, we see the same phenomenon in operation. There was hardly any city of importance in the tenth century BCE but the relation between the two kings and the tradition of Jerusalem as a holy place is nonetheless very strong, shrouded in a literary disguise of a narrative that goes from the transport of the Ark of the Covenant to Jerusalem (2 Samuel: 6), describing how the king is dancing in front of the movable sanctuary, until David's construction of a sanctuary on the threshing floor of Araunah (2 Samuel 24), which explains the reason for his inability to build a proper temple, a task his son Solomon takes upon himself – although Chronicles has it differently: In Chronicles David has prepared everything for the construction. It is just up to Solomon to put it all together (1 Chronicles 22).

In 1960, our "magic" year of unity among biblical scholars, the archaeologists had already, a long time before, joined forces with their biblical colleagues and were digging "for God and country" to find evidence of the

---

[99] Cf. on the problem of Jerusalem in the Persian period the review of the various positions involving both biblical scholars and archaeologists in Finkelstein 2006b reprinted with additional comments in Finkelstein 2018, 3–28. As argued by Finkelstein, most studies of Jerusalem in this period have mainly built on the information in the Old Testament, but it is really an archaeological problem. David Ussishkin 2006, 147–66 will say the same. On this discussion, and its consequences (where this writer differs from Finkelstein), cf. Lemche 2015b.

presence of these two Israelite kings.[100] Nobody doubted the basic correctness of the biblical evidence, so it was now up to the archaeologists to illustrate the biblical story with facts on the ground, and so they did. The years before World War II were the golden age for this kind of archaeology, and a series of the most important of the *biblical* places were selected for extensive archaeological campaigns, such as Megiddo, Shechem, Samaria, and Jericho.[101] Alas, this was not to last. Thus John Garstang, digging in the 1930s, had no problems identifying the Jericho of the time of Joshua, but when his successor, Kathleen M. Kenyon resumed the British excavations between 1952 and 1958, Joshua's Jericho was no more, meaning that there was no city on Tell es-Sultan, the Arabic name for Tel Jericho, any more; it had vanished as one of the results of Kenyon's excavation, which had overturned Garstang's earlier happy message of the confirmation of Joshua's conquest.[102] The new Italian-Palestinian excavations have not in any serious way made changes to Kenyon's conclusion regarding Jericho and Joshua.[103]

On the other hand, the establishment of the modern state of Israel in 1948 created a thirst for every possible confirmation of Jewish presence through history in Palestine, a name from now on banned from Israeli consciousness, and archaeology – hand in hand with the Bible (or should we rather say the Bible hand in hand with archaeology) – became the primary means to obtain this knowledge of ancient Israel.[104]

---

[100] Cf. the title of Neil Asher Silberman's *Digging for God and Country: Exploration, Archaeology, and the Secret Struggle for the Holy Land 1799–1917* (Silberman 1982).

[101] Megiddo: 1903 and 1905, Gottlieb Schumacher, and again 1926–1927, Clarence S. Fisher and more; Jericho; 1907–1909 and in 1911, Ernst Sellin and Carl Watzinger, and again 1930–1936, John Garstang; Shechem: Ernst Sellin from 1913 to 1914 and 1926–1934; Samaria: Gottlieb Schumacher in 1908 and then by George Andrew Reisner in 1909 and 1910 and again John W. Crowfoot between 1931 and 1935; with the assistance of, among others Kathleen M. Kenyon.

[102] Kenyon's excavation report became the standard by which every other report has been measured – *Excavations at Jericho*, I–V (Kenyon 1960–83). A popular report appeared already in 1957 (Kenyon 1957).

[103] First an exclusive Italian excavation led by Lorenzo Nigro and Nicolo Marchetti from 1997 to 2000; and from 2009 a combined Italian and Palestinian excavation under the direction of Lorenzo Nigro and Hamdan Taha. The quite comprehensive reports are available at the home page of the Jericho project: http://www.lasapienzatojericho.it/Bibplio.php. So far, these reports have only covered the early periods down to the end of the Early Bronze Age. For a more general overview cf. Lorenzo Nigro 2019, 175–214.

[104] On political archaeology, cf. Kletter 2006. It is also the subject in Oestigaard 2007. Terje Oestigaard (Terje Østigård), Docent at the Department of Archaeology and Ancient History, Uppsala University, Sweden, has done fieldwork in many parts of the world, from Bangladesh to Scandinavia, with an emphasis on Egypt. His book is a sad memento of the

When I argue that the Bible came first, then archaeology, the best illustration of how the Bible was known to identify archaeological discoveries is found in 1 Kings 9:15 where we have the following text:

This is the record of the forced labour which King Solomon conscripted to build the house of the LORD, his own palace, the Millo, the wall of Jerusalem, and Hazor, Megiddo, and Gezer (Trans. *New English Bible*).

For generations no critical questions were asked and the information in this place was, together with the notes about Solomon's activities in 1 Kings 10:26–29, accepted as the historical truth. King Solomon really was the mastermind behind this building activity which told us that he must have ruled over a rich kingdom and that he had in his possession the three cities mentioned here, Hazor, Megiddo, and Gezer. Otherwise, we would not have known that they were in Israelite possession. It is just taken for granted by the biblical author. It was therefore up to the archaeologists to substantiate the biblical claims, and so they did. Already during the Oriental Institute excavations at Megiddo such confirmations were found and duly noted when two complexes interpreted as stables turned up in the excavations, housing maybe between four hundred and fifty and five hundred horses – if they were indeed stables.[105] Similar structures were found already by Frederick J. Bliss at Tell el-Hesi in 1891 but also later by Yigael Yadin at Hazor and Yohanan Aharoni at Tel Beersheva. The position of Yadin and other archaeologists of the period was seen as confirmed by another feature that became

---

status of biblical (Syro-Palestinian) archaeology in other fields of archaeology. His preface to his book includes a very serious description of what biblical archaeology is: "The general attitude towards biblical archaeologists and Israel's past within the archaeological circles in Northern Europe is that the past is politically misused in the Middle East and that biblical archaeological research and Israeli nationalist archaeology are biased". Oestigaard refers to the influence of Gustav Kossinna (1858–1931), a German who is today a highly controversial figure in the theoretical foundation of archaeology with some very suspicious followers (including Heinrich Himmler). The mostly neglected study of Dermot Anthony Nestor, *Cognitive Perspectives on Israelite Identity* (Nestor 2010), also points to the dependence of Israeli national archaeology on assumptions which really have their home in Kossinna's but also V. Gordon Childe's ideas about archaeology, race and ethnicity (Nestor 2010, 68–76).

[105] Cf. A. Mazar 1990, 476–8. The complex on Megiddo and in similar places like Beersheva have alternatively been seen as warehouses or barracks. The basic question is: Do horses in Palestine need stables? The climate will allow horses to live in the open practically the whole year. The two cobbled galleries where the horses are supposed to have been kept would demand an enormous amount of hay and straw to make it comfortable for the horses but still the space in one of the "boxes" is much too small. Horses do lie down.

conspicuous during excavations in the 1950s and 1960s at Megiddo, Hazor, Gezer, Lachish, but also Ashdod: the six-chamber gate.[106] All of this Yadin, together with his followers, considered examples of Solomon's building activities (Yadin 1972, 147–64). The only problem which somehow disturbed the picture was the presence of such a gate at Ashdod, being a Philistine city, not really a place to be considered in this connection.[107]

The importance of the biblical connection was that in a typical kind of circular argumentation the chronological information in the books of Kings which would place David and Solomon in the tenth century BCE was used to create an archaeological scenario which, based on the biblical chronology, was also to be set in the tenth century BCE, and *vice versa*.[108] The biblical chronology relating to anything before the Assyrian Period beginning in the eighth century is notoriously unusable for chronological reconstructions with its use of round numbers with emphatic meanings: seven years, twenty years, forty years, and seventy years.[109] Were it not for the status of the Bible among modern Bible students the traditions of the United Monarchy might be related to conditions in Palestine at any time before, say, 950 BCE – in the same way as the King Arthur circle of legends relates to any time between the Roman withdrawal from the British Islands in the fifth century CE and the arrival of the Saxons some hundred years later,[110] or the *Niebelungenlied* may refer to conditions in central Europe around 500 CE,[111] and the Norse sagas to Scandinavia before 900 CE,[112] not to speak of Saxo Grammaticus' *Gestae Danorum*, tracing the history of the Danes from the hoary past to the present.[113] In short, to a totally legendary time with little (or at least a very

---

[106] For reference, A. Mazar 1990, 384.

[107] The gate was excavated by Moshe Dothan in 1970. For an early discussion of this type of gate, and of the importance of its presence at Lachish and Ashdod, see Ussishkin 1980.

[108] For a series of hilarious examples of this kind of circularity, cf. Finkelstein 2005, 31–42. But as indicated a number of times in this book, logic has never been a major issue among those who work with the Bible either textually or materially.

[109] Cf. on this Lemche 2001b. I plan to make an English translation of this article available as "Emphatic Time in the Old Testament" on the internet before too long.

[110] King Arthur: Halsall 2014. Date of the medieval legends probably twelfth century.

[111] Nibelungenlied, c. 1200 CE, Leinert 2015.

[112] Norse sagas, c. 1200: English translation: Snorri Sturluson 1991. For a discussion cf. Brown 2012.

[113] Saxo wrote at the same time as Snorri. His *Gestae Danorum* is similar to the Old Testament in the way Saxo proceeds from a total legendary past down to events of his own time, his hero being his master the archbishop Absalon the "founder" of Copenhagen – in reality Copenhagen is up to two hundred years older, but great persons like Absalon founded cities. English translation; Saxo Grammaticus 2008. A recent study in English: Muceniecks 2017.

dubious) basis in actual history. The references to these competing legends from Europe are not unimportant but in many ways revealing because they are all witnesses to the same phenomenon: the inventiveness of the human mind when constructing the past from legend.[114] As already stated, the question is simply: Without biblical information (I would prefer not to say "data") what would the archaeologist have to say about Palestine in the eleventh to ninth century BCE?

The problems of the Solomonic origins of the stables and of the six chamber gates seen in the light of a questionable historical analysis based on presumably late biblical sources soon came to the fore when Yadin, hand in hand with David Ussishkin, downdated the stables to the ninth and not the tenth century and attributed them to the activities of the Omrides.[115] Today it seems that this trend has continued as the stables are now dated to the eighth century BCE by Norma Franklin and ascribed to the policies of Jeroboam II.[116] One only has to ask: Who's next?

How fragile the whole situation is becomes apparent when we review the discussion about Jerusalem and the tenth century BCE among archaeologists over the last thirty years. If in any place it was here that the fate of the United Monarchy under David and Solomon was sealed, or so it is believed. It was not a minimalist project; it simply came about as primarily an archaeological subject. And yet it is still heavily debated not only among the archaeologists themselves and historians of this ancient society but also and perhaps especially in the media.[117] Among archaeologists two schools have emerged, one based at Tel Aviv University, the second at the Hebrew

---

[114] Which has not prevented biblical scholars of the Albright family to fable about an oral epic tradition as the prototype of later biblical prose narrative, an idea that seems to originate with Albright, but has been taken up by his student Frank Moore Cross (Cross 1973) and especially by some of the fourth generation Albrighteans, such as Ronald S. Hendel (1987). No more about this here. A more complete discussion will be included in my project *Cultural Memory is not a Paper Tiger*. For an idea of what may be going on, cf. the example of *Iflatun pınarı*, "the Well of Plato", in Lemche (forthcoming), about how an old Hittite border sign at the border to Arzawa was reinterpreted in the Middle Ages as a well which owed its existence to the magic of Plato (whose tomb was supposed to be in nearby Konya). This example shows how totally uncontrolled public memory is: everything may be invented or blended together from the most impossible sources. On the monument, cf. Harmanşah 2015, 54–82.

[115] Yigael Yadin on Megiddo: Yadin 1960. But compare with Yadin 1979, where at least the Solomonic date of the stables has been given up. The six-chamber gate at Megiddo had already been downdated by David Ussishkin (Ussishkin 1980).

[116] Franklin 2017, 103–14. See also Cantrell and Finkelstein 2006.

[117] Thus perhaps the most recent survey of the discussion was published in the magazine *The New Yorker* in the summer of 2020 by a journalist, Ruth Margalit, "In Search of King

University in Jerusalem. The group of archaeologists in Jerusalem headed by Amihar Mazar stands for an approach that seeks to save as much as possible of the biblical account, whereas the Tel Aviv group headed by Israel Finkelstein and David Ussishkin – at least in the traditional set-up of both groups; new generations are slowly taking over – is far more critical of the biblical information.

Archaeologically, the Tel Aviv group and the Jerusalem group seem far apart, although the main subject of the discussion has been chronology based on different interpretations of the pottery chronology, a highly technical discussion really only accessible fully to the specialist. However, for both groups the evidence of the Bible is of the highest importance: the discussion soon deteriorated into a fight for the historicity of David and Solomon. This is especially evident when we review the output of the spokesperson of the Tel Aviv group, Israel Finkelstein. Finkelstein was probably not the first to address the question of the historicity of these two Israelite kings. Neither was it any of the minimalists. The first instance of the historical critic of the biblical image of great kings residing in Jerusalem in the tenth century BCE was probably provided by G.J. Wightman who introduced a low chronology by pulling the rug out from under the historical Solomon (Wightman 1990). The issue of the low chronology was soon to become the mark of the Tel Aviv archaeologists, resulting in bitter strife with the Jerusalem team.[118] The Israeli public was informed in the most brutal way by Zeev Herzog, an archaeologist from Tel Aviv who, in the weekly magazine *Ha'aretz*, published an article titled, "Deconstructing the walls of Jericho" (Ha'aretz 29 October 1999). Here Herzog presented the following statement:

> Following 70 years of intensive excavations in the Land of Israel, archaeologists have found out: The patriarchs' acts are legendary, the Israelites did not sojourn in Egypt or make an exodus, they did not conquer the land. Neither is there any mention of the empire of David and Solomon, nor of the source of belief in the God of Israel. These facts have been known for years, but Israel is a stubborn people and nobody wants to hear about it.

David's Lost Empire", *The New Yorker*, June 22, 2020: "The Biblical ruler's story has been told for millennia. Archeologists are still fighting over whether it's true".

[118] Finkelstein 1996, 177–87. In the almost endless series of articles pro and contra this low chronology, cf. A. Mazar 2005, and Finkelstein 2005.

And certainly nobody wanted to hear such things. Herzog's words were intended as a provocation and they certainly were. As I wrote above, the secular Zionist Israeli cares little about the historicity of Abraham and Moses, but David is a different matter. To remove David from history is the same as to remove ancient Israel from history, which is also the same as to remove modern Israel's claim to be the legitimate successor state to ancient Israel in Palestine. This is dangerous business in a society like modern Israel, and also involves personal risks for persons formulating such ideas (as the Israeli historian Shlomo Sand was to find out a few years later when he published his studies on the invention of Israel and of the land of Israel, a reaction that also included physical abuse: Sand 2008, 2012). Israel Finkelstein escaped such problems, or hoped that he would escape them, by reintroducing David through the back door: He simply reinvented David as a chieftain roaming the Judean hills between Jerusalem and Hebron following a sociological model from the time of anthropological system theory which reckoned with a series of political changes from tribalism via chiefdoms to states.[119]

Here it becomes evident that the gap between Finkelstein and his opponents from Jerusalem may not be as wide as normally assumed. Of course the only extra-biblical scrap of evidence of this David is the reference in the Tel Dan inscription to "David's House" (if this is, indeed, the correct interpretation). Then the questions are:

1. Does this "David's House" refer to a patronage family of this name with an apical ancestor we can only date by using, in a rather naïve way, the chronological information in the Old Testament placing David in the tenth century BCE? Without this biblical framing he could just as well belong to the eleventh or the twelfth century BCE or, as a matter of fact, to any time predating the Tel Dan inscription; or he may be totally fictitious in the same way as King Arthur, Siegfried and all the other heroes known from folk literature.
2. Does it refer to a chiefdom supposed to have existed in Judah, a political construction on the way to becoming a state – something which Judah only became in the eighth or even the seventh century BCE?

---

[119] This idea of David as a kind of ḫabīru chieftain goes like a scarlet thread through Finkelstein's works. The idea is most eloquently formulated in Finkelstein and Silberman 2006. For a very harsh criticism, especially of Finkelstein's anthropological modeling, cf. Kletter 2004.

3   Does it refer to a state with ethnic uniformity already in the tenth century BCE?

In these three questions the problems for Finkelstein's reconstruction are exposed: He cannot break free from the biblical evidence. In talking about a society founded on the basis of specific ethnic sentiments, he is simply paraphrasing the Old Testament narratives about this period. But how does Finkelstein know that such sentiments were valid say around 1000 BCE? The truth is that he cannot know but resorts to age-old ideas about Israelite identity, which is definitely a problem for him as his acquaintance with the specialized anthropological literature is at best not very solid, which was already obvious when we discussed Finkelstein's model of the Israelite settlement. As Raz Kletter correctly remarks: Finkelstein's conception of the national state only became a historical reality a couple of hundred years ago – in Europe – after the fall of the French monarchy. It had as little meaning in ancient Palestine as it has today in most of the Middle East.[120]

The team of Eilat Mazar in Jerusalem didn't care about such minor matters. They opted for a full restoration of the biblical image of David (and Solomon). The battleground is Jerusalem itself, and it also involves the cooperation of the Israeli nationalistic organization ELAD, which in turn is supported by a Russian oligarch financing the establishment of the *City of David National Park* on the south-eastern hill.[121] By combining her excavations with those of Kathleen Kenyon and Yigael Shiloh and others, the Hebrew University archaeologist Eilat Mazar identified and supervised the reconstruction of the foundations of David's palace. At least this is what she believes (E. Mazar 2008 and 2015). Her interpretation has been taken down by other archaeologists, thus by Israel Finkelstein in cooperation with Zeev Herzog, Lili Singer-Avitz, and David Ussishkin, and by Margreet Steiner (Steiner 2016).[122]

---

[120] Cf. the very relevant criticism of Finkelstein's ideas in Kletter 2004. Kletter's criticism underscores a problem with interpretation, archaeological as well as historical: The interpretation will always be dependent on the state of knowledge of how societies function on many different levels. To use sociological models of, say fifty years ago, will simply deny the interpreter an enormous amount of possibilities and often exhibit the interpreter's "European" background. This was really what my *Early Israel* was about: To illustrate the many varieties to choose from, thereby providing a better understanding of the possibilities of interpretation.

[121] ELAD or *The City of David Foundation*: https://en.wikipedia.org/wiki/Ir_David_Foundation.

[122] Margreet Steiner is the curator of Kenyon's heritage and involved in the publication of the results of Kenyon's excavations in Jerusalem. On financing, see the Wikipedia article "Ir David Foundation" https://en.wikipedia.org/wiki/Ir_David_Foundation.

Margreet Steiner has also engaged with the general issue of a Jerusalem in the tenth century BCE in other places, and her verdict has been consistently the same: There was no Jerusalem at that time, sometimes in the presence of and in direct confrontation with archaeologists of the opposite opinion.[123]

It is a strange world. Israeli archaeology is not as bad as the remarks in Terje Oestigaard's essay about its premises might indicate, at least not all aspects of it. However, from a scientific angle there are problems. I would never say that the archaeologists from Tel Aviv are digging for "God and Country", emulating Neil Asher Silberman's book title (Silberman 1982). Neither are they trying to verify the claims of the Bible, although they are still constrained by assertions from the Bible, such as the nationality of the Israelites. They end up in a logical morass because they basically adopt the language of the Bible, making a distinction between the biblical "Israelites" and the rest of the population of ancient Palestine, typically dubbed "the Canaanites".[124] They are still a long away from understanding the issue of ethnicity, and blend in with it an idea of "nation" which is foreign to ancient peoples. In short, their understanding of anthropology is lagging behind their understanding of archaeological techniques. They definitely know the trade of their craft. Moreover, Finkelstein has, over many years, shown an understanding of the status of archaeology vis-à-vis textual information that accepts some of the many problems which the interconnection between facts on the ground and facts in books cause. Finkelstein has evidently looked for advice among leading European biblical scholars such as Thomas Römer, H. Michael Niemann, and Manfred Oeming. His dating of the pan-Israelite tradition to the period between the fall of Samaria in 722 BCE and of Jerusalem in 587 BCE and his references here and there to the activities of the deuteronomistic historiographers are recommended.[125] If this was common for all archaeologists, we would have more qualified interpretations of archaeological finds when put into a biblical perspective.

Alas, the same cannot be said about his colleagues in Jerusalem whose understanding of what is found in the Bible prevents them from escaping the accusation of digging with the Bible in one hand and the trowel in the other. In this way they are producing "good ole biblical archaeology" in a fashion that would have pleased Albright. Their problems with textual materials are

---

[123] Most outspoken in her conclusion to Jerusalem in the Late Bronze Age and Iron I Period, in Steiner 2003.
[124] This distinction is as fictitious today as it ever was. In ancient Palestine there was never an ethnic distinction between "Israelites" and "Canaanites". It is a biblical myth. On this Lemche 1991a.
[125] More about this in the following chapter.

self-evident, e.g., in Amihai Mazar's lecture at the *IOSOT* meeting in Munich in 2013.[126] Mazar's idea of biblical studies' contribution to history is, as a matter of fact, another form of "excavation" of the biblical texts, by "peeling off the literary, theological, and ideological layers of the texts ... the text may be evaluated as raw material for the extraction of historical data" (A. Mazar 2003, 94). Are we talking about "*Offenbarungsarchäologie*"?[127] The sad thing is that Amihai Mazar hasn't any clue as to how tradition works, and has never studied the subject in a serious way. A perusal of anthropologists such as Walter Ong and Jack Goody would have been a great help for him – or maybe not, perhaps rather a great surprise or even a shock.[128] He uncritically suggests that there must be memories embedded in biblical narrative but he has no method to control the information.

Conclusion

We are now at the end of the road to minimalism, and also a bit further than 1990. The development within biblical studies over the period from 1960 to 1990 moved us from the safe haven of accepted ideas to a world in turmoil. We might say that the only constant thing was the Hebrew of the texts of the Old Testament, and even this is not so assured as it was two generations ago. Basically, this has nothing to do with minimalism; or perhaps it is a consequence of the changing world of Old Testament studies caused by the minimalists.

The aim of this section is to show that minimalism did not, like another Athena, spring out of the foreheads of a few bizarre scholars with strange ideas and purposes. On the contrary, minimalism – which was not the way the group of scholars involved in the process of rethinking Israel's history considered their efforts – came into being step by step as biblical scholarship progressed. In 1960 we may speak of a general agreement about the essentials of this scholarship including an almost unified interpretation of the history of ancient Israel. Martin Noth and John Bright, the two antagonists, were not at all antagonists; they just represented two parts of the same cloth. Their world began to fall apart when it became obvious that their idea about the home of the twelve-tribe ideology in the Old Testament in a sacred league

---

[126] A. Mazar 2014. An earlier version is A. Mazar 2003.
[127] Cf. Diebner above, p. 4.
[128] Ong 2002; Goody 2010. To indicate Ong's importance the editor of the thirtieth-anniversary edition states that there was a world before Ong, and a new one after him.

belonging to the time of the judges had a home no longer. When their tribal league vanished, scholars only slightly changed the perspective and created a brave new world for this ideology, in the time of the United Monarchy of David and Solomon. There are good reasons for the strong although impossible defense of this monarchy, for without it the ideology of the twelve tribes has once more lost its home. This point has to be accepted by the minimalists as well and it will be our task to present alternative reasons for its existence, or at least to point to a new path towards the solution of the problem.

Archaeology as it is practiced in modern Israel is of little help: On the one hand it is too complicated to the non-specialist to be of much use and, on the other not, sophisticated enough in its application of methods not directly formulated by archaeologists – especially biblical studies in all its complexity, and social anthropology. Even the most sophisticated group of archaeologists in modern Israel situated around the towering figure of Israel Finkelstein is not up-to-date when it comes to anthropology. William G. Dever has accused the minimalists of relying on a sociological approach called "processual anthropology" – we are now talking about post-processual anthropology, he argues, but is he right? If you read some of his archaeological recommendations you will get the opposite impression that the minimalists – or at least this one – are not following the unhelpful ways of processual archaeology and social anthropology. On the contrary, they left processual anthropology (and thereby also processual archaeology and processual historical studies) a long time ago. Our/my approach is definitely post-processual.

But Israel Finkelstein's approach is not! His theorizing about the emergence of ancient Israel is definitely founded in the same type of anthropology which was developed by Elman R. Service who was the anthropological mentor of George E. Mendenhall. He also includes a number of features belonging to previously followed forms of social anthropology, such as a somewhat imprecise understanding of the concept of ethnicity. The study of traditions is another field where he needs an update. In many ways Finkelstein is much more the likely target of Dever's criticism than Dever's despised minimalists, but perhaps there is too little space in the centre where Dever believes himself to be – together with the two archaeologists Israel Finkelstein and Amihai Mazar.

The next and last section will try to indicate the next steps on the road to wherever the end will be – or maybe because there is never an end, then a road that will lead biblical scholarship in new directions.

3   Back to Reason

Back in 1992, when he had heard my lecture on "The Old Testament: A Hellenistic Book?" which I delivered in Copenhagen in March 1992,[1] the late Frederick H. Cryer immediately responded: "This is the most important lecture since Frederick Winnett's presidential address to the *Society of Biblical Literature* in December 1964" (Winnett 1965). This was quite a response to a lecture which I planned as a reaction to the development which was the subject of the previous part and which had removed any possibility of an early date for the historical literature in the Old Testament. Planning the lecture, I decided to pull out all the stops: How would it look if I simply skipped the nitpicking and the endeavours to place this historiography at various points in Israel's history, a history which had shown itself to be more and more elusive, or as I put it at the time: Showing a *systemic* – not a systematic – lack of congruence with what happened in ancient Palestine in the Bronze and Iron Ages? As an answer I proposed to see the writings of the Old Testament as a product originating in the Hellenistic Age. The idea was to begin where we have the first physical evidence of the books which have been included in the Old Testament, and the *first evidence of the existence of the Hebrew books are the Dead Sea Scrolls,* indicating that in general this literature was in existence around 100 BCE. Following Winnett, we have here the evidence. This literature existed c. 100 BCE. Furthermore, if there was no compelling reason to date it, or part of it earlier, a date earlier than the second century BCE would exclusively rely on assumptions. The question is simply: do we really believe in an early date for something which we only know of from a late, i.e., Hellenistic date?

The normal procedure was, and still is, to propose a date for a piece of literature in the Bible by extracting from the very text itself the information which would place it in a certain period.[2] If part of the historiography describes the reform of King Josiah, well, then this reform must have taken place, or so it is

---

[1] The lecture was in Danish and held in March 1992. Published the same year as Lemche 1992c, and translated into English as Lemche 1993.

[2] A quite hilarious example of this way of arguing can be found in Friedman 1989. He opens with a longish résumé of the (biblical) portrait of the history of Palestine between the tenth and the seventh century, and then he continues by presenting dates for the

assumed. Otherwise, we would have no story about it. The procedure would make sense only if it was possible to control the information of this text, if it was possible to verify that the text was really talking about something that happened. As it is, this is normally not the case with biblical historiographic texts; we only have the evidence of the text itself. This creates an awkward situation when these texts are used to confirm themselves. Here we are back to the rationalistic paraphrase: remove what is unlikely and retain the rest and consider it a first-class witness. The examples presented earlier, including Sennacherib's attack on Jerusalem or Shishak's plundering of the temple, were eye openers in this connection because they showed how totally arbitrary biblical historiographers handled their stories even in such cases where there was a historical background. The procedure of self-confirmation does not work; it is totally arbitrary.

Proposing a Hellenistic date for the historiography meant that this is the logical starting point for any analysis. The *Dead Sea Scrolls* are factual, indisputable. They are the *terminus ante quem* for the dating of biblical literature. They are not necessarily the *terminus a quo* although they show a more complex situation than the status of the Hebrew texts a few centuries later, as it is clear that more than the forerunners of the later Masoretic tradition are present here. It is, however, here we have to begin, and not at the other end when a dating relies on nothing except assumptions suggesting that the tradition leading to a certain text began somewhere in the past – we of course don't know when it began – and it developed over the next many years – maybe hundreds of years – until it achieved its present form.[3] As we were taught at the university sixty years ago: It took a thousand years to produce the Old Testament.

By saying a *systemic lack of congruence* and not a systematic one the meaning was (and still is) that this lack of congruence was intended: The historiographer (a collective person) had no interest in telling us how it really was (as if he should have known); his plan was to tell us why we are here and for that purpose he constructed a history which he deemed fit to forward his purpose: To tell his readership, the people of God, the sons of Israel, why they were the chosen people and why they belonged in this specific country of theirs. As is the case with all history writing, it is done with a purpose which is not only to entertain its readership (which is of course no fault if it does), but also to

---

literature in which he found his reconstructed Israel. The technique is the same as in Bright's *History* but the subject has changed to the date of the literature.

[3] The biblical fragments have been excellently collected and edited by Eugene Ulrich (Ulrich 2013).

create a feeling of belonging together, a kind of ethnicity which in modern times has often been converted into nationalism. It was not without reason that history as a subject of the curriculum of the primary school was one of the victims of the 1968 students' rebellion in Europe. The leftist/Marxist leaders of the rebellion knew well that if they made the primary school "forget" history, the next generation would grow up without any national identity, or a much weakened nationality, making it much more likely to be engulfed by the Marxist *international*. And they, to a large extent, succeeded, at least in Europe where national history is no longer really something "everybody" knows by heart.[4]

Historiography is an identity-creating project, and so it was also in antiquity. As such, ethnicity is shared by those who are part of a specific history, whether we are talking about the members of a small group living in a cavern thousands of years ago creating a border with the group living in the next cavern by having different stories to tell, or members of a modern national state. The stories told all help to bind together the group which shares the stories. Moving to biblical historiography, this is exactly what the intention behind the creation of this history was – and still is today. A shared history creates an ethnicity of some kind, something that can be shared – whether in church, at the football ground, within the family, in your village, city, or country. It was perhaps the catharsis of the American Civil War that created a feeling among Americans of belonging together on the ruins of various projects of creating diversity. Similarly, the European Union is the product of the two great wars in Europe during the twentieth century, when it was realized that the traditional European tribal wars had to end as the consequences had become too serious and threatened the whole of European civilization. A common European history was needed, but the opposite happened. Now local histories are threatening even this project. Ethnicity is a highly dynamic issue and the

---

[4] Being the citizen of the oldest modern state in Europe officially founded more than eleven hundred years ago and still ruled by what is ideologically the same royal family I can really subscribe to the impact of such ideologies. When I took Rainer Albertz, a well-known German *Alttestamentler*, to the Castle of Fredensborg to visit the National Museum there and its huge collection of historical paintings (mostly from the nineteenth century – the period when European nationalism was formed with its soon-to-be catastrophic consequences) – he was duly impressed and at the same time surprised and exclaimed when we left: "Now, I understand why Lemche says that ancient Israel was not a nation. To a Dane there is only one nation, Denmark!" The core area of Denmark has also remained the same during all this time, although many changes have occurred along the fringes.

stories on which it is based have constantly to be reformulated, at least as far as interpretation goes.⁵

Seen in this light, biblical historiography should not be evaluated according to the extent to which it conforms with a real past, which is a foreign country, as it is put by David Lowenthal, but according to how far it lives up to its task of being a tool for identity creation (Lowenthal 2015). This should not be problematic, and was not problematic when the biblical historiography was put to paper (skin or parchment or whatever), but it definitely became a problem when the mood of the readership changed from a primary interest in the narratives themselves to the alleged periods they were describing. This change came late, but can be followed in art with the increasing interest in "historical" staging becoming more and more evident as the Renaissance changed into the Enlightenment and after that into the Modern Age.⁶ Simultaneously, the problems for biblical readership arose as critical voices began to be heard among European intellectuals, creating a gap between what is related and what really happened.⁷ A concept like fundamentalism only emerged when it became clear that academic critical study was lost as a subject for fundamentalists, and a movement arose which simply was named after a collection of writings, *The Fundamentals*, which was published in twelve volumes between 1910 and 1915. Of course the phenomenon was much older, almost present everywhere and at any time within Christianity, but the phenomenon found its identity expressed in these writings. And it is to this very day

---

⁵ So are we speaking about history as a myth? We can definitely say that ancient history reached back into a mythological landscape. It is perhaps even more interesting the way this mythical landscape has been translated by modern historiography into a historical *mythical* landscape through the phenomenon of *metahistory* in the sense of Hayden White (White 1973) allowing the mythology to live on. Humankind does not easily let go of its memories.

⁶ At the beginning of this period – between c. 1350 and 1800 – the figures depicted were dressed in contemporary clothing. Later, a world of fantasy took over and the figures often appeared in imagined dress. At the end of this development they were dressed in historically correct (as it appeared at the time of painting) garments.

⁷ It is to be stressed: Among intellectuals understood to be people educated on a higher level. Ordinary people of today do not care. If in doubt, it is recommended to review some of the esoteric literature of freemasonry, including subjects like Egyptomania, alchemy, magic, cabbala, even astrology, all taken seriously by non-academic masons. It is not a matter of what is historically correct; it's a matter of what sells best, i.e., what tickles the fancy of the reader. Another source of information about what normal people go for will be to watch programs such as those on the *History Channel*. Here programs on Egypt and the pyramids are good examples. Again it has to be stressed: normal people have no tools enabling them to control information from such "sources", and they probably live happily ever after.

obvious that it still has a very strong hold on parts of academic theology, and there are no signs of it losing its grip on popular culture.

However, leaving this discussion aside for the moment, we may ask why Winnett's lecture was so important, and why my lecture was compared to it. Winnett gave his lecture at a time when the dating of biblical historiography had assumed almost a canonical status: The oldest part, traditionally called the *Yahwist*, or simply "J", belonged to the early Israelite monarchy, i.e. the time of David and Solomon.[8] The second part was called the *Elohist* or E, either understood to be an independent document or a revision to the Yahwist and stemming from the eighth century BCE. Then we had the *deuteronomistic* literature reckoned to belong to the late monarchy and spiritually related to the reform of King Josiah in 623 BCE, which was often supposed to be based on the content of the fifth book of Moses, *Deuteronomy*, from which it took its name. Originally considered an ideology represented in a number of biblical books, the status of the deuteronomistic literature changed when Martin Noth proposed the viewing of this literature – from the Book of Joshua to the Second Book of Kings (with or without the fifth book of Moses) – as one piece of historiography partly independent from the historiography found in the Yahwist and in the Elohist.[9] The date of this work, often indicated by just a "D", would operate with Josiah's reform dated to 622 BCE as it's *terminus a quo*.[10] The identity of this deuteronomistic document has for many years been duly discussed among biblical scholars trying to dissolve it into several layers or even to blow up the idea of such a coherent work of historiography, often considering its oldest layer pre-exilic and its final redaction exilic.[11] The

---

[8] The "canonical" opinion was formulated by no less than Gerhard von Rad – although he did not propose these dates as the first. Cf. von Rad 1944.

[9] Noth 1943. The English edition (Noth 1981) represents an amputated edition of Noth 1943, as the German original included two separate but comparative analyses, first of the deuteronomistic history, second the Chronicler's work. This last part was only made available in English much later in Noth 1997.

[10] It was for many years the *veritas communis opinionis* that the Book of Deuteronomy in its early form as *Urdeuteronomium* was the very law book said to have been found in the temple during its restoration and the course of the reform itself (2 Kings 22:8–11). The first to oppose this idea was probably Östreicher 1923, but this has not prevented the discussion from continuing to this very day.

[11] Worth including here will be the so-called "Göttinger Schule" of Rudolf Smend (Smend 1971), followed by Dietrich (1972), and Veijola (1975, 1977, and 1982), dividing the deuteronomistic history into two, successively three redactional layers, and, the Frank Moore Cross circle including (apart from Cross himself, cf. Cross 1973), also Richard A. Nelson (Nelson 1981), splitting it into two strata (litt.). A direct rejection of Noth's thesis: among others Römer 2007.

final document or layer is the *Priestly Writer* or "P", which almost everybody considered post-exilic.

The "history" of Old Testament historiography was challenged by Winnett in his famous lecture, arguing for a much later dating of these documents, being in his view exilic or even-postexilic. The foundation of his view is simple and clear: If we date this historiography late it is because of internal evidence, i.e. evidence from the text itself. If we date it early it is on the basis of assumptions. The usual example of this, as also provided by Winnett, is the home of Abraham in Ur in Chaldea, which would not have been the case before the Chaldeans were present in Ur, i.e., from the eighth century BCE and onwards. The *terminus a quo* would therefore be the eighth century and not the tenth. Normally such information has been considered a late intrusion into an earlier text, but to follow up Winnett, this only works on the assumption that the text in question (the Abraham story) is earlier. So, the weighing of evidence versus assumptions in cases like this simply points in the direction of a late date of the Abraham story in Genesis, a statement which is of course poison to normal biblical scholarship which has expertly, over many generations, built houses of cards by joining assumptions to assumptions. If Winnett is right, the whole construction of the series of documents illuminating Israel's history from the earliest times to the exile has simply lost its *Sitz im Leben*. It is simply no more than based on a series of assumptions which have been linked together by dubious reasoning which is basically founded on the assumption (another one) that a text relates to the events which it recounts, which is simply the fundamental logical mistake that has governed Old Testament scholarship for many generations. It is a mistake because, logically, a text is not an event. Simply because we read something in a text we cannot assume that what we read really happened. The assumption is particularly strange especially because the assumption emerged in a time when other fields were skipping this naïve kind of reasoning.

Winnett's challenge was taken up by his student John Van Seters in a comprehensive series of studies beginning with the already mentioned study of the Abraham tradition, which, by the way, is dedicated to Winnett (Van Seters 1975). Van Seters' Abraham studies simply tears apart almost everything written before him about how traditions relate to an imagined past, an imagination based on the same sources which are analyzed as the result of the past being remembered – as we would perhaps prefer to say today – by the present; in classic Old Testament study an often repeated kind of circular argumentation. What Van Seters writes comes very close to the basic ideas of minimalism:

Consequently, without any such effective historical controls of the tradition one cannot use any part of it in an attempt to reconstruct the primitive period of Israelite history (Van Seters 1975, 309).

And it goes very well with what is standard procedure in all fields of folklore studies, except when it comes to the Bible. We have often seen the complaint being formulated by conservative maximalists that the critical scholars, with their hypercritic approach (whatever this is supposed to mean[12]) are treating the Bible differently from all other texts from ancient time.[13] This is not correct. As a matter of fact the conservative maximalists are those who demand a special reading of biblical texts – after all, they believe in what is written there, something which is not a problem they have with other texts. Kenneth Kitchen has been a keen proponent of such an attitude, a very critical scholar within his own field, Egyptology, but at the same time naively believing in whatever the biblical stories tell him.[14]

It is impossible to control stories originating in a milieu without logical thinking, with no control of "facts". Van Seters knows that and it is for that reason that he, in his *Abraham in History and Tradition,* includes a serious discussion of oral tradition and folklore. He draws attention especially to the laws of popular literature formulated by the Danish folklorist Axel Olrik (1864–1917)[15] If we study the "history" of early Denmark by Saxo Grammaticus (c. 1200 CE), we will find a history with many similarities to biblical historiography, not least the chapters on the Kings from Lejre close to Roskilde on Sealand, including characters like Rolf Krake. The royal establishment at Lejre has been excavated. But even so, because there are no texts going back to the days of Rolf before the medieval sources (including as the most important

---

[12] As I have said many times, there is only one stance for a critical scholar and that is to be one hundred percent critical. If you are not one hundred percent critical you don't belong among the critical scholars, evidently because you are influenced by factors which have nothing to do with critical scholarship. There is no possibility of gradation here. This also implies that there is no difference – nor should there be – between the methods and criteria employed by biblical scholars and any other field within academia.

[13] Let's remember the introduction to Iain Provan's attacks on minimalism (Provan 1995).

[14] Cf. above on Kitchen and fundamentalism p. 29.

[15] Olrik 1992. Van Seters did not have access to the English translation when he wrote his study on the Abraham tradition but used the German version of Olrik 1908; 1909. Olrik formulated his "laws" on the basis of a comprehensive number of studies of Scandinavian folk literature resulting in such works as *Danske Danmarks heltedigtning: en oldtidsstudie.* Bind 1 *Rolf Krake og den ældre Skjoldungrække* (1903), and *Danmarks heltedigtning: en oldtidsstudie.* Bind 2 *Starkad den Gamle og den yngre Skjoldungrække* (1910), alas practically exclusively in Danish.

Saxo's *Gestae Danorum*, which is at least three hundred years later than any putative dating of Rolf), he still belongs to the realm of myth and legends and Rolf's time is still a part of a mythical pre-history of Denmark.[16]

The same will be the case wherever we look for similar legends found all over Europe. These do not belong to the genre of history; they represent folk literature, and it is impossible to control the information contained in such legends if no further information can be found. A name will not be considered sufficient. The Viking chief Ragnar Lodbrog won his first wife by killing a dragon, but he is probably also mentioned by Frankish chronicles from the middle of the ninth century CE as leading the Viking raids on Paris in 845 CE. Early Medieval sources put him in many various contexts, in England, as well as Ireland, France, and the Netherlands. In spite of all that, a historian could conclude as late as 2003: "Although his sons are historical figures, there is no evidence that Ragnar himself ever lived and he seems to be an amalgam of historical figures and literary invention" (Holman 2003, 220). If Ragnar had been a biblical figure, he would have been hailed as one of the great heroes of ancient Israel, and his historicity would not have been questioned – after all it only took a dubious mention of his "house" (?) to establish that David was a historical person. Furthermore, even if David was a historical person of the Early Iron Age, we have a way to go before deciding if any of the traditions attached to him have any bearing on historical events. This is indeed a reminder to biblical scholars: The name of a person will logically have to be separated from the stories told about this person. The stories belong to literature, whether oral or written, whereas a person is a physical entity.

Van Seters wrote his Abraham study – as did Thompson – in the light of the then prevailing North American paradigm postulating a historical background for Abraham and his descendants. And it still works this way: Any possible – and impossible – reference to anything that could be Abraham is immediately taken up by the popular press and turned into a proof of his existence. A tragicomic example of this occurred when Giovanni Pettinato, followed by Mitchell Dahood more than forty years ago, found Abraham and several other names and localities related to Abraham and Palestine – or somebody whom he took to be Abraham – mentioned among the then newly discovered texts from Ebla in northern Syria. The time horizon of these texts is some time around 2300 BCE, meaning that it would fit well with the biblical

---

[16] Other medieval texts include the *Chronicon Lethrense* (Lejrekrøniken) from the 12th century. He is mentioned in the epic *Beowulf*, 9th century CE (?), and other texts. Scholars have accordingly assumed that he might be a historical person, but what we know about him is all sagas and legends.

dates for this patriarch (Dahood 1979).[17] After several years of intense discussion the Assyriologist Robert D. Biggs concluded his article on "Ebla Texts" in the *Anchor Bible Dictionary* by quoting Jonas C. Greenfield: "Suffice it to say that Ebla has no bearing on the prophets minor or major" (Biggs 1992, 265). We might add: Even if Abraham's name turned up in an Ebla text, it only means that the name existed, not that the patriarch of this name has got more life in the real world because of the appearance of the name in a different context from the Bible. In the same manner: Even if David's name turned up in an inscription, as is the case of the Tel Dan inscription, whether genuine or not, the David of the Bible has not appeared in person, which again means that none of the fairy tales told about him and his dynasty in the Books of Samuel and Kings have changed status from being legendary tales to become proper historical descriptions of what happened in David's time.[18]

Dealing with the historiography of the Old Testament this is of the greatest importance and the examples illuminating the problems can be doubled many times. We thus have examples of well-known historical persons such as Charlemagne where there is no reason to doubt the historicity of the person. The emperor nevertheless became entangled in a web of romantic tales and epics, creating a whole world of narratives without providing more historicity to Charles himself. Thus, we have a whole circle of tales relating to his household including, as the most famous Roland, mention once by Einhard around 800 CE as killed in action at Roncesvalles in 778. With the memory of Roland and his master Charles the Great an extensive range of literature emerged which was still alive when Ludovico Ariosto (1474–1533), more than seven hundred years later, created his epic *Orlando furioso* (1516). In some way the memory of Charles and his heroes never died but was continuously presented in new forms and in different media. At the end it was only a name and the simple fact that the carrier of the name of Roland died in 778 CE.

---

[17] See also the triumphal – or rather not so triumphal article by David Noel Freedman (Freedman, 1978), 143–64. What was announced as the most spectacular find ever – almost – was already partly denied by Freedman in a note to his article: A letter to him from Dahood was published which partly retracted what had been previously maintained by Dahood – and Pettinato.

[18] It is as expected when Van Seters write about David as *The Biblical Saga of King David* (Van Seters 2009). Van Seters' way of handling the stories about David, separating between a deuteronomistic version and the two narrative complexes devoted to David's career and his succession respectively is coming close to my ideas of how to handle popular literature without falling in trap of discussing historicity, really an intruder into ancient legends and sagas which owes its presence to a modern sentiment of historicity.

If we have no other information to check such literature we cannot control it. There are no limits as to how it may develop, there are no limits as to how many "traditions" and fairy tale motifs, have been incorporated into it. It is, accordingly, of no importance that a fair number of tales centre on David as a person; they do not make him a historical person, although there might have existed a "David" once in the past – such an assertion is gratuitous; it cannot be falsified. The problem for biblical scholars has always been their preoccupation with the project of *propaganda fide*. This obsession has been their fate and the fate of their scholarship which in any other similar context of today would be considered "unreasonable", against reason. In this way a large section of biblical scholarship is impossible to distinguish from the reception among uneducated people of sagas and legends like those referred to here; the Norse sagas and the epic of Charlemagne and his heroes. Ordinary people will go to any length to accept any imaginative reference to such legends in popular media including "historical" novels. Academically trained biblical scholars should be able to distinguish between "fact and fiction", but they evidently often cannot since they have been trapped by a discipline where far too much is simply accepted as fact.

If we make an overview of the historiography of the Old Testament, we are entitled to ask: Is this historiography intended; i.e. does it go back to an author with specific motives and aims directing his writing, or are we talking about collections of stories put together by an editor from many sources difficult to place in time and milieu? Although this is not a moot question, there is no need to present a longish overview of the discussion, whether there are one or many deuteronomistic historians at work, or whether the Yahwist was such an editor or a writer with a purpose, to create a "national" history of ancient Israel.[19] Nor is there any reason to doubt that even if we are talking about historiographical works allowing for at least three such or more: the deuteronomistic one, the Yahwist, the Chronicler, we are not excluding other hands at work. In spite of minimalism, it is still possible to carry on with source criticism in the Pentateuch (Lemche 2011b). The discussion is unending and will, most likely for a very long time, continue from one generation of biblical scholars to the next (which does not mean that it is unnecessary).

However, the question of whether we should talk of historiography coming from a single author, or limited circle of authors, or of tradition literature which has, like a black hole, swallowed up whatever tradition which seemed fit to enter a collection of tales from the past is important, as it has

---

[19] "Editor" written with the tongue in cheek in light of John Van Seters' *The Edited Bible* (Van Seters 2006).

consequences for the understanding of the background of the historiographical works of the Old Testament. It could be said that a collection of tales would demand that somebody put this collection together. It could be done primarily for entertainment purposes, as was probably the main reason for the medieval European legendary collection such as those mentioned here; the tales of King Arthur could be added as just another example, or the reason might be to endorse a political constellation such as the appearance of a new dynasty or a changing system of government. Saxo's chronicle was an example of the first, created at a time when Denmark had been through a period of severe internal wars between different pretenders to the crown but had settled down to a strong centralized monarchy. And if we look for an example of the latter, we might understand Livy's history of ancient Rome as produced to create a historical legitimization for Rome's new status under Augustus. Herodotus's history could be seen in a similar light as a celebration of a once emerging Greek consciousness of belonging together in the wake of the victory over Persia but also as a reflection on the Greek disunity which soon followed: Its basic tone is pessimistic. And, in the same vein, the many new national histories of the 19th century might be seen as a necessary process of assimilating a new political – post-monarchical – order in Europe when the previous national symbol *per se* – the king – lost his head to the guillotine. Although it is a foreign country it is often necessary to invoke the past to create national unity.[20] It was also the original reason for the dating of the Yahwist to the time of the United Monarchy: A new political order demanded a national historical work to legitimize it.

The deuteronomistic history – and here it should be stressed that this author belongs among those dinosaurs who still speak about the deuteronomistic history in fundamentally the same meaning as Martin Noth did – does not legitimize anything. It is not written in response to the establishment of a new order but rather as an explanation for a catastrophe which had already happened. If anything, it carries the mood of a tragic past that led to the present. In its attitude to the past when history becomes the carrier of a tragic message, the similarities between the deuteronomistic history and Herodotus's "investigations" is striking as explained by Flemming A.J. Nielsen (Nielsen

---

[20] To avoid any misunderstanding: "National" does not mean "nationalistic" understood to be a concept which developed over the last two centuries. The modern conflation of concepts has led to it being almost impossible, except in certain right-wing organizations, to speak about "nations", "nationalities", in short anything deriving from Latin *nation* with its many possibilities of translation: "gens", "nation", "tribe", "people", "race", "Volk".

1997).²¹ The deuteronomistic history explains why Israel was thrown out of its land by Yahweh its god and this is indeed a tragic tale.

Van Seters considers following Hans Heinrich Schmid and his student Martin Rose the deuteronomistic history to precede the Yahwist historiography in time.²² The deuteronomistic version is a tragic history of the failure of Israel to attend to the will of its god. In contrast, the Yahwist is a history of promise which brings its readership to the brink of the Holy Land, envisaging a new future here. It could almost be seen as a response to the story told by the deuteronomistic history. It is obvious why the deuteronomistic history had to follow the Yahwist when put together as part of the *Enneateuch* – the collection of historiography from Genesis to 2 Kings.²³ It is also obvious why it has normally been considered later than the Yahwist: It is simply a matter of psychology. In the Old Testament the deuteronomistic history is placed *after* the Pentateuch. Per instinct, people living in our age will see this as a sign that coming after means being later and the priority is given to the Yahwist. This is beguiling because such a sequence is not automatically present when we are thinking of individual scrolls where each "book" has its own life before being joined together in a book. The person(s) who gave priority to the Yahwist was (were) the ancient scholar(s) who joined the Pentateuch together with the deuteronomistic history; the Yahwist must have told stories about events that logically must have preceded the story of the deuteronomistic history. This decision does not force us to accept the priority of the Yahwist as based on anything other than literary and historiographical considerations.

Van Seters bases his comprehensive analyses of the Yahwistic historiography on his seminal overview of ancient historiography including Greek, Mesopotamian, Hittite, Egyptian and Israelite historiography (Van Seters 1983). Within this context the biblical historiography definitely comes closest to the Greek one, which is also Van Seters' conclusion. He accordingly places biblical historiography within temporal and cultural reach of the Greek variety, especially Herodotus and his precursors. Again, it is an example of

---

²¹ When we talk about Herodotus's "investigations" this is the correct meaning of the Greek *historia*.

²² Cf. H. Schmid 1976 and Rose 1981. John Van Seters and the Yahwist: Van Seters 1992, 1994, and the final summary: Van Seters 2013a.

²³ The Enneateuch is definitely one of the most neglected areas of Old Testament studies, although it has always lurked in the background because the seams between the Pentateuch and the deuteronomistic history are so obvious and at the same time problematic. Reinhard G. Kratz has in many ways made up for this in Kratz 2000. Without necessarily following Kratz, he has defined the problems and thus prepared the way for a more extensive occupation with it.

the Winnett approach: Go for internal evidence which can be controlled and dismiss external arguments which are only assumptions. Both the deuteronomistic history and the Yahwist display such a range of commonality with Greek authors that they mentally belong in an environment created by their Greek colleagues. The only issue is: The Greek historiographers of the sixth to fifth centuries BCE can only be considered a *terminus a quo*; they only give an upper date for the biblical parallels. I have before argued that the closest parallel is not Herodotus but Titus Livius, but Livy represents Hellenistic history writing which is otherwise not well-known for the simple reason that almost nothing is preserved from the fourth century BCE and what we have from the third and second centuries BCE such as Polybius has a different purpose and content. All three histories, Herodotus, Livy, and the Yahwist were writing universal history which was, in the course of the narrative, turned into a national history.

The "Hellenistic" End of the Line

The problem which arose as the empire of David vanished from history is simple. Now there is no basis for the ideology of the twelve tribes of Israel in David's or Solomon's time, the legitimate question has to be asked: Is there another time or place for this ideology? Can we point at a new reason for it?

If we insist that the talk about a twelve-tribe system implies that all twelve tribes of Israel were united when the ideology came into being, the answer must be: It never happened. There was never a historical organization which embraced all the tribes of Israel. Furthermore, above I questioned the relevance of this idea of tribes as the basis of the Israelite unity, the tribe being a useful metaphor for a society without a king, i.e., a useful element in the literary construction of a past but hardly relevant to the actual process that may have led to a centralized socio-political system in central Palestine. One such example of the artificial use of tribes on such a connection was the idea of the twelve tribes of Israel which dominated so much Old Testament scholarship two generations ago. As I explained in *The Israelites in History and Tradition* more than twenty years ago, the amphictyony is still there although it has no place in any *real* history of Israel. It is simply a dominant feature in connection with the wanderings of the tribes in the desert organized as twelve tribes surrounding the tabernacle. Historically it never was, but in literature its presence is heavily felt (Lemche 1998b, 97–107).

However, the very model of the amphictyony forming the background of this organization of Israel in the desert dates the tradition. As the model of this organization undoubtedly was Greek, it presupposed a Greek model, and historically this cannot be the case earlier than the eighth or more likely the seventh century BCE (further Lemche 1976); a fact which lends support to the late dating of not only the ideology of the twelve tribes but also of the historical works which embrace this idea.

It goes without saying that dating biblical historiography to the Hellenistic Age did not stop with the twelve-tribe league. Today we see a growing interest in such a date, and the Hellenistic Age is surely a candidate because in its great centres of learning, especially Alexandria, we have all the ingredients necessary to create this historiography, a mixture of oriental and Greek tradition – today many will say *memories* but what are memories if not traditions, which means that memory represent the adaption and reformulation of tradition? Recent studies involve motifs found in the Pentateuch, not least in Genesis, but also rather convincingly the reliance of the Torah as a constitution on Plato's works, especially the laws; we are only at the beginning of an ongoing reevaluation of the origins of biblical literature.[24] In Alexandria, say around 200 BCE, everything was there: the international heritage reflected in biblical traditions, and the learned company of scholars and scrolls and places to study, the *Museion* and the *Serapeion*.[25] There were similar institutions all over the Hellenistic world, and another candidate for production of memory literature of the kind found in biblical historiography could be Babylon – my original choice (Lemche 2001a). Should we, perhaps, think of both Babylon and Alexandria in mutual competition? The historiography of the Old Testament points in both directions. Thus the old problem of the incorporation of the Sinai Complex in the story of the Exodus which Gerhard von Rad discussed in 1938 might be seen in this light (von Rad 1938). The law given at Sinai opens with a "Babylonian" law book, the Book of Covenant.[26]

---

[24] Cf. the following studies: Wesselius 2002, Gmirkin 2006, and 2017, and Wajdenbaum 2011. Gnuse 2020 did not become available to me before this work was finished.

[25] Indispensable for the study of the libraries of especially the Hellenistic world is König, Oikonomopoulou and Woolf 2013. The opening sentence on the front page says everything: "The circulation of books was the motor of classical civilization". On Alexandria and its library in particular, cf. Pollard and Reid 2006, and MacLeod 2004. We should also not overlook the Hellenistic elite's interest in historiography as a mean to solidify the new Greek rulers of the Near East. Here, a study like Strootman 2014 is highly relevant.

[26] Kratz has misunderstood the function of law in the ancient Near East (Kratz 2015, 84–87). Law was never settled in official lawbooks, secular or religious or both. Laws were collections of judgments in court. There never was a Codex Hammurabi. The "codex" is a collection of judgments which the king presents to his god as a proof of how just his government is. Thus the Codex begins with a paragraph telling us that if a person accuses another person of murder and is right, the accused person must die. But if the accusation

Such observations inspire to introduce also geographical considerations in the discussion of the origins of different parts of biblical historiography and may in this way also be an introduction to a different study of the origins of Judaism which should be traced, not in one place, but in the Persian and especially the Hellenistic world at large.

Thus, in connection with these studies of the formation of biblical literature, placing its beginning not in the first part of the first millennium BCE but instead at the end of this millennium, we will have to review probably most of our ideas about how Judaism arose, and it is a must to inquire how the northern tradition of historical Israel lived on and was incorporated in a so-called southern, but certainly Jerusalem oriented constructed memory which borrowed heavily not only from Palestinian traditions to such a degree that it ended up erasing the memory of ancient Palestine, but also from cultural loans from other parts of the Ancient Near East and Greece.

The idea originating with Albrecht Alt: that when Samaria fell to the Assyrians in 722 BCE refugees from Samaria brought their traditions – and probably more than that, their documents – with them as they fled to Jerusalem. In more recent times Alt's assumption was taken up by, among others, Israel Finkelstein in various places not least in connection with his plea for remembering a forgotten kingdom, the House of Omri, also called Samarina after its capital, but also Israel.[27] Finkelstein bases his theory on the rise in size of the population of Jerusalem at the end of the eighth century, a fact not to be denied; but there might be other reasons than the one proposed by Finkelstein, such as Jerusalem becoming a refuge to people living in southwestern Palestine after the destruction caused by Sennacherib during his campaign in 701 BCE. The hypothesis of a mass migration from Samaria to Jerusalem after 722 BCE, which is, as a matter of fact, without support in the biblical historiography may be useful in one respect. It has, from of old, been a problem that Judaism – with its preference for Jerusalem and Judah, the last giving its name

---

is wrong, the accusator must die. There is no paragraph saying that if a person kills another person, the murderer must die. Why? Because everybody knew that; it didn't have to be written down. Written "law" in Mesopotamia was for academic use, not laws to be followed in court. This has been clear in ancient Near Eastern studies since Kraus 1960. See also for a short discussion Roth 1997, 4–7. On the missing laws in Western Asia, cf. Lemche 1995b.

[27] Cf. Alt 1953a, Finkelstein 2013a. I announced my opposition not to the existence of the kingdom which was forgotten – we may say: it became the victim of a *damnatio memoriae* – but to the gratuitous speculation about people from Samaria moving to Jerusalem after 722 BCE in order to establish a new home for their memories of the past but now lost world in Lemche 2010b.

to the Jews, the *Yehudim* – in its traditions includes so much information which has no bearing on Judah at all. Therefore, some may accept this theory of Alt as a likely explanation of the presence of these – northern – elements. There are, however, serious problems attached to this hypothesis – if it should not simply be degraded to an assumption. If the tradition of ancient Israel was implanted in Jerusalemite society as early as in the years after 722 BCE and resulted in a "pan-Israelite" ideology that included all of the land of biblical Israel from Dan to Beersheba and made everyone an "Israelite" (as seen in the historiography of the Old Testament), why does this not have any effect until many hundreds of years later? According to a traditionally favourite theory of biblical scholars, the first notable result of the transplantation of northern traditions, including the memory of its religion, was the reform of King Josiah in 623 BCE. But did this reform really happen?[28] If it did, it had no effect at all. That is actually what the biblical historiographer says. The reform was forgotten and did not save Jerusalem from its fate. It is thus remarkable that after 722 BCE the name of Israel does not turn up again in a political context before the time of the two Jewish rebellions against the Romans in 66–70 and 132–135 CE except in contexts where the biblical idea of the people of Israel lurks in the background. It has been noted that as late as six hundred years after the fall of Samaria and the putative migration of its citizens to the south, the Hasmonean rulers who definitely had aspirations of becoming rulers of all of the "land of the Bible" – well, under Roman surveillance, but nevertheless – did not use the title "king of Israel" but called themselves leaders of the assembly of the Jews.[29] Another indication that "Israel" was definitely not part of the cultural memory of people living in the sixth and fifth centuries BCE could be the name of the city of origin of some of the persons mentioned in the David Sofer collection, URU *šá ia-a-ḫu-du-a-a*, URU *ia-'u-du* (and variants) (Pearce and Wunsch 2014). Neither did the people living in Elephantine call themselves "Israelites" but *Yehudin* (the Aramaic form and not *Yehudim*, the Hebrew form as sometimes argued, since the Elephantine letters are in Aramaic). Not before the first century CE do we encounter the name of Israel as representing anything other than the *biblical* nation of Israel.[30]

---

[28] Among the skeptics belong Lemche 2010a, and now Handy 2020.

[29] Cf. Lemche 2017; also Lemche 2012c.

[30] The contributions to Kartveit and Knoppers 2020 show a willingness to part with the traditional history of the relations between Jerusalem and Samaria, which as Konrad Schmid describes the situation, Sub-Deuteronomism and Sub-Chronicism is about how ancient historiography has totally dominated modern historiography which has only recently shown evidence of freeing itself from the grasp of the ancients (K. Schmid 2020). As John Strange, during a seminar on 1 and 2 Kings back in 1967, expressed in his characteristic

While the political independence of historical Israel undoubtedly ended with the Assyrian conquest of 722 BCE, this does not mean that anything "Israelite" ceased to exist in the former territory of Omri's state. Even Finkelstein has to admit it. A fair part of the population, about 40,000 souls, were transported to Mesopotamia, some by Tiglathpileser III in 727 BCE, others ("27,280") by Salmanasser V or Sargon II in 722 BCE – according to Finkelstein's calculation about twenty percent of the population – and some resettlement took place. It was, by later biblical historiographers, seen as an intolerable punishment, but was it really? Sargon ends his description of the fall of Samaria by expressing the fact that the inhabitants of the province were "Assyrians". The military garrison of Samaria, and especially the chariotry, were incorporated into the Assyrian army.[31] All of this makes good sense. A standing problem for Assyria was the limited size of its population, far too small to sustain a mighty empire for its duration. The Assyrians did not want to create more enemies than necessary. It needed these new "Assyrians". The situation was probably the same after Jerusalem's fall less than a hundred and forty years later. When we meet deportees from Palestine in Achaemenid Babylonia, it is not as slaves but as citizens living in named localities around Babylon. In memory, the exile – whether Israelite or Judean – was a hell; in practice, life in these centres was much easier than in distant Palestine. Palestine was always a poor country with too little to eat. Famine was normal. In Mesopotamia this was not the case. On the contrary, a culture based on irrigation such as the Mesopotamian one would always be a haven of safety for people living there.

At the end of the day nothing supports a date of biblical historiography as a whole preceding the Babylonian conquests in 597/587 BCE, apart from the self testimony of the literature itself. This will hardly count as proof of anything. It is, on the other hand, just as clear that the historiographers were drawing on accounts going back to the kings of Assyria and Babylonia and used them for their own purpose. An overview of such references, most likely found in Assyrian and Babylonian archives, presents us with glimpses of the history of Palestine before the Persians simply because an antiquarian culture such as that found in Ashurbanipal's Assyria and Nebuchadnezzar's Babylonia preserved records from the past; it did not destroy them deliberately.

---

way: "We have all been brainwashed by the Deuteronomists". In spite of indicating this problem of "brainwashing", Konrad Schmid is still enticed by biblical historiography. Thus he still speaks of a post-exilic period, which is definitely a biblical construction as the exile never ended. See also Lemche 2015b.

[31] Cf. the "Great Summary" Inscription, in Hallo and Younger 2000, 296.

The hatred for the inhabitants of the former state of Samerina which we find expressed in 2 Kings 17 where the people living there are denounced as an unclean population consisting of foreigners without any relation to the land of Israel, and the negative evaluation of its kings in deuteronomistic historiography leading to the cancellation of the north in the historiography of Chronicles will, in any case, represent a view of the civilization of Northern Palestine that makes most sense as expressions of the aspirations of Jerusalem and its rulers in the Hellenistic Period to control all of Palestine which ultimately led to the destruction of the sanctuary on the top of Mount Gerizim. Recent Samaritan or better *Samarian* studies has revealed a rich culture that lasted until the Hasmonean onslaught. The inscriptions from their sanctuary at Gerizim have shown themselves to be extraordinary rich and informative. A reevaluation of the connection between Jerusalem and Gerizim is mandatory and already underway.[32]

Endgame

Contrary to the image painted by the self-proclaimed maximalists, the minimalists are not minimalists; they are reasonable, i.e., directed by reason. When the vice chancellor of the University of Copenhagen in 1879 during the celebrations of the university's four-hundredth anniversary demanded from the theologians that they followed the same scientific procedures as all other disciplines, it almost led to the faculty of theology leaving the university. What an insolent demand! It is, however, what the minimalists have demanded: Biblical scholars of all kinds, including biblical archaeologists, are bound to use the same procedures and methods as are current in contemporary scholarship at large. I have here presented my case, and it has constantly been indicated that biblical scholars are not following normal procedures whenever historical matters are under considerations.

Today we see many literary studies of a very high quality and a readiness to embrace all kinds of modern literary theory, whether structuralist, semiotic, reader-response, or deconstructuralist; there is no end to it. When historical questions come up, all of this is forgotten as soon as the historical paradigm inherited from the Bible takes over. Maybe it was our destiny in a world that has, for two hundred years or more, been obsessed with the past as a historical

---

[32] Cf. Hjelm 2004. Also the chapter on Jewish archives in Kratz 2015, 133–96, and the remarks in Kratz 2015, 197–208. Cf. also Kartveit and Knoppers 2020. On the inscriptions, see Gudme 2013.

reality. Maybe it is impossible not to demand from pre-modern tales the same kind of historical exactness as is requested from modern historians, but it has led to a basic flaw in the study of biblical historiography which is simply that we, today, almost exclusively think according to a pattern which is founded on the assumption of its historicity. To find out whether something is a historical fact or "just" an invention is not only the goal of historical studies of the modern age, it is, so-to-speak, the very essence of historical studies. But being practitioners of an academic pursuit, scholars of our background do not realize that those for whom they write – when it is not for their peers – are not in possession of the same apparatus of critical methodology which is a prerequisite of academic scholarship. Non-academics will simply accept whatever they are told if they like the message. It was like this in ancient times, and it still is apart from the very few who are trained as academics. Herodotus was not loved in antiquity because of the historicity of what he told. Every educated person – those who could read him – knew that he was not to be trusted when it came to the exactitude of what he wrote, but they loved him for the way he presented the past and admired him for his style and ethos. They knew that Thucydides was of another caliber when it came to the exactness of his writings about the Peloponnesian War, but he was also a high-ranking officer with the mind of such a person, demanding that reports should be as exact as possible. It is quite a different genre.[33]

The ethics of the pursuit of biblical historical studies is dubious. The discipline has been usurped by a series of considerations which are really foreign to the discipline itself. Thus we have religious demands made of the scholars, that their investigations should be seen as a support for the right beliefs. The reaction from religious groups to biblical studies has always been dominated by mistrust, and it is very easy to win support for conservative ideas of biblical historicity from religious people chasing around in the mountains of Asia Minor or Iran to find Noah's ark. There is nothing new here. Here religious people are like doubting Thomas: They want hard evidence. Critical scholars have problems but hardly the maximum conservative ones. They can easily produce what goes for evidence.

There is every possibility that conservative evangelical biblical scholarship will just carry on without recourse to reason. It is, however, a scandal when critical scholarship does not follow reason. Biblical scholarship takes place within a grey zone, but pretending that it is rational it should at least be aware

---

[33] Military reports are highly formalized and simple. We talk of a system of five points: When? Where? What? The enemy? You? Every commander of even the smallest unit knows this. I have myself authored scores of such reports. Officers do not write literature.

of the pitfalls which are constantly here: that reason is sacrificed to biblical truth. Maybe there are too many parameters which have to be exchanged for other ideas; maybe the change recommended here is impossible. But we are in a situation where it is time to look at the options. As Mario Liverani pointed out many years ago, historians of ancient cultures are inherently lazy, meaning that if they find historical records in ancient documents, they complacently paraphrase these records without trying to analyze them critically and thus the story told in such documents is adopted as the real history (Liverani 1077).[34] Liverani wrote this in a study on the decree of Telipinus (c. 1460 BCE) which is introduced with an overview of previous Hittite history before his accession. The historical overview presents history in such a way that Telipinus emerges as a kind of Messiah who brought peace to troubled Ḫatti. He did not, but this version was accepted by modern specialists for far too many years. It was propaganda written to support the new usurper of the Hittite throne who had put away his competitors in the usual Hittite manner.

Since the beginning of modern historical–critical scholarship, scholars have followed the same line by blindly accepting most of the historiography from ancient times as their guide to the history of now – in this case ancient Palestine. They have only changed position when, as is shown here, it becomes impossible to uphold traditional positions. We don't need more of this paraphrasing; we need a new approach where everything is "on the table", including and *especially* the inconvenient information. Ingrid Hjelm has, together with Hamdan Taha, Ilan Pappe, and Thomas L. Thompson, started the "Palestine History and Heritage Project" to make ground for an independent history of Palestine, i.e. a history which is not almost exclusively at the mercy of biblical historiography and its modern paraphrasers.[35]

The impact of the canonical history has been so decisive that even traces of alternative information not incorporated in the official version are normally brushed aside, although they may be present here and there in the official version. One such example is the mentioning of Abraham's relation to the Damascene Eliezer in Genesis 15:2. In its present context, this verse makes

---

[34] Translated in Liverani 2004, 28 as "Laziness is common among historians. When they find a continuous account of events for a certain period in an 'ancient' source, one that is not necessarily contemporaneous with the events, they really adopt it. They limit their work to paraphrasing the source, or, if needed to rationalization".

[35] So far only an introductory volume has appeared (Hjelm, Taha, Pappe and Thompson 2019). When I tried to present a history of ancient Palestine without recourse to biblical historiography, "The History of Israel or the History of Palestine?" (Lemche 2008, 393–453) I was able to conclude that it worked perfectly. The problems only begin when biblical historiography gets the first or only word.

absolutely no sense. However, if we refer to the story of Abraham's relation to Damascus as a late source, according to which he arrived with an army at Damascus and ruled there as a king, we suddenly have a quite different idea of who Abraham might have been outside of the biblical narrative.[36] However, this other Abraham may be the same as present in Genesis 14, in the tale of Abraham's battle against the four great kings. This chapter has always been considered a kind of intruder into the patriarchal story of Abraham, leaving interpreters without a clue. The question remains whether it could in fact be an intruder from a quite different story of Abraham, which could have just as must legitimacy (from a historian's point of view) as the canonical Abraham.[37]

Other examples of loose ends, which point in the direction of alternative stories not found worthy to be included in the canonical version of the biblical historiography, have often been noted, such as divergences in the historical overview in Deuteronomy, which has a quite different idea about the unity of the Sinai episode – in Deuteronomy Horeb and not Sinai – and the formulation of the Law of Moses which is, in Deuteronomy, not part of a Sinai revelation but proclaimed for Israel by Moses in the land of Sihon and Og (Deut. 4:44–49; 5). In the version in Deuteronomy the common element is the list of the Ten Commandments, but the law itself only comes later (Deut. 6 ff.). Then it is a minor issue that we, in the Book of Judges, find a reference to an incident which is not included in the narrative, a reference that leaves its reader in the dark (Judges 8:18–21). The missing link is used to legitimize the execution of two Midianite princes who killed Gideon's brothers, but we have no mention of this event anywhere else. The narrator is obviously playing on his audience's knowledge of other traditions than the ones told by him.

It is to be hoped that the future will see a change in attitude to biblical historiography, a change of perspective where the task is no longer to go for elements which may (or may not) be historical reminiscences, but to investigate the stories and motifs included in this historiography. A beginning was made when Thomas L. Thompson published his *The Bible in History: How*

---

[36] Cf. above p. 46, fn. 41.
[37] Ancient writers sometime play with their reader in such a way. We call it "re-writing", but we sometimes get the feeling that they knew very well that their readership also knew other versions. One such example is the role of the raven in the story of the flood in Genesis (Gen 8:7). It has absolutely no part in the biblical story, but in *Gilgameš* it is the third bird which Utnapištim sends out, and never returns. The raven is an unclean animal, so its role has been reduced in the Genesis version. But in this way the author tells the reader: "You see! I know my Gilgameš!" See more in Lemche 2012d.

Writers Create a Past.[38] It is my hope that it will not be the end. Minimalism has, hopefully, paved the way to a study of biblical historiography which does not reduce it to casual glimpses from the past, but to a piece of literature which must be studied in and of itself, and not because of what may have been stored there from an elusive foreign world, the past. Instead of making the Old Testament relevant to a modern readership, as was the project of biblical archaeology and its practitioners, the Albright family, this project has made the Old Testament almost redundant within Christian theology and has produced an amputation of modern Christianity which has made it much poorer than necessary. As any classical Christian dogmatician would say: Everything is present in the Old Testament; the New Testament only adds to the details.

---

[38] In this he was following a path that led him from his magnus opus *Early History of the Israelite People: From the Written and Archaeological Sources* (Thompson 1992) – as a matter of fact the first draft of the project of writing the history not of Israel but of Palestine, to his *The Bible in History: How Writers Create a Past* (Thompson 1999). The North-American title – *The Mythic Past: Biblical Archaeology and The Myth of Israel* – is unfortunate because it is most imprecise and misleading, and also because it automatically causes opposition seemingly claiming that the Bible is a myth, which to a North-American public means that it is a lie. This prevented it from becoming publicly well-known in North America. Thompson, in a truly Wellhausenian manner, undeterred, continued with the study of Jesus in the New Testament, *The Messiah Myth: The Near Eastern Roots of Jesus and David* (Thompson 2005), the closest companion to Mowinckel's *He That Comes* (Mowinckel 2005/1951) ever seen.

Bibliography

Ahlström, G.W. 1975. "Some Comments on John Bright's 'History of Israel'", *Journal of the American Oriental Society* 95, pp. 236–41.

Albertz, R. 1992. *Religionsgeschichte Israels in alttestamentlicher Zeit*, I–II. ATD Ergänzungsreihe Band 7, 1–2. Göttingen: Vandenhoeck & Ruprecht.

——1994. *A History of Israelite Religion in the Old Testament Period*, I–II. London: SCM Press.

——2018. "Review of William G. Dever, *What Did the Biblical Writers Know and When Did They Know It?* (2001) and *Who Were the Early Israelites and Where Did They Come From?*" (2003), in Grabbe 2018, pp. 99–113.

Albertz, R. and R. Schmitt. 2012. *Family and Household Religion in Ancient Israel and the Levant*. Winona Lake, Indiana: Eisenbrauns.

Albright, W.F. 1937. "Further Light on the History of Israel from Lachish and Megiddo", *Bulletin of the American Schools of Oriental Research* 68, pp. 22–6.

——1938. "The Present State of Syro-Palestinian Archaeology", *Haverford Symposium on Archaeology and the Bible*, pp. 1–46.

——1939. "The Israelite Conquest of Canaan in the Light of Archaeology", *Bulletin of the American Schools of Oriental Research* 74, pp. 11–23.

——1940. *From the Stone Age to Christianity: Monotheism and the Historical Process*. Baltimore: The John Hopkins Press.

——1949. *The Archaeology of Palestine*. Penguin Books: Harmondsworth, 1949. 2nd edn. 1963.

——1950–51. "A Catalogue of Early Hebrew Lyric Poems (Psalm LXVIII)", *Hebrew Union College Annual* 23,1, pp. 1–39.

——1953. "Notes on Psalms 68 and 134", in Niels Alstrup Dahl and Arvid Kapelrud (eds.), *Interpretationes ad Vetus Testamentum Pertientes Sigmundo Mowinckel septuagenario missae*. Oslo: Forlaget Land of Kirke, pp. 1–12.

——1957. *From the Stone Age to Christianity: Monotheism and the Historical Process*. 2nd edn New York: Doubleday & Anchor Books.

——1959. "The Psalm of Habakkuk", in H.H. Rowley (ed.), *Studies in Old Testament Prophecy presented to Theodore H. Robinson*. Edinburgh: T & T Clark, pp. 1–18.

——1961. "Abram the Hebrew a New Archaeological Interpretation", *Bulletin of the American Schools of Oriental Research*, 163, pp. 36–54.

——1963. *The Biblical Period from Abraham to Ezra: A Historical Survey*. New York: Harper Torchbooks.

Alt, A. 1925. *Die Landnahme der Israeliten in Palästina*. Reformationsprogram der Universitäts Leipzig. Repr. in Alt 1959, 1, pp. 89–125.

———1929. "*Der Gott der Väter*", in Alt, 1959, pp. 1-78.

———1939. "Erwägungen über die Landnahme der Israeliten in Palästina", *Palästinajahrbuch* 38, pp. 8-63. Reprinted in Alt 1959, pp. 126-75.

———1953a. "Die Heimat des Deuteronomiums", in Alt 1953 II, pp. 250-75.

———1953b. *Kleine Schriften zur Geschichte des Volkes Israel*. I-II. München: C.H. Beck'sche Verlagsbuchhandlung.

———1959. *Kleine Schriften zur Geschichte des Volkes Israel*. III. Herausgegeben von Martin Noth. München: C.H. Beck'sche Verlagsbuchhandlung.

———1989a. *Essays on Old Testament History and Religion*. Transl. R.A. Wilson. Sheffield: JSOT Press, 1989

———1989b. "The Gott of the Fathers", in Alt 1989a, 1-78.

———1989c. "The Settlement of the Israelites in Palestine", in Alt, 1989a, pp. 133-70.

Amit, Y., E. Ben Zvi, I. Finkelstein and O. Lipschits (eds.). 2006. *Essays on Ancient Israel in Its Near Eastern Context: A Tribute to Nadav Na'aman*. Winona Lake: Eisenbrauns.

Anonymous. 1903. *Danmarks heltedigtning: en oldtidsstudie*. Bind 1 *Rolf Krake og den ældre Skjoldungrække*. København: Gad.

———1910. *Danmarks heltedigtning: en oldtidsstudie*. Bind 2 *Starkad den Gamle og den yngre Skjoldungrække*. København: Gad.

Antoun, R.T. 1972. *Arab Village: A Social Structural Study of a Transjordanian Peasant Community*. Bloomington: Indiana University Press.

Athas, G. 2003. *The Tel Dan Inscription: A Reappraisal and a New Interpretation*. Copenhagen International Seminar, 12. Journal for the Study of the Old Testament Supplement Series, 360. London: Sheffield Academic Press.

Avalos, H. 2007. *The End of Biblical Studies*. Amherst, New York.

Bächli, O. 1977. *Amphiktyonie im Alten Testament: Forschungsgeschichtliche Studie zur Hypothese von Martin Noth*. Basel: Verlag Friedrich Reinhardt.

Baker, D.W. and B.T. Arnold (eds.). 1999. *The Face of Old Testament Studies: A Survey of Contemporary Approaches*. Grand Rapids, Michigan: Baker Books.

Barr, J. 1961. *The Semantics of Biblical Language*. Oxford: University Press.

———1977. *Fundamentalism*. London: SCM Press.

———1984. *Escaping from Fundamentalism*. London: SCM Books.

———2000. *History and Ideology in the Old Testament. Biblical Studies at the End of a Millennium*. Oxford: University Press.

Barth, F. 1964. *Nomads of South Persia: The Basseri Tribe of the Khamseh Confederacy*. Oslo: Universitetsforlaget.

———1969. "Introduction", F. Barth (ed.), *Ethnic Groups and Boundaries*. Oslo; Universitetsforlaget, pp. 9-37.

———1973. "A General Perspective on Nomads-Sedentary Relations in the Middle East", in Nelson 1973, pp. 11-21.

Bates, D.G. 1973. *Nomads and Farmers: A Study of the Yörük of Southeastern Turkey*. Museum of Anthropology, University of Michigan, 52. Ann Arbor, Michigan: The University of Michigan.

Beckman, G. 1999. *Hittite Diplomatic Texts*. Edited by Harry A. Hoffner. Society of Biblical Literature Writings from the Ancient World Series, 7. Atlanta, Georgia: Scholars Press. 2nd edn.

Ben-Tor, A. 1992. *The Archaeology of Ancient Israel*. New Haven: Yale University Press.

Biggs, R.D. 1992. "Ebla Texts", in Friedman 1992, pp. 263-70.

Binger, T. 1997. *Asherah: Goddesses in Ugarit, Israel and the Old Testament*. Journal for the Study of the Old Testament Supplement Series, 232. Copenhagen International Seminar, 2. Sheffield: Sheffield Academic Press.

Binford, L. 1972. *An Archeological Perspective*. New York: Seminar Press.

Biran, A. and J. Naveh. 1993. "An Aramaic Stele Fragment from Tel Dan", *Israel Exploration Journal* 43, pp. 81-98.

—— 1995. "The Tel Dan Inscription: A New Fragment", *Israel Exploration Journal* 45, pp. 1-18.

Blenkinsopp, J. 2013. *David Remembered: Kingship and National Identity in Ancient Israel*. Grand Rapids, Michigan: William B. Eerdmans Publishing Company.

Bottéro, J. (ed.). 1954. *Le problème des ḫabīru à la 4ᵉ Rencontre assyriologique international*. Cahiers de la Société Asiatique, 12. Paris: Imprimerie nationale.

Bright, J. 1956. *Early Israel in Recent History Writing: A Study in Method*. Studies in Biblical Theology, 19. London: SCM Press.

—— 1959. *A History of Israel*. Philadelphia: Westminster Press.

—— 1966. *Geschichte Israels. Von den Anfängen bis zur Schwelle des neuen Bundes*. Düsseldorf: Patmos.

—— 2000. *A History of Israel*. 4th edn. with an Introduction and an appendix by William P. Brown. Louisville, Kentucky: Westminster John Knox Press.

Brown, N.M. 2012. *Song of the Vikings: Snorri and the Making of Norse Myths*. New York: St. Martin's Press (Kindle).

Bruneau, P. 1982. "'Les Israelites de Delos' e la Juiverie Delienne", *Bulletin de Correspondance Hellenique* 106, pp. 465-504.

Bryce, T. 2005. *The Kingdom of the Hittites*. New edn. Oxford: University Press.

Buccellati, G. 1966. *The Amorites of the Ur III Period*. Pubblicazioni del Seminario di Semitica Ricerche. 1. Naples: Istituto Orientale di Napoli.

Buhl, F. 1915. *Wilhelm Gesenius' Hebräisches und Aramäisches Handwörterbuch über das Alte Testament*. Leipzig: Verlag von F.C.W. Vogel.

Bultmann, R. 1921. *Die Geschichte der synoptischen Tradition*. Forschungen zur Religion und Literatur des Alten und Neuen Testaments. Göttingen: Vandenhoeck & Ruprecht.

Burke, A.A. 2020. *The Amorites and the Bronze Age Near East: The Making of a Regional Identity*. Cambridge: University Press.

Burrows, M. 1957. *What Mean These Stones: The Significance of Archaeology for Biblical Studies*. London: Meridian Books / Thames and Hudson.

Cantrell, Deborah O. and I. Finkelstein. 2006. "A Kingdom for a Horse: The Megiddo Stables and Eighth Century Israel", in Finkelstein, Ussishkin and Halpern 2006, pp. 643-65.

Carlson, R.A. 1964. *David, the chosen King: A Traditio-Historical Approach to the Second Book of Samuel*. Stockholm: Almqvist & Wiksell.

Carroll, R.P. 1997. "Madonna of Silence: Clio and the Bible", in Lester L. Grabbe (ed.) 1997, pp. 84-103.

Carstens, P., T.B. Hasselbalch, and N.P. Lemche (eds.). 2012. *Cultural Memory in Biblical Exegesis*. Piscataway: Gorgias Press.

Carter, C.L. and C.L. Meyers (eds.). 1996. *Community, Identity, and Ideology. Social Sciences Approaches to the Hebrew Bible*. Sources for Biblical and Theological Studies, 6; Winona Lake, Indiana, Eisenbrauns.

Causse, A. 1937. *Du groupe éthnique à la communauté religieuse : La problème de la religion d'Israël*. Paris : Librairie Felix Alcan.

Chadwick, H.M. 1912. *The Heroic Age*. Cambridge: Cambridge University Press.

Charlesworth, J.H. (ed.). 1985. *The Old Testament Pseudepigrapha*, II. New York: Doubleday.

Climo, J.J. and M.G. Cattell (eds.). 2002. *Social Memory and History: Anthropological Perspectives*. Walnut Creek: Altamira Press.

Cline, E.H. 2009. *Biblical Archaeology: A Very Short Introduction*. Oxford: University Press.

Cody, Aelred. *A History of Old Testament Priesthood*. Analecta Biblica, 35. Rome: Pontifical Biblical Institute, 1969.

Cole, D.P. 1975. *Nomads of the Nomads: The Āl-Murrah Bedouin of the Empty Quarter*. Works of Man: Studies in Cultural Ecology. Chicago: Aldine Publishing Company.

Coote, R.B. and K.W. Whitelam. 1987. *The Emergence of Early Israel in Historical Perspective*. The Social World of Biblical Antiquity Series, 5. Sheffield: The Almond Press.

Cowley, C.E., 2005. *Aramaic Papyri of the Fifth Century B.C.* Ancient Texts and Translations (1919). Eugene, Oregon: Wipf & Stock, Publishers, 2005.

Cross, F.M. 1973. *Canaanite Myth and Hebrew Epic: Essays in the History of the Religion of Israel*, Cambridge, Massachusetts: Harvard University Press.

Cryer, F.H. 1994. "On the Recently-Discovered 'House of David' Inscription", *Scandinavian Journal of the Old Testament* 8, pp. 3-19.

——1995a. "A 'Betdwad' Miscellany: Dwd, Dwd' or David?", *Scandinavian Journal of the Old Testament* 9, pp. 52-8.

——1995b. "King Hadad", *Scandinavian Journal of the Old Testament* 9, pp. 223-35.

——1996. "Of Epistemology, Northwest-Semitic Epigraphy and Irony: The 'BYTDWD/House of David'", *Journal for the Study of the Old Testament* 69, pp. 3-17.

Cubitt, G. 2007. *History and Memory*. Manchester: Manchester University Press.

Dahood, M. 1979. "Ebla, Ugarit and the Old Testament", in Emerton 1977, pp. 81–112

Dassow, E. von. 2008. *State and Society in the Late Bronze Age: Alalaḫ under the Mitanni Empire*. Edited by David I. Owen and Gernot Wilhelm. Studies on the Civilization and Culture of Nuzi and the Hurrians, 17. Bethesda, Maryland: CDL Press.

Davidovich, T. (ed.). 2012. *Plogbillar & svärd: En festskrift till Stig Norin*. Uppsala: Molin & Sorgenfrei.

Davies, P.R. 1983. The Damascus Covenant: An Interpretation of the "Damascus Document". *Journal for the Study of the Old Testament Supplement Series*, 25. Sheffield: JSOT Press.

——1992. In Search of "Ancient Israel". *Journal for the Study of the Old Testament Supplement Series*, 148. Sheffield: Sheffield Academic Press.

——1994. "BYTDWD and SWKT DWYD: A Comparison", *Journal for the Study of the Old Testament* 64, pp. 23–4.

——1995. "Method and Madness: Some Remarks on Doing History with the Bible", *Journal of Biblical Literature* 114, pp. 699–705.

—— 2002. "Minimalism, 'Ancient Israel', and Anti-Semitism", in *Bible and Interpretation*: https://web.archive.org/web/20081021140010/http://w-w.bibleinterp.com/articles/Minimalism.htm.

—— 2012. "A Brief Note for Yosi Garfinkel" (June 2012), *Bible and Interpretation* https://bibleinterp.arizona.edu/articles/dav368018.

Davies, P.R. and D.V. Edelman (eds.). 2010. *The Historian and the Bible: Essays in Honour of Lester L. Grabbe*. Library of Hebrew Bible/Old Testament Studies, 530; London: T&T Clark / Continuum.

Davis, T.W. 2004. *Shifting Sands: The Rise and Fall of Biblical Archaeology*. Oxford: University Press (Kindle).

Derrida, J. 1978. *Writing and Difference*. Routledge Classics, London: Routledge.

Dever, W.G. 1977. "The Patriarchal Traditions", in Hayes and Miller 1977, pp. 70–120.

—— 1985. "Syro-Palestinian and Biblical Archaeology", in D.A. Knight and G.M. Tucker (eds.), *The Hebrew Bible and Its Modern Interpreters*. Philadelphia: Fortress Press, pp. 31–74.

—— 1993. "What Remains of the House that Albright Built", *Biblical Archaeologist Review* 56, pp. 25–35.

—— 1995. "Will the Real Israel Please Stand Up! Archaeology and Israelite Historiography: Part I," *Bulletin of the American Schools of Oriental* Research 297, pp. 61–80.

—— 2000. "Save us from postmodern Malarkey", *Biblical Archaeologist Review* 26, pp. 28–35, 68–69.

—— 2001. *What Did the Biblical Writers Know and When Did They Know It? What Archaeology Can Tell Us about the Reality of Ancient Israel*. Grand Rapids, Michigan: William B. Eerdmans Publishing Company.

—— 2003. *Who Were the Early Israelites and Where Did They Come From?* Grand Rapids, Michigan: William B. Eerdmans Publishing Company.

—— 2005. *Did God Have a Wife? Archaeology and Folk Religion in Ancient Israel.* Grand Rapids, Michigan: William B. Eerdmans Publishing Company.

—— 2017. *Beyond the Texts: An Archaeological Portrait of Ancient Israel and Judah.* Atlanta: SBL Press.

—— 2018. "Response to Rainer Albertz", in Grabbe 2018, pp. 114–18.

—— 2020. *My Nine Lives: Sixty Years in Israeli and Biblical Archaeology.* Atlanta, Georgia: SBL Press.

Dever, W.G. and S. Gitin (eds.). 2003. *Symbiosis, Symbolism and the Power of the Past: Canaan Ancient Israel and their Neighbors from the Late Bronze Age through Roman Palestine.* Winona Lake, Indiana: Eisenbrauns.

Dibelius, M. 1906. *Die Lade Jahves: Eine religionsgeschichtliche Untersuchung.* Inaugural-Dissertation der Universität zu Tübingen. Göttingen: Druck der Univ.-Buchdruckerei von E.A. Huth, 1906

—— 1919. *Die Formgeschichte des Evangeliums.* Tübingen: Mohr Siebeck, 1919.

Diebner, B.J. 1984a. "Wieder die 'Offenbarungs-Archäologie' in der Wissenschft von Alten Testament: Grundsätzliches zum Sinn alttestamentlicher Forschung im Rahmen der Theologie", *Dielheimer Blätter zum Alten Testament* 18, pp. 30–53.

—— 1984b. "'Es last sich nicht beweisen – Tatsache aber ist: Sprachfigur statt Methode in der kritischen Erforschung des AT", *Dielheimer Blätter zum Alten Testament* 18, pp. 138–46.

Dietrich, W. 1972. *Prophetie und Geschichte: Eine redaktionsgeschichtliche Untersuchung zum deuteronomistischen Geschichtswerk.* Forschungen zur Religion und Literatur des Alten und Neuen Testaments. Göttingen: Vandenhoeck & Ruprecht.

Dietrich, W. and M.A. Klopfenstein (eds.). 1994. *Ein Gott allein? JHWH-Verehrung und biblischer Monotheismus im Kontext der israelitischen und altorientalischen Religionsgeschichte.* Bern: Schweizerische Akademie der Wissenschaften.

Donner, H. 1984. *Geschichte des Volkes Israel und seiner Nachbaren in Grundzügen.* 1–2. Grundrisse zum Alten Testament, 4/1–2. Göttingen: Vandenhoeck & Ruprecht.

Doughty, C.M. 1888. *Travels in Arabia Deserta.* Cambridge: University Press.

Durand, J.-M. 1998–2002. *Les documents épistolaires du palais de Mari.* I–III. Littératures anciennes du Proche-orient, 16–18. Paris: Éditions du Cerf.

Edelman, D.V. (ed.). 1991. *The Fabric of History: Text, Artifact and Israel's Past.* Journal for the Study of the Old Testament Supplement Series, 127. Sheffield: Sheffield Academic Press.

—— 2005. *The Origins of the "Second" Temple: Persian Imperial Politics and the Rebuilding of Jerusalem.* London: Equinox, 2005.

Ehmann, D. 1975. *Baḫtiyāren: Persische Bergnomaden im Wandel der Zeit.* Beihefte zum Tübinger Atlas der Vorderen Orient Reihe B, nr. 15. Wiesbaden: Dr. Ludwig Reichert.

Eichrodt, W. 1961. *Theology of the Old Testament*. I–II. Philadelphia: Westminster Press, 1961.

—— 1962–1964. *Theologie des Alten Testaments*, I–III. 7. Durchgesehene Auflage. Stuttgart: Ehrenfried Klotz Verlag.

Eissfeldt, O. 1935. "Der geschichtliche Hintergrund der Erzählung von Gibeahs Schandtat (Richter 19–21)". Repr. Otto Eissfeldt, *Kleine Schriften*, II (Tübingen: J.B.C. Mohr, 1963), 64–80.

Emerton, J. 1971. "'The Riddle of Genesis XIV'", *Vetus Testamentum* 21, pp. 403–39.

—— 1978. *Congress Volume Göttingen 1977*. Leiden: Brill.

—— 1991. *Congress Volume Leuven 1989*. Supplements to *Vetus Testamentum* 43.

Engel, H. 1979a. *Die Vorfahren Israels in Ägypten*. Frankfurter Theologische Studien, 27; Frankfurt a/M: Josef Knecht.

—— 1979b. "Die Siegestele des Merenptah: Kritische Überblick über die verschiedenen Versuche historischer Auswertung des Schlussabschnitts", *Biblica* 60, pp. 373–99.

English, P.W. 1966. *City and Village in Iran. Settlement and Economy in the Kirman Basin*. Madison: University of Wisconsin Press.

Engnell, I. 1945. *Gamla Testamentet: En traditionshistorisk inledning*. Första delen. Stockholm: Svenska Kyrkans Diakonissstyrelsens Bokförlag.

—— 1969. *A Rigid Scrutiny: Critical Essays on the Old Testament*. Nashville: Vanderbilt University Press.

Eriksen, T.H. 1993. *Ethnicity & Nationalism: Anthropological Perspectives*. London: Pluto Press (3rd edn 2010).

—— 2015. *Fredrik Barth: An Intellectual Biography* (Anthropology, Culture and Society) Pluto Press.

Fenton, S. 2010. *Ethnicity*. Second Edition. Cambridge: Polity.

Ferdinand, K. 1993. *Bedouins of Qatar*. The Carlsberg Foundation's nomad research project, 1. Copenhagen: Rhodos.

—— 2006. *Afghan Nomads: Caravans, Conflicts, and Trade in Afghanistan and British India 1800–1980*, The Carlsberg Foundation's nomad research project, 13. Copenhagen: Rhodos.

Finkelstein, I. 1988. *The Archaeology of the Israelite Settlement*. Jerusalem. Israel Exploration Society.

—— 1996. "The Archaeology of the United Monarchy: an Alternative View", *Levant* 28, 177–87.

—— 2005. "A Low Chronology Update: Archaeology, History and Bible", in Levy and Higham 2005, pp. 31–42.

—— 2006a. "The Last Labayu: King Saul and the Expansion of the First North Israelite Territorial Entity", in Yairah Amit, Ehud Ben Zvi, Israel Finkelstein and Oded Lipschits (eds.), *Essays on Ancient Israel in Its Near Eastern Context: A Tribute to Nadav Na'aman* (Winona Lake, Michigan: Eisenbrauns, 2006), pp. 171–87.

—— 2006b. "Jerusalem in the Persian (and Early Hellenistic) Period and the Wall of Nehemiah", *Journal for the Study of the Old Testament* 32 (2006), 501–20.

—— 2008. "Jerusalem in the Persian (and Early Hellenistic) Periods and the Wall of Nehemiah", in Finkelstein 2018, pp. 3–27.

—— 2013a. *Le Royaume biblique oublié*. Paris: Odile Jacob, 2013.

—— 2013b. *The Forgotten Kingdom: The Archaeology and History of Northern Israel*. Ancient Near East Monographs. Society of Biblical Literature).

—— 2018. *Hasmonean Realities Behind Ezra, Nehemiah, and Chronicles*. Ancient Israel and Its Literature. Atlanta, Georgia: SBL Press.

Finkelstein, Israel and Alexander Fantalkin. 2012. "Khirbet Qeiyafa: An Unsensational Archaeological and Historical Interpretation", *Tel Aviv* 39, pp. 38–63.

Finkelstein, Israel and Neil Asher Silberman. 2001. *The Bible Unearthed: Archaeology's New Vision of Ancient Israel and the Origins of Its Sacred Texts*. New York: The Free Press.

—— 2006. *David and Solomon: In Search of the Bible's Sacred Kings and the Roots of the Western Tradition*. New York: Free Press.

Finkelstein, I, D. Ussishkin and B. Halpern (eds.). 2006. *Megiddo IV: The 1998-2002 Seasons*. Monograph Series Tel Aviv University, Sonia and Marco Nadler Institute of Archaeology, 24.

Fohrer, G. 1966. "'Amphiktyonie' und 'Bund'", 1966, reprinted in Georg Fohrer 1969, pp. 84–119.

—— 1969 *Studien zur alttestamentliche Theologie und Geschichte*. Beiheft zur Zeitschrift für die alttestamentliche Wissenschaft, 115. Berlin: Walter de Gruyter

—— 1988. "Methoden und Moden in der alttestamentlichen Wissenschaft", *Zeitschrift für die alttestamentliche Wissenschaft* 100, pp. 243–74.

Franklin, N. 2017. "Entering the Arena: The Megiddo Stables Reconsidered", in Lipschits, Gadot and Adams (eds.) 2017, pp. 103–14.

Freedman, D.N. 1978. "The Real Story of the Ebla Tablets: Ebla and the Cities of the Plain", *Biblical Archaeologist* 41, pp. 143–64.

—— 1992. *The Anchor Bible Dictionary I-VI* (New York: Doubleday.

Freedman, D.N. and David Frank Graf (eds.). 1983. *Palestine in Transition: The Emergence of Ancient Israel*. The Social World of Biblical Antiquities Series. Sheffield: The Almond Press.

—— 1998. *The Leningrad Codex: A Facsimile Edition*. Grand Rapids, Michigan: W.B. Eerdmans Publishing Company.

Frerichs, Ernest S. and Leonard H. Lesko (eds.). 1997. *Exodus: The Egyptian Evidence*. Winona Lake, Indiana: Eisenbrauns.

Frevel, Christian. 2016. *Geschichte Israel*. Kohlhammer Studienbücher Theologie. Stuttgartt: Verlag W. Kohlhammer.

Fried, M. 1975. *The Concept of Tribe*. Menlo Park, Calif: Cummings Pub. Co.

Friedman, R.E. 1989. *Who Wrote the Bible?* New York: HarperOne.

Friedrich, J. 1926-1930. *Staatsverträge des Ḫatti-Reiches in hethitischer Sprache*, I–II. Mitteilungen der Vorderasiatisch-Ägyptischen Gesellschaft 31 and 34. Leipzig: Hinrichs.

Fritz, V. and P.R. Davies (eds.). 1996. *The Origins of the Israelite States*. JSOT Supplement Series 228; Sheffield.

Galling, K. 1928. *Die Erwählungstraditionen Israels*. Beihefte zur Zeitschrift für die alttestamentliche Wissenschaft, 48. Giessen: Verlag von Alfred Töpelmann.

—— 1937. *Biblisches Reallexikon*. Handbuch zum Alten Testament, erster Reihe I. Tübingen: Verlag von J.C.B. Mohr (Paul Siebeck) (2nd edn. 1977).

—— 1950. *Textbook zur Geschichte Israels*. Tübingen: Mohr Siebeck (3rd edn. 1979).

Garbini, G. 1960. *Il Semitico di Nord-Ovest*. Quaderni della sezione linguistica degli annali, 1. Napoli: Istituto universitario orientale di Napoli.

—— 1978. "Il Cantico di Debora", (1978), in Garbini 2010, pp. 32–60.

—— 1988a. *Il Semitico nordoccidentale: Studi di storia linguistica*. Studi Semitici, Nuova serie. 5. Dipartimento di Studi Orientali. Roma: Università degle Studi 'La Sapienza'.

—— 1988b. *History and Ideology in Ancient Israel*. London: SCM Press.

—— 1994. "L'iscrizione aramaica di Tel Dan", *Atti della Academia Nazionale dei Lincei*, 391, pp. 461–71.

—— 2003a. "Abraham and Damascus", in Garbini 2003b, pp. 22–36.

—— 2003b. "Myth and History in the Bible". *Journal for the Study of the Old Testament Supplement Series*, 362. London: Sheffield Academic Press.

—— 2006. *Introduzione all'epigrafia semitica*. Brescia: Paideia.

—— 2008. *Scrivere la storia d'Israele*. Brescia: Paideia.

—— 2010. *Letteratura e politica nell'Israele antico*. Brescia: Paideia.

Gernot, W. 1982. *Grundzüge der Geschichte und Kultur der Hurriter*. Grundzüge, 45. Darmstadt: Wissenschaftliche Buchgesellschaft.

Geus, C.H.J. de. 1976. *The Tribes of Israel: An Investigation into some of the Presuppositions of Martin Noth's Amphictyony Hypothesis*. Studia Semitica Neerlandica, 18. Assen-Amsterdam: Van Gorcum.

Gilbert, F. 1987. "What Ranke Meant", *The American Scholar* 56, pp. 393–97.

Gmirkin, R. 2002. "Tool Slippage and the Tel Dan Inscription", *Scandinavian Journal of the Old Testament* 16, pp. 293–302.

—— 2006. *Berossus and Genesis, Manetho and Exodus: Hellenistic Histories and the Date of the Pentateuch*. Copenhagen International Series, 15. Library of the Hebrew Bible Old Testament Studies, 433. New York London: T & T Clark.

—— 2017. *Plato and the Creation of the Hebrew Bible*. Copenhagen International Seminar. London: Routledge: 2017.

Gnuse, Robert K. 2020. *Hellenism and the Primary History: The Imprint of Greek Sources in Genesis – 2 Kings*. Copenhagen International Seminar. London: Routledge.

Goldman, S. 2009. *Zeal for Zion: Christians, Jews, & the Idea of The Promised Land*. Chapel Hill, The University of North Carolina Press.

Goody, J. 2010. *Myth, Ritual and the Oral*. Cambridge: University Press.

Gottwald, Norman K. 1979. *The Tribes of Yahweh: A Sociology of the Religion of Liberated Israel 1250-1050 B.C.E*. Maryknoll, New York: Orbis Books.

Grabbe, L.L. 1997. (ed.). *Can a 'History of Israel' Be Written?* European Seminar in Historical Methodology, 1. Journal for the Study of the Old Testament Supplement Series, 245. Sheffield: Sheffield Academic Press.

—— 2001. (ed.). *Did Moses Speak Attic? Jewish Historiography and Scripture in the Hellenistic Period*, Journal for the Study of the Old Testament Supplement Series 317; Sheffield: Academic Press.

—— 2002. "The 'Comfortable Theory', 'Maximal Conservatism', and Neo-fundamentalism Revisited", in Alistair G. Hunter and Philip R. Davies (eds.), *Sense and Sensitivity: Essays on Reading the Bible in Memory of Robert Carroll*. Journal for the Study of the Old Testament Supplement, 348. Sheffield: Academic Press, pp. 174-93.

—— 2003. (ed.). "'Like a Bird in a Cage'. The Invasion of Sennacherib in 701 BCE". *Journal for the Study of the Old Testament Supplement Series*, 245; European Seminar in Historical Methodology, 4, Sheffield.

—— 2007. *Ancient Israel: What Do We Know and How Do We Know It?* London: T & T Clark (revised edition 2017).

—— 2011. (ed.). *Enquire of the Former Age: Ancient Historiography and Writing the History of Israel*. Library of Hebrew Bible/Old Testament Studies, 554; T&T Clark.

—— 2018. (ed.). *'Even God Cannot Change the Past': Reflections on Seventeen Years of the European Seminar in Historical Methodology*. European Seminar in Historical Methodology, 11. Library of Hebrew Bible Old Testament Studies, 663. London: T & T Clark.

—— 2019. (ed.). *The Hebrew Bible and History: Critical Readings*. London: T & T Clark.

Griffin, H.M. 1993. "Not the Way It Essentially Was", *The Journal of Pacific History* 28, pp. 69-74.

Grønbæk, J.H. 1971. *Die Geschichte vom Aufstieg Davids (1. Sam. 15-2. Sam. 5): Tradition und Komposition*. Acta Theologica Danica, X. Copenhagen: Prostant apud Munksgaard.

Grotefend, G.Fr. 1802. *Erste Nachricht von seiner Entzifferung der Keilschrift*. Zum Abdruck gebracht W. Meyer. Repr. Darmstadt: Wissenschaftliche Buchgesellschaft, 1972.

—— 1837. *Neue Beiträge zur Erläuterung der persepolitanischen Keilschrift nebst einem Anhange über die Vollkommenheit der ersten Art derselben bei der ersten Secularfeier der Georgia Augusta in Göttingen Hannover*. Hannover: Im Verlage der Hahn'schen Hofbuchhandlung.

Gruen, E.S. (ed.). 2011. *Cultural Identity in the Ancient World*. Getty Research Institute. Issues & Debates. Los Angeles: Getty Research Institute.

—— 2018. *The Construct of Identity in Hellenistic Judaism: Essays on Early Jewish Literature and History*. Deuterocanonical and Cognate Literature Studies, 29. Berlin: De Gruyter.

—— 2020. *Ethnicity in the Ancient World – Did It Matter?* Berlin: De Gruyter.

Gubser, P. 1973. *Politics and Change in al-Karak, Jordan. A study of a Small Arab Town and Its District*. Middle Eastern Monographs, 11. Oxford: University Press.

Gudme, A.K. de Hemmer. 2013. *Before the God in This Place for Good Remembrance: A Comparative Analysis of the Aramaic Votive Inscriptions from Mount Gerizim*. Beihefte zur Zeitschrift für die alttestamentliche Wissenschaft, 441. Berlin: De Gruyter.

Gulick, J.J. 1955. *Social Structure and Cultural Change in a Lebanese Village*. Viking Fund Publications in Anthropology No. 21. New York: Wenner-Gren Foundation for Anthropological Research.

Gunkel, H. 1917. *Genesis Übersetzt und erklärt*. Vierte unveränderte Auflage. Göttinger Handkommentar zum Alten Testament, I, 1. Göttingen: Vandenhoeck & Ruprecht.

—— 1968. *Die Psalmen*. Fünfte Auflage. Göttinger Handkommentar zum Alten Testament, II, 2. Göttingen: Vandenhoeck & Ruprecht.

Gunn, D.M. 1978. "The Story of King David: Genre and Interpretation". *Journal for the Study of the Old Testament Supplement Series*, 6. Sheffield: Department of Biblical Studies, the University of Sheffield.

Hagelia, H. 2006. *The Tel Dan Inscription: A Critical Investigation of Recent Research on Its Palaeography and Philology*. Acta Universitatis Upsaliensis. Studia Semitica Upsaliensia, 22. Uppsala: Universitetet.

Hallbäck, G. and N.P. Lemche (eds.). 2001. *"Tiden" i bibelsk belysning*. Forum for Bibelsk Eksegese 11.

Hallo, W.W. and K. L. Younger (eds.). 2000. *The Context of Scripture. The Context of Scripture. Volume Two. Monumental Inscriptions from the Biblical World*. Leiden: Brill.

Halpern, B. 1999. "Erasing History: The Minimalist Assault on Ancient Israel", in Long 1999, pp. 415–26.

—— 2001. *David's Secret Demons: Messiah, Murderer, Traitor, King*. Grand Rapids, Michigan: William B. Eerdmans Publishing Company

Halsall, G. 2014. *Worlds of Arthur*. Oxford: University Press (Kindle).

Handy, L.K., 2020. *Josiah: From Improbable Stories to Inventive Historiography*. Worlds of the Ancient Near East and Mediterranean. Sheffield: Equinox.

Harmanşah, Ö. 2015. *Place, Memory, and Healing: An Archaeology of Anatolian Rock Monuments*. London: Routledge.

Hayes, J.H. and J. M. Miller (eds.). 1977. *Israelite and Judaean History*. Old Testament Library. London: SCM Press.

Heimpel, W. 2003. *Letters to the King of Mari: A New Translation, with Historical Introduction, Notes, and Commentaries*. Mesopotamian Civilizations, 12. Winona Lake, Indiana: Eisenbrauns.

Hempel, J. and L. Rost (eds.). 1958. *Von Ugarit nach Qumran: Beiträge zur Alttestamentlichen und Altorientalischen Forschung*. Beihefte zur Zeitschrift für die alttestamentliche Forschung, 77; Berlin: De Gruyter.

Hendel, R.S. 1987. *The Epic of the Patriarch: The Jacob Cycle and the Narrative Traditions of Canaan and Israel*. Harvard Semitic Monographs, 42. Atlanta, Georgia: Scholars Press.

Herrmann, S. 1962. "Das Werden Israels", *Theologische Literaturzeitung* 87, pp. 561–74.

Hesse, F. 1971. *Abschied von der Heilsgeschichte*. Theologische Studien, 108. Zürich: TVZ.

Hjelm, I. 2004. *Jerusalem's Rise to Sovereignty: Zion und Gerizim in Competition*. Copenhagen International Seminar, 14. Journal for the Study of the Old Testament Supplement Series, 404. London: T & T Clark International.

Hjelm, I., Hamdan Taha, Ilan Pappe and Thomas L. Thompson (eds.). 2019. *A New Critical Approach to the History of Palestine*. Palestine and Heritage Project, 1. London: Equinox.

Hjelm, I. and T.L. Thompson. 2002. "The Victory Song of Merneptah, Israel and the People of Palestine", *Journal for the Study of the Old Testament* 27, pp. 3–18.

—— 2016. *History, Archaeology and The Bible Forty Years After "Historicity"*. Changing Perspectives, 6. London: Routledge.

Hodder, I. and S. Hudson. 2003. *Reading the Past: Current Approaches to Interpretation in Archaeology*. 3rd edition. Cambridge: University Press.

Hoftijzer, J. and K. Jongeling. 1995. *Dictionary of the North-West Semitic Inscriptions*, I. Handbuch der Orientalistik, I: 21. Leiden: E.J. Brill.

Holman, K., 2003. *Historical Dictionary of the Vikings*. Lanham, Maryland: Scarecrow Press.

Hunt A. (ed.). 2012. *Second Temple Studies IV: Historiography and History*. Library of the Hebrew Bible Old Testament Studies, 550. London: T & T Clark.

Hutchinson, J. and A.D. Smith (eds.). 1996. *Ethnicity*. Oxford: University Press.

Hütteroth, W.-D. 1978. *Palästina und Transjordanien im 16. Jahrhundert: Wirtschaftsstruktur ländlicher Siedlungen nach osmanischen Steuerregistern* (*Beihefte zum Tübinger Atlas des Vorderen Orients. Reihe B: Geisteswissenschaften*. Nr. 33). Reichert, Wiesbaden.

Hutton, P.H. 1993. *History as an Art of Memory*. Hanover: University Press of New England.

Kant, Immanuel. 1793. *Die Religion innerhalb der Grenzen der blossen Vernunft*. Königsberg: Bei Friedrich Nicolovius.

Kartveit, M. and G.N. Knoppers (eds.). 2020., *The Bible, Qumran, and the Samaritans*. Studia Samaritana, 10; Berlin: De Gruyter.

Kaufmann, Y. 1953. *The Biblical Account of the Conquest of Palestine*. Jerusalem: At the Magnes Press.

Kenyon, K.M. 1960–83. *Excavations at Jericho*. I–V. London: Council for British Research in the Levant.

—— 1957. *Digging up Jericho*. London: Ernest Benn.

—— 1965. *Archaeology in the Holy Land*. London: Methuen, 1965.

—— 1966. *Amorites and Canaanites*. The Schweich Lectures of the British Academy 1963. London: Published for the British Academy. The Oxford University Press.

—— 1979. *Archaeology in the Holy Land*. London Methuen, 1965. 4th edition.

Kimbrough, S.T., 1978. *Israelite Religion in Sociological Perspective: The Work of Antonin Causse*. With a Foreword by Edmond Jacob. Studies in Oriental Religions, 4. Wiesbaden: Otto Harrassowitz.

Kitchen, K.A. 1966. *Ancient Orient and Old Testament*. London: The Tyndale Press.

—— 2003. *On The Reliability of the Old Testament*. Grand Rapids, Michigan: William B, Eerdmans Publishing Company.

Kittel, R. 1883. *Geschichte des Volkes Israel*. 1–III/2. Several editions and revisions between 1883 and 1929, partly published in Gotha: Leopold Klotz Verlag, partly in Stuttgart: W. Kohlhammer.

Kletter, R. 2004. "Chronology and United Monarchy A Methodological Review", *Zeitschrift des deutschen Palästinavereins* 120, pp. 13–54.

—— 2006. *Just Past: The Making of Israeli Archaeology*. London: Equinox.

Knauf, E.A. 1991. "From History to Interpretation", in Diana V. Edelman 1991, pp. 26–64.

—— 1994. *Die Umwelt des Alten Testaments*. Neue Stuttgarter Kommentar Altes Testament, 29. Stuttgart: Katholisches Bibelwerk.

Knauf, E.A. and P. Guillaume. 2016. *A History of Biblical Israel: The Fate of the Tribes and Kingdoms from Merenptah to Bar Kochba*. Worlds of the Ancient Neat East and Mediterranean. Sheffield: Equinox.

Knauf, E.A. and H.M. Niemann. 2021. *Geschichte Israels und Judas im Altertum*. Berlin: De Gruyter.

Knauf, E.A., A. de Pury and T.R. Römer 1994. "*BaytDawīd* ou *BaytDōd?*", *Biblische Notizen* 72, pp. 60–69.

Knudtzon, J.A., 1907/1915. *Die El-Amarna Tafeln mit Einleitung und Erläuterungen*. I–II. Vorderasiatische Bibliothek. Nachdruck, Aalen: Otto Zeller Verlagsbuchhandlung, 1964.

Koenen, Klaus, 1998. *Unter dem Dröhnen der Kanonen. Arbeiten zum Alten Testament aus der Zeit des Zweiten Weltkriegs* (Neukirchen-Vluyn: Neukirchener Verlag, 1998).

Kofoed, Jens Bruun. 2005. *Text and History: Historiography and the Study of the Biblical Text*. Winona Lake, Indiana: Eisenbrauns.

—— 2011. "Factualizing the Evasion: A Response to Niels Peter Lemche", in Grabbe 2011, pp. 164–78.

König, Jason, Katerina Oikonomopoulou, Greg Woolf (eds.). 2016. *Ancient Libraries*. Cambridge: University Press.

Korošec, V. 1931. *Hethitische Staatsverträge: ein Beitrag zu ihrer juristischen Wertung*, Leipzig: T. Weicher.

Kratz, R.G. 2000. *Die Komposition der erzählende Bücher des Alten Testaments: Grundwissen der Bibelkritik.* Göttingen: Vandenhoeck & Ruprecht.

—— 2013. *Historisches und biblisches Israel: Das Überblick zum Alten Testament.* Tübingen: Mohr Siebeck

—— 2015. *Historical and Biblical Israel: The History, Tradition, and Archives of Israel and Judah.* Oxford: University Press.

Kraus, F.R. 1960. "Ein zentrales Problem des altmesopotamischen Rechts: Was ist der Codex Hammu-rabi?" *Geneva* 8, pp. 283-96,

Kuhn, Thomas S. 2012. *The Structure of Scientific Revolutions.* With an Introductory Essay by Ian Hacking. Chicago: The Chicago University Press.

Kupper, J.-R. 1957. *Les nomads en Mésopotamie au temps des rois de Mari.* Bibliothèque de la Faculté de Philosophie et Lettres de l'Université de Liège, 142. Paris: Société d'Édition "Les Belles Lettres".

Lancaster, W. 1981.*The Rwala Bedouin Today.* Changing Cultures. Cambridge: University Press (2nd. Edn, Long Growe, Illinois: Waveland Pr Inc., 1997).

Larsen, M.T. 1995. "The 'Babel/Bible' Controversy and Its Aftermath", in Sasson 1995: II, pp. 95-106.

Le Goff, J. 1992. *History and Memory.* New York: Columbia University Press.

Leach, E. 1976. *Culture and Communication: The Logic by which Symbols Are Connected. An Introduction to the Use of Structuralist Analysis in Social Anthropology.* Themes in the Social Sciences. Cambridge University Press.

Leinert, E. 2015. *Mittelhochdeutsche Heldenepik: Eine Einführung.* Grundlagen der Germanistik, 58. Berlin: Erich Schmidt Verlag GmbH & Co.

Lemaire A. and M. Sæbø (eds.). 2000., *Congress Volume Oslo 1998.* Vetus Testamentum Supplements, 80; Leiden: Brill.

Lemche, N.P. 1968. *Forudsætningerne for Davids imperium inden for og uden for Israel,* University of Copenhagen (unpublished thesis).

—— 1972. *Israel i Dommertiden. En oversigt over diskussionen om Martin Noths 'Das System der zwölf Stämme Israels'.* Tekst og Tolkning. Monografier udgivet af Institut for Bibelsk Eksegese 4. København: G. E. C. Gad.

—— 1975, "'The Hebrew Slave'. Comments on the Slave Law Ex xxi 2-11", *Vetus Testamentum* 25, pp. 129-44. New edn. in Lemche 2013b, pp. 11-25.

—— 1976. "The Greek 'Amphictyony', Could it be a Prototype for the Israelite Society in the Period of the Judges?" *Journal for the Study of the Old Testament* 4, pp. 48-59. New edn. in Lemche 2013b, pp. 61-8.

—— 1978. "David's Rise". *Journal for the Study of the Old Testament* 10, pp. 2-25.

—— 1979. "Hebrew as a National Name for Israel", *Studia Theologica* 33, pp. 1-23. New edn. in Lemche 2013b, pp. 77-94).

—— 1982. "Det revolutionære Israel. En præsentation af en moderne forskningsretning", *Dansk teologisk Tidsskrift* 45, pp. 16-39.

—— 1984a. "On the Problem of Studying Israelite History: Apropos Abraham Malamat's View on Historical Research", *Biblische Notizen* 24, pp. 94-124.

—— 1984b. "Israel in the Period of the Judges: The Tribal League in Recent Discussion", *Studia Theologica* 38, pp. 1-28.

—— 1984c. *Det Gamle Israel: Det israelitiske samfund fra sammenbruddet af bronzealderkulturen til hellenistisk tid.* Århus: ANIS.

—— 1985. *Early Israel: Anthropological and Historical Studies on the Israelite Society Before the Monarchy.* Supplements to Vetus Testamentum, 37. Leiden: E.J. Brill.

—— 1987. "Rachel and Lea. Or: On the Survival of Outdated Paradigms in the Study of the Origin of Israel": I. *Scandinavian Journal of the Old Testament* 2/1987: 127-53.

—— 1988a. "Rachel and Lea. Or: On the Survival of Outdated Paradigms in the Study of the Origin of Israel": II: *Scandinavian Journal of the Old Testament* 1/1988, 39-65. New edn. in Lemche 2013b, pp. 95-132.

—— 1988b. *Ancient Israel: A New History of Israelite Society.* The Biblical Seminar. Sheffield: JSOT Press. Repr. with a new introduction: *Ancient Israel: A New History of Israel.* Second edition. London: Bloomsbury T&T Clark, 2015.

—— 1990. "On the Use of 'System Theory', 'Macro Theories' and Evolutionistic Thinking in Modern OT Research and Biblical Archaeology", *Scandinavian Journal of the Old Testament* 1990/2, pp. 73-88, reprinted in Carter and Meyers 1996, pp. 273-86.

—— 1991a. *The Canaanites and their Land. The Idea of Canaan in the Old Testament* Journal for the Study of the Old Testament Supplement Series, 110; Sheffield: Academic Press. 2nd edition 1999.

—— 1991b. "The Development of the Israelite Religion in Light of Recent Studies on the Early History of Israel", in J.A. Emerton (ed.), *Congress Volume Leuven 1989.* Supplements to Vetus Testamentum 43, pp. 97-115,

—— 1992a. "ḫabīru / Hebrews", in Friedman 1992: III, pp. 95 and 106-12.

—— 1992b. "History of Israel (Pre-Monarchic Period)", in Friedman 1992: III, pp. 526-45.

—— 1992c. "Det gamle Testamente som en hellenistisk bog", *Dansk Teologisk Tidsskrift* 55, pp. 81-101.

—— 1993. "The Old Testament—A Hellenistic Book?" *Scandinavian Journal of the Old Testament* 7, pp. 163-93; Repr. with corrections in Grabbe 2001, pp. 287-318, and again in Lemche 2013b, pp. 133-57.

—— 1994. "Is It Still Possible to Write a History of Ancient Israel?" *Scandinavian Journal of the Old Testament* 8, pp. 163-88. Reprinted in Lemche 2013b, pp. 169-88.

—— 1995a. "Syrian-Palestinian History: An Overview", Sasson 1995: II, pp. 1195-218.

—— 1995b. "Justice in Western Asia in Antiquity, Or: Why No Laws Were Needed!" *Chicago Kent Law Review* 70, pp. 1695-716.

—— 1995c. "Kings and Clients: On Loyalty Between the Ruler and the Ruled in Ancient 'Israel'", *Semeia* 66, pp. 119-32.

—— 1995d. "Bemerkungen über eines Paradigmenwechsels auf Anlaß einer neuenddeckte Inschrift", in Weippert and Timm 1995, pp. 99-108.

—— 1996a. "From Patronage Society to Patronage Society", in Fritz and Davies 1996, pp. 106–20.

—— 1996b. "Pedersen, Johannes", *Theologische Realenzyclopädie* XXVI, pp. 162–64.

—— 1997. "Clio is Also Among the Muses. Keith W. Whitelam and the History of Palestine: A Review and a Commentary", in Grabbe 1997, pp. 123–55.

—— 1998a. "Greater Canaan: The Implications of a Correct Reading of EA 151:49–51", *Bulletin of the American Schools of Oriental Research* 310, pp. 19–24.

—— 1998b. *The Israelites in History and Tradition*. Library of Ancient Israel. Louisville: Westminster John Knox Press.

—— 1999. "The Relevance of Working with the Concept of Class Society in the Study of Israelite Society in the Iron Age", in Sneed 1999, pp. 89–98.

—— 2000. "Ideology and the History of Ancient Israel", *Scandinavian Journal of the Old Testament* 14, pp. 165–94.

—— 2001a. "How does One Date an Expression of Mental History? The Old Testament and Hellenism", in Grabbe 2001, pp. 200–24.

—— 2001b. "Prægnant tid i Det Gamle Testamente", in G. Hallbäck and N.P. Lemche (eds.), *"Tiden" i bibelsk belysning*. Forum for Bibelsk Eksegese 11, pp. 29–47.

—— 2003a. "On the Problems of Conservative Scholarship – Critical Scholarship: Or How Did We Get Caught by This Bogus Discussion: On Behalf of the Dever-Davies Exchange", *The Bible and Interpretation* http://www.bibleinterp.com/index.htm.

—— 2003b. "Reconstructing Pre-Hellenistic Israelite (Palestinian) History", in Grabbe 2003, pp. 150–67, reprinted in Grabbe 2019, pp. 100–15.

—— 2003c. "'House of David'. The Tel Dan Inscription", in Thompson 2003, pp. 46–67.

—— 2003d. "'House of David'", Arabic edition, in *Jerusalem in Ancient History and Tradition*, Beirut: Qadmus Publications: 77–105.

—— 2003e. "Conservative Scholarship-Critical Scholarship: Or How Did We Get Caught by This Bogus Discussion: On Behalf of the Dever-Davies Exchange", *Bible and Interpretation* Sep 2003.

—— 2005. "Conservative Scholarship on the Move", *Scandinavian Journal of the Old Testament* 19, pp. 203–52.

—— 2008. *The Old Testament between Theology and History*. Louisville, Kentucky, 2008.

—— 2010a. "Did a Reform like Josiah's Happen?" in Davies and Edelman 2010, pp. 11–9.

—— 2010b. "The Deuteronomistic History: Historical Reconsiderations", in K.L. Noll and B. Schramm (eds.), *Raising Up a Faithful Exegete: Essays in Honor of Richard D. Nelson*. Winona Lake, Eisenbrauns, pp. 41–50.

—— 2011a. "Evading the Facts: Notes on Jens Bruun Kofoed's *Text and History: Historiography and the Study of the Biblical Text* (2005)", in L.L. Grabbe 2011, pp. 139–63.

—— 2011b. "Does the Idea of the Old Testament as a Hellenistic Book Prevent Source Criticism of the Pentateuch?" *Scandinavian Journal of the Old Testament* 25, pp. 75-92.

—— 2012a. "Cultural Amnesia", in Carstens, Hasselbalch and Lemche 2012, pp. 159-72.

—— 2012b. "The Greek Israelites and Gerizim", in Tal Davidovich 2012, pp. 147-54.

—— 2012c. "Writing Israel Out of the History of Palestine", *Bible and Interpretation* Oct 2012 https://bibleinterp.arizona.edu/articles/lem368022.

—— 2012d. "Gammeltestamentlige tekster som genskrevet litteratur", in Jesper Høgenhaven and Mogens Müller, *Bibelske Genskrivninger* (Forum for Bibelsk Eksegese 17; København: Museum Tusculanum, 2012), pp. 51-73.

—— 2013a. "Power and Social Organization: Some misunderstanding and some proposals: or Is It all a Question of Patrons and Clients?" Lemche 2013b, pp. 158-68.

—— 2013b. *Biblical Studies and the Failure of History, 3: Changing Perspectives.* Copenhagen International Seminar, London, Equinox.

—— 2015a. "Locating the Story of Biblical Israel" in Thelle, Stordalen and Richardson 2015, pp. 217-29.

—— 2015b., "Exile as the Great Divide: Would There Be an 'Ancient Israel' without an Exile?" In Anne Kathrine Gudme and Ingrid Hjelm (eds.), *Myths of Exile: History and Metaphor in the Hebrew Bible.* Copenhagen International Seminar. London: Routledge, pp. 13-27.

—— 2015c. *Ancient Israel: A New History of Israel.* Second edition. London: Bloomsbury T&T Clark, 2015

—— 2017. "A Sectarian Group Called Israel: Historiography and Cultural Memory", in West and Crossley 2017, pp. 72-96.

—— 2020. "What People Want to Believe: Or Fighting Against 'Cultural Memory'", in Niesiołowski-Spanò and Pfoh 2020, pp. 22-34.

—— (forthcoming). 'Social Anthropology of Biblical Memory', in Emanuel Pfoh (ed.), *The T & T Clark Handbook of Anthropology and the Hebrew Bible.* London: Bloomsbury T & T Clark.

—— (in preparation) *Cultural Memory is not a Paper Tiger.* Copenhagen International Series; London: Routledge.

Leonard-Fleckman, M. 2016. *The House of David: Between Political Formation and Literary Revision.* Minneapolis: Fortress Press.

Levy, T.E. and T. Higham (eds.). 2005. *The Bible and Radiocarbon Dating: Archaeology, Text and Science.* London: Equinox.

Lévi-Strauss, C. 1989. *The Savage Mind.* 5th impr. London: Weidenfeld and Nicolson [orig. French edn: *La pensée sauvage*, Paris: Plon, 1962].

Lipschits, O., Y. Gadot and M.J. Adams (eds.). 2017. *Rethinking Israel; Studies in the History and Archaeology of Ancient Israel in Honor of Israel Finkelstein.* Winona Lake, Indiana: Eisenbrauns.

Lipschits, O. and M. Oeming (eds.). 2006. *Judah and the Judeans in the Persian Period.* Winona Lake: Eisenbrauns.

Liverani, Mario. 1965. "Il fuoriuscitismo in Siria nella tarda età del bronzo", *Rivista Storica Italiana* 77, pp. 315-36 (ET: "Refugees in Syria in the Late Bronze Age" in Liverani 2021, pp. 222-40).

—— 1966. "Problemi e indirizzi degli studi storici sul Vicino Oriente antica", *Cultura e Scuola* 20, pp. 72-9

—— 1969. "Introduzione" to Mario Liverani (ed.), *La Siria nel Tardo Bronzo*. Orientis Antiqvi Collectio, 9. Roma: Centro per le Antichità e la storià dell'arte del Vicino Oriente , pp. 3-14.

—— 1974. "L'histoire de Joas", *Vetus Testamentum* 24, pp. 438-453 (ET: "The Story of Joash", in Liverani 2004, pp. 147-59).

—— 1976. "Review of de Vaux", *Oriens Antiquus* 15, pp. 145-59.

—— 1977. "Storiografia politica Hittita - II: Telepinu, ovvero: Della Solidarietà", *Oriens Antiquus* 16, pp. 105-131 (ET: Liverani 2004, pp. 27-52).

—— 1979a. "Farsi ḫabīru", Vicino Oriente 2, pp. 65-77 (ET: "Becoming ḫabīru", in Liverani 2021, pp. 241-53).

—— 1979b. "Messaggi, donne, ospitalità: Communicazione intertribale in Giud. 19-21", *Studi Storico-Religiosi*, pp. 303-41 (ET: "Messages, Women and Hospitality: Inter-Tribal Communication in Judges 19-21", in Liverani 2004, pp. 160-92).

—— 1998-1999. *Le lettere di el-Amarna. I-II*. Testi del Vicino Oriente, 3, 1-2. Brescia: Paideia.

—— 1999. "Nuovi sviluppi nello studio della storia dell'Israele biblico", *Biblica* 80, pp. 488-505 (ET: "New developments in the study of the history of biblical Israel", in Liverani 2021, pp. 274-90).

—— 2003. *Oltre la Bibbia: Storia antica di Israële*. Roma-Bari: Editori Laterza, 2003.

——2004. *Myths and Politics in Ancient Near Eastern Historiography*. Eds. Zainab Bahrani and Marc Van de Mieroop. London: Equinox.

—— 2005. *Israel's History and the History of Israel*. London: Equinox, 2005.

—— 2014. *The Ancient Near East: History, Society and Economy*. London: Routledge.

—— 2021. *Historiography, Ideology and Politics in the Ancient Near East and Israel: Changing Perspectives 5*. Eds. Niels Peter Lemche and Emanuel Pfoh. Copenhagen International Seminar. London: Routledge.

Long, B. 1968. *The Problem of Etiological Narrative in the Old Testament*. Beihefte zur Zeitschrift für die alttestamentliche Wissenschaft, 108. Berlin: De Gruyter.

—— 1997. *Planting and Reaping Albright: Politics, Ideology, and Interpreting the Bible*. University Park, Pennsylvania: The Pennsylvania State University Press.

Long, V.P. (ed.). 1999. *Israel's Past in Present Research: Essays on Ancient Israelite Historiography*. Sources for Biblical and Theological Study. Winona Lake, Indiana: Eisenbrauns.

Long, V.P., D.W. Baker and G.J. Wenham (eds.). 2002. *Windows into Old Testament History*. Grand Rapids, Michigan.

Lowenthal, D. 2015. *The Past is a Foreign Country - Revisited*. Cambridge: University Press, 2015.

Luckenbill, D.D. 2005. *The Annals of Sennacherib*. Ancient Texts and Translations. 1924. Reprint: Eugene, Oregon: Wipf & Stock Publishers.

MacLeod, Roy (ed.). 2004., *The Library of Alexandria: Centre of Learning in the Ancient World*. London, New York: I.B. Tauris.

Maidman, M.P. 1995. "Nuzi: Portrait of an Ancient Mesopotamian Provincial Town". In Sasson: 1995: II, pp. 931–47.

—— 2010. *Nuzi Texts and Their Uses as Historical Evidence*. Edited by Ann K. Guinan, Society of Biblical Literature. Writings from the Ancient World, 18. Atlanta: Society of Biblical Literature.

Maier, C.M. (ed.). 2014. *Congress Volume Munich 2013*. Vetus Testamentum Supplements, Leiden: E.J. Brill, 2014.

Mandell, S. 2012. "Response to Niels Peter Lemche's 'How to Do History?'". In Hunt 2012, pp. 17-25.

Ma'oz, M. (ed.). 1975, *Studies on Palestine During the Ottoman Period*. Jerusalem: Magen Press.

Margueron, J.-C. 2014. *Mari: Capital of Northern Mesopotamia in the Third Millennium. The Archaeology of Tell Hariri on the Euphrates*. Oxford: Oxbow Books.

Marx, E. 1967. *Bedouin of the Negev*. Manchester: University Press.

Masalha, Nur. 2007. *The Bible and Zionism: Invented Traditions, Archaeology and Post-Colonialism in Israel-Palestine*, London: Zed Books.

Matthews, V.H. 1978. *Pastoral Nomadism in the Mari Kingdom (ca. 1830-1760 B.C.)*, American Schools of Oriental Research Dissertation Series, 3. Cambridge, Massachusetts: Harvard University Press.

Mayer, W. 2003. "Sennacherib's Campaign of 701 BCE: The Assyrian View", in Grabbe 2003, pp. 168–200.

Mayes, A.D.H. 1974. *Israel in the Period of the Judges*. Studies in Biblical Theology, 29. London: SCM Press.

—— 1977, "The Period of the Judges and the Rise of the Monarchy", in Hayes and Miller 1977, pp. 285–331.

Mazar, A. 1990. *Archaeology of the Land of the Bible 19,000–586 B.C.E.* The Anchor Bible Reference Library. New York: Doubleday.

—— 2003. "Remarks on Biblical Traditions and Archaeological Evidence Concerning Early Israel", in Dever and Gitin 2003, pp. 85–98.

—— 2005. "The Debate over the Chronology of the Iron Age in the Southern Levant: Its History, the Current Situation, and a suggested resolution", in Levy and Higham 2005, pp. 15–30.

—— 2014. "Archaeology and the Bible: Reflections on Historical Memory in the Deuteronomistic History", in Maier 2014, pp. 347–69

Mazar, E. 2008. *Preliminary Report on the City of David Excavations 2005 at the Visitors Center Area*. Jerusalem: Shalem Press.

—— 2015. "The Stepped Stone Structure", in *The Summit of the City of David - Excavations 2005-2008*. Final Reports, I. Jerusalem: Shoham: 169–88.

McCarthy, D.J. 1963. *Treaty and Covenant*. Analecta Biblica, 21. Rome: Pontifical Biblical Institute.

McInerney, J. (ed.). 2014. *A Companion to Ethnicity in the Ancient Mediterranean*. Blackwell Companions to the Ancient World. Chichester, West Sussex: John Wiley & Sons.

Mendels, D. 1987. *The Land of Israel as a Political Concept in Hasmonean Literature: Recourse to History in Second Century B.C. Claims to the Holy Land*. Texte und Studien zum Antiken Judentum, 15. Tübingen: J.C.B. Mohr (Paul Siebeck).

—— 1992. *The Rise and Fall of Jewish Nationalism*. The Anchor Bible Reference Library. New York: Doubleday.

—— 1998. *Identity, Religion and Historiography: Studies in Hellenistic History*. Journal for the Journal of the Pseudepigrapha Supplement Series, 24. Sheffield: Sheffield Academic Press.

Mendenhall, G.E. 1962. "The Hebrew Conquest of Palestine", *The Biblical Archaeologist* 25 (1962), 66–87.

—— 1964. "Covenant Forms in Israelite Tradition", *Biblical Archaeologist* 17 (1964), 50–76.

—— 1973. *The Tenth Generation: The Origins of the Biblical Tradition*. Baltimore: The Johns Hopkins University Press.

—— 1983. "Israel's Hyphenated History", in Freedman and Graf 1983, pp. 95–104.

Merlo, P. 1998. *La dea Ašratum – Aṯiratu – Ašera: Un contributo alla storia della religion semitica del Nord*. Mursia: Ponteficial Università Lateranense.

Meyer, E. 1884–1902. *Geschichte des Altertums* I–V, Stuttgart: J.G. Cotta.

—— 1906. *Die israeliten und ihre Nachbarstämme*. Halle: Max Niemeier. Reprinted Darmstadt: Wissenschaftliche Buchgesellschaft, 1967.

Miller, J. M. and J.H. Hayes, 1986. *A History of Ancient Israel and Judah*. Philadelphia: The Westminster Press.

—— 2006. *A History of Ancient Israel and Judah*. Philadelphia: The Westminster Press. 2nd edn.

Moore, M.B. and B.E. Kelle. 2011. *Biblical History and Israel's Past: The Changing Study of the Bible and History*. Grand Rapids, Michigan: William B. Eerdmans Publishing House.

Moran, W.L. 1992. *The Amarna Letters*. Baltimore: The Johns Hopkins Press.

Mowinckel, Sigmund. 1951. *Offersang og sangoffer: Salmediktning i Bibelen*. Oslo: Forlagt af H. Aschehoug & Co. (W. Nygaard).

—— 1951. *Han som kommer: Messiasforventningen i Det Gamle Testamente og på Jesu Tid*. København: G.E.C. Gads Forlag.

—— 1958. "'Rahelstämme' und 'Leastämme'", in Hempel and Rost 1958, pp. 129–50.

—— 1966. *Psalmenstudien I–VI*. 1921–1924. Reprint in two volumes. Amsterdam: Verlag P. Schippers N.V.

—— 2004. *The Psalms in Israel's Worship*. Grand Rapids, Michigan: William B. Eerdmans Publishing Company 2004.

—— 2005. *He that Cometh: The Messiah Concept in the Old Testament and Later Judaism*. Grand Rapids, Michigan: William B. Eerdmans Publishing Company.

Muceniecks, A. 2017. *Saxo Grammaticus: Hierocratical Conceptions and Danish Hegemony in the Thirteenth Century.* Carmen Monographs and Studies. York: Arc Humanities Press.

Müller, M. and T.L. Thompson (eds.). 2005. *Historie og Konstruktion: Festskrift til Niels Peter Lemche I anledning af 60 års fødselsdagen den 6. september 2005.* Forum for Bibelsk Eksegese; Copenhagen: Museum Tusculanums Forlag.

Musil, A. 1928. *The Manners and Customs of the Rwala Bedouins.* New York: American Geographical Society.

Na'aman, N. 1986. "Ḫabiru and Hebrews: The Transfer of a Social Term to the Literary Sphere", *Journal of Near Eastern Studies* 45, pp. 271–88.

Nelson, C. (ed.). 1973. *The Desert and the Sown: Nomads in the Wider Society.* Berkeley: University of California: Institute of International Studies.

Nelson, R.A. 1981. *The Double Redaction of the Deuteronomistic History.* Journal for the Study of the Old Testament Supplement Series, 18. Sheffield: JSOT Press.

Nestor, D.A. 2010. *Cognitive Perspectives on Israelite Identity.* Library of Hebrew Bible / Old Testament Studies, 519. London: T&T Clark.

Nicolaisen, Johannes. 1963. *Ecology and Culture of the Pastoral Tuareg.* Nationalmuseets Skrifter. Etnografisk Række, IX. København: The National Museum of Copenhagen, 1963.

Niebuhr, B.G. 1811-1812. *Römische Geschichte.* 3 vol., Berlin: Realschulbuchhandlung, 1811–1812). http://www.deutschestextarchiv.de/book/show/niebuhr_roemische01_1811 and http://www.deutschestextarchiv.de/book/show/niebuhr_roemische02_1812.

Nielsen, E. 1952. "Mundtlig Tradition I–III", *Dansk Teologisk Tidsskrift* 15, pp. 19–37, 88–106, 129–46.

—— 1956. *Oral Tradition: A Modern Problem in Old Testament Introduction.* Studies in Biblical Theology, 11. London: SCM Press, 1956.

Nielsen, F.A.J. 1997. *The Tragedy in History: Herodotus and the Deuteronomistic History.* Copenhagen International Seminar, 4. Journal for the Study of the Old Testament Supplement Series, 251. Sheffield: Sheffield Academic Press.

Niesiołowski-Spanò, Ł. 2011. *Origin Myths and Holy Places in the Old Testament: A Study of Aetiological Narratives.* Copenhagen International Seminary. London: Equinox.

Niesiołowski-Spanò, Ł. and E. Pfoh (eds.). 2020. *Biblical Narratives, Archaeology and Historicity. Essays in Honour of Thomas L. Thompson.* Library of Hebrew Bible Old Testament Studies, 680. London: T & T Clark.

Nigro, L. (ed.). 2005. *Tell es-Sultan/Gerico alle soglie della prima urbanizzazione: il villaggio e la* necropoli del Bronzo Antico I (3300–3000 a.C.),* with contributions by Andrea Polcaro and Maura Sala. Rome 'La Sapienza' Studies òn the Archaeology of Palestine & Ttransjordan, 1. 'La Sapienza' Dipartimento di Sciene Storiche Archeologiche e Antropologiche dell'Anticità sezione Vicino Oriente Expedition to Palestine & Jordan.

—— 2010. *Tell es-Sultan/Jericho in the Early Bronze II (3000-2700 BC): the rise of an early Palestinian city. A synthesis of the results of four archaeological expeditions*. Studies on the Archaeology of Palestine & Transjordan, 5. Roma. Università di Roma 'La Sapienza' Dipartimento di Scienze dell'Antichità. Sezione di Orientalistica Expedition to Palestine and Jordan.

—— 2019. "The Italian-Palestinian Expedition to Tell es-Sultan, Ancient Jericho (1997-2015): Archaeolohy and Valrosation of Material and Immaterial Heritage", Sparks etc. 2019, pp. 175-214.

Nigro, Lorenzo and Hamdan Taha (eds.). 2006. *Tell es-Sultan/Jericho in the Context of the Jordan Valley: Site Management, Conservation and Sustainable Development*. Studies on the Archaeology of Palestine & Transjordan, 2. Università di Roma 'La Sapienza' Dipartimento di Sciene Storiche Archeologiche e Antropologiche dell'Anticità sezione Vicino Oriente Expedition to Palestine & Jordan.

Noll, K.L. 2002. *Canaan and Israel in Antiquity: An Introduction*. Biblical Seminar, 83; London: Continuum International Publishing Group Ltd. 2nd enlarged version *Canaan and Israel in Antiquity: A Textbook on History and Religion*. London: Bloomsbury, 2013.

Noth, M. 1929. *Das System der Zwölf Stämme Israels*. Beiträge zur Wissenschaft vom Alten und Neuen Testament, 4,1.

—— 1938a. *Das Buch Joshua*. 1938. Zweite, verbesserte Auflage, 1953. Handbuch zum Alten Testament, erste Reihe, 7. Tübingen: Verlag von J.C.B. Mohr (Paul Siebeck).

—— 1938b. "Grundsätzliches zur geschichtliche Befunde auf dem Boden Palästinas", *Palästinajahrbuch* 34, pp. 7-22, repr. Noth 1971: I, pp. 3-16.

—— 1943. *Überlieferungsgeschichtliche Studien: Erster Teil: Die sammelnden und bearbeitenden Geschichtswerke im Alten Testament*, repr. Darmstadt: Wissenschaftliche Buchgesellschaft, 1963

—— 1948. *Überlieferungsgeschichte des Pentateuch* (Stuttgart: Kohlhammer). Repr. Darmstadt: Wissenschaftliche Buchgesellschaft, 1966)

—— 1950a. *Geschichte Israels*. Göttingen: Vandenhoeck & Rupprecht, 1950

—— 1950b. "Das Amt des 'Richter Israel'", in *Festschrift Alfred Bertholets*, pp. 404-17. Repr. in Noth 1969, pp. 71-86.

—— 1960a. *The History of Israel*. Second edition. London: Adam & Charles Black.

—— 1960b. "Der Beitrag der Archäologie zur Geschichte Israel", *Vetus Testamentum Supplements* 7. Leiden: Brill, pp. 262-82. Repr. in Noth 1971, pp. 34-51. Theologische Bücherei, 39, München: Chr. Kaiser, 1969.

—— 1971a. *Aufsätze zur biblischen Landes- und Altertumskunde*. I-II. Herausgegen von Hans Walter Wolff. Neukirchen: Neukirchener Verlag.

—— 1971b. "Beiträge zur Geschichte des Ostjordanlandes", in Noth 1971: I, pp. 345-543 ("Das Land Gilead als Siedlungsgebiet israelitischer Sippen" (1941), "Israelitische Stämme zwischen Ammon und Moab" (1944), "Die Nachbarn der israelitischen Stämme im Ostjordanlande" (1946), "Jabes-Gilead. Ein Beitrag zur Methode alttestamentlicher Topographie" (1953), and "Gilead und Gad" (1959).

—— 1972. *A History of Pentateuchal Traditions*. Upper Saddle River, New Jersey: Prentice Hall.

—— 1981. *The Deuteronomistic History*. Journal for the study of the Old Testament, Supplement series, 15. Sheffield, UK: JSOT, 1981).

—— 1997. *The Chronicler's History. Journal for the study of the Old Testament, Supplement series*. Sheffield: Sheffield Academic Press, 1997.

Nyberg, H.S. 1935. *Studien zum Hoseabuche*. Uppsala Universitets Årsskrift.

Oestigaard, Terje. 2007. *Political Archaeology and Holy Nationalism: Archaeological Battles over the Bible and Land in Israel and Palestine from 1967-2000*. Göteborg: Göteborg University. Department of Archaeology. Gotarc Serie C, No. 67.

Olrik, A. 1908. "Episke love i folkedigtningen", *Danske Studier* 5, pp. 69-89.

—— 1909. "Epische Gesetze der Volksdichtung", *Zeitschrift für deutsches Altertum* 51, pp. 1-12.

—— 1992. *Principles for Oral Narrative Research*, Bloomington, IN: Indiana University Press, 1992.

Olyan, S.M. 1988. *Asherah and the Cult of Yahweh in Israel*. SBL Monograph Series, 34. Atlanta, Georgia: Scholars Press.

Ong, W.J. 2002. *Orality and Literacy: The Technologizing of the Word*. 30th Anniversary Edition with additional chapters by John Hartley. London: Routledge.

Oppenheim, M. Freiherr von. 1939-68. *Die Beduinen* I-IV (Leipzig-Wiesbaden: Otto Harrassowitz.

Orlinski, H. 1962. "The Tribal System of Israel and Related Groups in the Period of the Judges", *Oriens* Antiquus 1, pp. 11-20.

Östreicher, T. 1923, *Das deuteronomische Grundgesetz*. Beitrage zur Förderung christlicher Theologie, 27/4. Gütersloh: Bertelsmann.

Pappe, Ilan, 2014. *The Idea of Israel: A History of Power and Knowledge*. London: Verso.

Parpola, S. and K. Watanabe. 1988. *Neo-Assyrian Treaties and Loyalty Oaths*. State Archive of Assyria, II. Helsinki: Helsinki University Press.

Pasto, J. 1998. "When the end is the beginning? Or when the biblical past is the political present: Some thoughts on ancient Israel, 'post-exilic Judaism', and the politics of biblical scholarship", *Scandinavian Journal of the Old Testament* 12 (1998), 157-202.

Pearce, L.E. and C. Wunsch. 2014. *Documents of Judean Exiles and West Semites in Babylonia in the Collection of David Sofer*. Cornell University Studies in Assyriology and Sumerology, 28. Bethesda, Maryland: CDL Press.

Pedersen, J. 1926-47. *Israel, Its Life and Culture*, I-II. I: Oxford: H. Milford, Oxford university press: 1926), II-IV: London: Cumberlege, 1947.

—— 1934. "Passafest und Passahlegende", *Zeitschrift für die alttestamentliche Wissenschaft* 52, pp. 161-76.

Perlitt, L. 1965. *Vatke und Wellhausen: Geschichtsphilosoph. Voraussetzungen u. historiograph. Motive f.d. Darstellung d. Religion u. Geschichte Israels durch Wilhelm*

Vatke u. Julius Wellhausen. Beiheft zur Zeitschrift für die alttestamentlische Wissenschaft, 94. Berlin: Töpelmann.

—— 1969. *Bundesteologie im Alten Testament*. Wissenschaftliche Monographien zum Alten und Neuen Testament, 36. Neukirchen: Neukirchener Verlag.

Pfoh, E. 2009a. "Some Remarks on Patronage in Syria-Palestine during the Late Bronze Age", *Journal of the Economic and Social History of the Orient* 52, pp. 363–81.

—— 2009b. *The Emergence of Israel in Ancient Palestine: Historical and Anthropological Perspectives*. Copenhagen International Seminar. London: Equinox.

—— 2016. *Syria-Palestine in the Late Bronze Age: An Anthropology of Politics and Power*. Copenhagen International Seminar. London: Routledge.

Pioske, D.D. 2015. *David's Jerusalem: Between Memory and History*. London: Routledge.

Pitard, W.T. 1987. *Ancient Damascus: A Historical Study of the Syrian City-State from Earliest Times until its Fall to the Assyrians in 732 B.C.E.*. Winona Lake, Indiana: Eisenbrauns.

Pollard, J. and H. Reid. 2006. *The Rise and Fall of Alexandria: Birthplace of the modern World*. London: Penguin Books.

Pritchard, J.B. (ed.). 1955. *Ancient Near Eastern Texts Relating to the Old Testament*. Second edition corrected and enlarged. Princeton, New Jersey: Princeton University Press.

Provan, I. 1995. "Ideologies, Literary and Critical: Reflections on Recent Writing on the History of Israel", *Journal of Biblical Literature* 114, pp. 585–606.

—— 2002. "In the Stable with the Dwarves: Testimony, Interpretation, Faith and the History of Israel", in Lemaire and Sæbø 2000, pp. 281–319. Repr. in Long, Baker and Wenham 2002: 161–97.

Provan, I., V.P. Long, T. Longman III. 2003. *A Biblical History of Israel*. Louisville: Westminster John Knox Press.

Rad, G. von. 1938. *Das formgeschichtliche Problem des Hexateuchs*. Beiträge zur Wissenschaft vom Alten und Neuen Testament, IV/26. Stuttgart: W. Kohlhammer. Repr. in his *Gesammelte Studien zum Alten Testament*. Theologische Bücherei, 8. München: Chr. Kaiser, 1958, 9–86.

—— 1944. "Der Anfang der Geschichtsschreibung im Alten Testament", *Archiv für Religionsgeschichte* 32 (1944), pp. 1–42. Reprinted in von Rad 1958, pp. 148–89. ET: "The Beginning of Historical Writing", in von Rad 1966, pp. 166–204.

—— 1957–60. *Theologie des Alten Testaments, 1–2*. München: Chr. Kaiser Verlag. ET : *Old Testament Theology*. I–II. London: SCM Press, 1975.

—— 1958. *Gesammelte Studien zum Alten Testament*. Theologische Bücherei Altes Testament, 8. München: Chr. Kaiser Verlag, 1965.

—— 1966. *The Problem of the Hexateuch and Other Essays*. London: SCM Press, 1966.

—— 1975. *Old Testament Theology*. I–II. London: SCM Press, 1975.

Rainey, A.F. 1996. "Who is a Canaanite? A Review of the textual Evidence", *Bulletin of the American Schools of Oriental Research* 304, pp. 1–15.

—— 2008. "Who were the Early Israelites?" *Biblical Archaeological Review* 34:06, Nov/Dec 2008, 51–55.

—— 2015. With the assistance of Z. Cochavi-Rainey and W. Schnidewind: *The El-Amarna Correspondence: A New Edition of the Cuneiform Letters from the Site of E-Amarna based on Collations of all Extant Tablets*. I–II. Handbuch of Oriental Studies. Section I, Ancient Near East, 110. Leiden: Brill.

Redman, C. 1978. *Rise of Civilization: From Early Farmers to Urban Society in the Ancient Near East*. San Francisco: W.H. Freeman & Co Ltd.

Renfrew, C. and P. Bahn. 2020. *Archaeology: Theories, Methods and Practice*. 8th edition. London: Thames & Hudson.

Renz, J. 1995. *Die althebräischen Inschriften. I: Text und Kommentar*. Handbuch der althebräischen Epigraphik, I. Darmstadt: Wissenschaftliche Buchgesellschaft.

Richter, W. 1965. "Zu den 'Richter Israels'", *Zeitschrift für die alttestamentliche Wissenschaft* 77, pp. 40–72.

Ricœur, P. 2004. *Memory, History, Forgetting*. Chicago: The University of Chicago Press.

Römer, T. *The So-Called Deuteronomistic History: A Sociological, Historical and Literary Introduction*. London: T&T Clark, 2007.

Rose, M. 1981. *Deuteronomist und Jahwist: Untersuchungen zu den Berührungspunkten beider Literaturwerke*. Abhandlungen zur Theologie des Alten und Neuen Testaments, 67. Zürich: TVZ.

Rost, L. 1926. *Die Überlieferung von der Thronnachfolge Davids* (1926). Repr. in Rost 1965, pp. 119–253.

—— 1956. "Das kleine Geschichtliche Credo". Repr. in Rost 1965, pp. 11–24.

—— 1965. *Das kleine Credo und andere Studien zum Alten Testament*. Heidelberg: Quelle & Meyer.

Roth, M. (1997), *Law Collections from Mesopotamia and Asia Minor*. Second edition. With a contribution by Harry A. Hoffner. Volume editor Piotr Michalowski. Society of Biblical Literature Writings from the Ancient World Series, 6. Atlanta, Georgia: Scholars Press.

Rowton, M.B., 1973a. "Autonomy and Nomadism in Western Asia", *Orientalia* NS 42, pp. 247–58.

—— 1973b. "Urban Autonomy in a Nomadic Environment", *Journal of Near Eastern Studies* 23, pp. 201–15.

—— 1974. "Enclosed Nomadism", *Journal of the Economic and Social History of the Orient* 17, pp. 1–30.

—— 1976. "Dimorphic Structure and the Tribal Elite", in *al-Bahit, Festschrift Joseph Henninger*. Studia Instituti Anthropos 28. St. Augustin bei Bonn: Verlag des Anthropos-Instituts, pp. 219–57.

Running, L.G. and D.N. Freedman. 1975. *William Foxwell Albright: A Twentieth Century Genius*. Berrien Springs, Michigan: Andrews University Press.

Said, E.W. 1979. *Orientalism*. New York: Vintage Books.

Salzman, P.C. 1980. *When Nomads Settle: Processes of Sedentarization as Adaption and Response*. New York: Holt, Rinehart and Winston Inc.

Sand, S. 2008. *Comment le people juif fut inventé: De la Bible au sionisme*. Paris: Fayard, 2008.

—— 2009. *The Invention of the Jewish People*. London: Verso.

—— 2012. *The Invention of the Land of Israel: From Holy Land to Homeland*. London: Verso.

Sasson, Jack. M. (ed.) 2005. *Civilizations of the Ancient Near East*. John Baines, Gary Beckman, Karen S. Rubinson associate editors. I–IV. New York: Charles Scribner's Sons MacMillan Library Reference USA Simon & Schuster MacMillan.

Saxo Grammaticus, 2008. *The History of the Danes*. Books I–IX. Translation Peter Fisher. Woodbridge: D.S. Brewer.

Schmid, H.H. 1976. *Der sogenannte Jahwist: Beobachtungen und Fragen zur Pentateuchforschung*. Zürich: TVZ Verlag.

Schmid, Konrad. 2020. "Overcoming the Sub-Deuteronomism and Sub-Chronicism of Historiography in Biblical Studies: The Case of the Samaritans", Kartveit and Knoppers. 2020, pp. 17–29.

Service, E.R. 1962. *Primitive Social Organization*. New York; Random House.

Shanks, H. 1997. "Face to face: Biblical Minimalists Meet Their Challengers", *Biblical Archaeological Review* 23.4, pp. 26–42.

—— 2010. *Freeing the Dead Sea Scrolls and Other Adventures of an Archaeology Outsider*. London: Bloomsbury.

Sherrard, B. 2011. *American Biblical Archaeologists and Zionism: The Politics of Historical Ethnography*. PhD Diss., College of Arts and Sciences, The Florida State University.

—— 2016 "American Biblical Archaeologists and Zionism: How Differing Worldviews on the Interaction of Cultures Affected Scholarly Constructions of the Ancient Past", *Journal of the American Academy of Religion* 84, pp. 234–59.

Silberman, N.A. 1982. *Digging for God and Country: Exploration, Archaeology, and the Secret Struggle for the Holy Land 1799-1917*. New York: Alfred A. Knopf.

—— 1994. *The Hidden Scrolls: Christianity, Judaism & the War for the Dead Sea Scrolls*. A Grosset/Putnam Book. New York: Published by G.P. Putnam's Sons.

Smend, R. 1971. "Das Gesetzt und die Völker: Ein Beitrag zur deuteronomistischer Redaktionsgeschichte", in Wolf 1971, pp. 494–509.

—— 1989. *Deutsche Alttestamentler in drei Jahrhunderten*. Göttingen: Vandenhoeck & Ruprecht.

Smith, S. 1949. *The Statue of Idrimi*. With an introduction by Sir Leonard Woolley. Occasional Publications of the British Institute of Archaeology in Ankara, 1. London: The British Institute of Archaeology in Ankara.

Sneed, M. (ed.).1999. *Concepts of Class in Ancient Israel*. South Florida Studies in the History of Judaism 201, Atlanta GA.

Snorri Sturluson. 1991. *Heimskringla: History of the Kings of Norway*. Translated by Lee M. Hollander. University of Texas Press.

Soggin, J.A. 1967. *Das Königtum in Israel: Ursprünge, Spannungen, Entwicklung*. Beiheft zur Zeitschrift für die alttestamentliche Wissenschaft, 178. Berlin: Verlag Alfred Töpelmann.

—— 1977. "The Davidic-Solomonic Kingdom", in Hayes and Miller 1977, pp. 332-380.

—— 1984. *A History of Israel from the Beginnings to the Bar Kochba Revolt AD 135*. London: SCM Press.

—— 1993. *An Introduction to the History of Israel and Judah: Second, completely revised and updated edition*. London: SCM Press.

Sparks, R.T., B. Finlayson, B. Wagemakers, J.M. Briffa (eds.). 2019. *Digging Up Jericho: Past, Present and Future*. Oxford: Archaeopress.

Speiser, Ephraim E. 1931-32. "Ethnic Movements in the near East in the Second Millennium B. C. The Hurrians and Their Connections with the ḫabiru and the Hyksos", *The Annual of the American Schools of Oriental Research* 13, pp. 13-54.

—— 1964. *Genesis: Introduction, Translation, and Notes*. The Anchor Bible, 1. New York: Doubleday & Company, Inc.

Steiner, Margreet. 2001. *Excavations by Kathleen M. Kenyon in Jerusalem 1861-1867, Volume III: The Settlement in the Bronze and Iron Ages*. Copenhagen International Series, 9. London: Sheffield Academic Press.

—— 2003. "The Evidence from Kenyon's Excavations in Jerusalem: A Response Essay", in Vaughan and Killebrew 2003, pp. 347-64.

—— 2014. "One Hundred and Fifty Years of Excavating Jerusalem", in Wagemakers 2014, pp. 24-37.

—— 2016. "From Jerusalem with Love", in Hjelm and Thompson 2016, pp. 71-84.

—— 2020. "The City of David as a Palimpsest", in Niesolowski-Spanò and Pfoh 2020, pp. 3-10.

Stinespring, W. 1957. "Review of John Bright, *Early Israel in Recent History* Writing", in *Journal of Biblical Literature* 76, pp. 249.

Strange, John. 2015. *Tall al-Fukhar: Result of Excavations in 1990-93 and 2002*. Proceedings of the Danish Institute in Damascus, 9; Aarhus University Press.

Strootman, Rolf. 2014. *Courts and Elites in the Hellenistic Empires: The Ancient Near East After the Achaemenids, c. 330 to 30 B.C*. Edinburgh Studies in Ancient Persia. Edinburgh: University Press

Sweet, L.E. 1960. *Tell Toqaan: A Syrian Village*. Anthropological Papers No. 14. Ann Arbor: University of Michigan.

Taha, H. and G. van der Kooij. 2014. *The Tell Balata Archaeological Guidebook*. Publications of the Tell Balata Archaeological Park. Ramallah: Ministry of Tourism and Antiquities. Department of Antiquities and Cultural Development.

—— 2020. "Tell Balata (Shechem): An Archaeological and Historical Reassessment", In Niesołowski-Spanò and Pfoh 2020, pp. 62-75.

Thelle, R., T. Stordalen and M.E.R. Richardson (eds.). 2015. *New Perspectives on Old Testament Prophecy and History. Essays in Honour of Hans M. Barstad*. Vetus Testamentum, Supplements, 168; Leiden: E.J. Brill.

Thompson, R.J. 2013. *Terror of the Radiance: Assur Covenant to YHWH Covenant*. Orbis Biblicus et Orientalis, 258. Fribourg Academic Press, Fribourg: Göttingen: Vandenhoeck & Ruprecht.

Thompson, T.L. 1974. *The Historicity of the Patriarchal Narratives: The Quest for the Historical Abraham*. Beihefte zur Zeitschrift für die alttestamentliche Wissenschaft, 133. Berlin: Walter de Gruyter

—— 1992. *Early History of the Israelite People: From the Written and Archaeological Sources*. Studies in the History and Culture of the Ancient Near East, 4. Brill: Leiden, 1992

—— 1995. "A Neo-Albrightean School in History and Biblical Scholarship?", *Journal of Biblical Literature* 114, pp. 683–98.

—— 1996. "Historiography of Ancient Palestine and Early Jewish Geography: W.G. Dever and the not so New Biblical Archaeology", in Fritz and Davies 1996, pp. 26–43.

—— 1999. *The Bible in History: How Writers Create a Past*. London: Jonathan Cape, 1999.

—— 2001. "A view from Copenhagen: Israel and the History of Palestine", *The Bible and Interpretation*. https://bibleinterp.arizona.edu/articles/view-copenhagen-israel-and-history-palestine.

—— 2003. *Jerusalem in Ancient History and Tradition*. Journal for the Study of the Old Testament Supplement Series, 381 / Copenhagen International Seminar, 12. London: T&T Clark International.

—— 2005. *The Messiah Myth: The Near Eastern Roots of Jesus and David*. New York: Basic Books.

Toll, C. 1990–91. "H.S. Nyberg". In *Svensk Bibliografisk Lexikon*, 27, p. 643. https://sok.riksarkivet.se/sbl/Presentation.aspx?id=8431

Tumblety, J. (ed.). 2013. *Memory and History: Understanding Memory as Source and Subject*. Routledge Guides to Using Historical Sources. London: Routledge.

Ulrich, Eugene (ed.). 2013. *The Biblical Qumran Scrolls: Transcriptions and Textual Variants*. Volume I-III. Leiden: Brill.

Ussishkin, D. 1980. "Was the 'Solomonic' City Gate at Megiddo Built by King Solomon?" *Bulletin of the American Schools of Oriental Research* 239, pp. 1–18.

—— 1982. *The Conquest of Lachish by Sennacherib*. Tel Aviv: Tel Aviv University, the Institute of Archaeology.

—— 2006. "The Borders and De Facto Size of Jerusalem in the Persian Period", in O. Lipschits and M. Oeming 2006, pp. 147–66.

Van Seters. J. 1975 *Abraham in History and Tradition*. New Haven: Yale University Press.

—— 1983. *In Search of History: Historiography in the Ancient World and the Origins of Biblical History*. New Haven: Yale University Press, 1983.

—— 1992. *Prologue to History: The Yahwist as Historian in Genesis.* Louisville, Kentucky: Westminster John Knox Press, 1992

—— 1994. *The Life of Moses: The Yahwist as Historian in Exodus-Numbers.* Kampen, the Netherlands: Kok Pharos Publishing House, 1994

—— 2006. *The Edited Bible: The Curious History of the 'Editor' in Biblical Criticism.* Winona Lake, Indiana: Eisenbrauns, 2006.

—— 2009. *The Biblical Saga of King David.* Winona Lake, Indiana: Eisenbrauns.

—— 2013a. *The Yahwist: A Historian of Israelite Origins.* Winona Lake, Indiana: Eisenbrauns, 2013.

—— 2013b. "Introduction", in Lemche 2013b, pp. 1–10.

—— 2018. *My Life and Career as a Biblical Scholar.* Eugene, Oregon: Cascade Books, 2018 (Kindle).

Vaughan, A.G. and A.F. Killebrew. 2003. *Jerusalem in Bible and Archaeology: The First Temple Period.* Society of Biblical Literature Symposium Series, 18. Atlanta: Society of Biblical Literature.

Vaux, Roland de, 1971. *Histoire ancienne d'Israël: Des origines à l'installation en Canaan.* Ètudes bibliques. Paris: Librairie Lecoffre J. Gabalda et Cie Éditeurs.

—— 1973. *Histoire ancienne d'Israël: La période des juges.* Études bibliques. Paris: Librairie Lecoffre J. Gabalda et Cie Éditeurs.

—— 1978. *The Early History of Israel to the Period of the Judges*, II. London: Darton, Longman & Todd.

Veijola, T. 1975. *Die ewige Dynastie: David und die Entstehung seiner Dynastie nach der deuteronomistischen Darstellung.* Annales Academiæ Scientiarum Fennica. Helsinki: Suomalainen Tiedeakatemia.

—— 1977 *Das Königtum in der Beurteilung der deuteronomistichen Historiographie: Eine redaktionsgeschichtliche Untersuchung.* Annales Academiæ Scientiarum Fennica, 198. Helsinki: Suomalainen Tiedeakatemia.

—— 1982. *Verheissung in der Krise: Studien zur Literatur und Theologie der Exilszeit anhand des 89. Psalms.* Annales Academiæ Scientiarum Fennica, 220. Helsinki: Suomalainen Tiedeakatemia.

Wagemakers, B. (ed.). 2014. *Archaeology in the 'Land of Tells and Ruins': A History of Excavations in the Holy Land Inspired by the Photographs and Accounts of Leo Boer.* Oxford: Oxbow Books.

Wajdenbaum, P. 2011. *Argonauts of the Desert: Structural Analysis of the Hebrew Bible.* Copenhagen International Seminar. London: Equinox.

Weidner, E.F. 1923. *Politische Dokumente aus Kleinasien: Die Staatsverträge in akkadischer Sprache aus dem Archiv von Boghazköi.*: Reprint Hildesheim: Georg Olms, 1970.

Weinfeld, M. 1972. *Deuteronomy and the Deuteronomic School*, Oxford: Clarendon.

Weinrich, H. 2005. *Lethe: Kunst und Kritik des Vergessens.* München: Verlag C.H. Beck, 2005.

Weippert, H. 1988. *Palästina in vorhellenistischer Zeit.* Handbuch der Archäologie. Vorderasien II.I. München: C.H. Beck'sche Verlagsbuchhandlung.

Weippert, M. 1967. *Die Landnahme der israelitischen Stämme in der neueren wissenschaftliche Diskussion: Ein kritischer Bericht*. Forschungen zur Religion und Literatur des Alten und Neuen Testaments, 92. Göttingen: Vandenhoeck & Ruprecht.

Weippert, M and S. Timm (eds.). 1995. *Meilenstein. Festgabe für Herbert Donner, Ägypten und Altes Testament* 30, Wiesbaden, 1995.

Wellhausen, Julius. 1878 [1886]. *Prolegomena zur Geschichte Israels*. Dritte Ausgabe. Berlin: Druck und Verlag von Georg Reimer, 1886. First published as *Geschichte Israels*, I. Berlin: Georg Reimer,.

—— 1883. *Prolegomena to the History of Ancient Israel*, with a reprint of the article *Israel* from the Encyclopedia Britannica. Preface by W. Robertson Smith. Reprint Cleveland and New York: Meridian Books. The World Publishing Company, 1965.

—— 1887. *Reste arabischen Heidentums: Gesammelt und erläutert*. Dritte unveränderte Auflage. Berlin: Walter de Gruyter, 1961.

—— 1902. *Das arabische Reich und sein Sturz*. Berlin: Georg Reimer, 1902.

Wesselius, J.-V. 2002. *The Origin of the History of Israel: Herodotus' Histories as Blueprint for the First Book of the Bible*. Journal for the Study of the Old Testament Supplement Series, 345. Sheffield: Sheffield Academic Press.

West, J. and J. Crossley (eds.). 2017. *History, Politics and the Bible from the Iron Age to the Media Age. Essays in Honour of Keith W. Whitelam*. Library of the Hebrew Bible/Old Testament Studies, 651; Bloomsbury T&T Clark, London.

Wette, W.M.L. de. 1806–1807. *Beiträge zur Einleitung in das Alte Testament*. I–II. Halle: Bey Schimmelpfenning und Compagnie. Reprint: Darmstadt: Wissenschaftliche Buchgesellschaft, 1971.

White, Hayden. 1973. *Metahistory: The Historical Imagination in Nineteenth-Century Europe*. Fourtieth-Anniversary Edition. Baltimore: Johns Hopkins University Press, 2014.

Whitelam, K.W. 1979. *The Just King: Monarchical Judicial Authority in Ancient Israel*. Journal for the study of the Old Testament supplement series. Sheffield: JSOT Press.

—— 2012. "The Death of Biblical History", in Duncan Burns and J.W. Rogerson (eds.), *Far From Minimal: Celebrating the Work and Influence of Philip R. Davies*. Library of Hebrew Bible / Old Testament Studies, 484. London: T & T Clark, pp. 484–504.

Whiting, Robert M. 1995. "Amorite Tribes and Nations of Second-Millennium Western Asia", in Sasson 1995: II, pp. 1231–42.

Whybray, R.N. 1968. *The Succession Narrative: A Study of II Samuel 9–20; I Kings 1 and 2*. Studies in Biblical Theology Second Series, 9. London: SCM Press.

Wiggins, S.A. 1993. *A Reassessment of 'Asherah': A Study According to the Textual Sources of the First Two Millennia B.C.E.* Alter Orient und Altes Testament, Band 235. Kevelaer: Verlag Butzon & Bercker; Neukirchen-Vluyn: Neukirchener Verlag.

Wightman, G. J. 1990. "The Myth of Solomon", *Bulletin of the American Schools of Oriental Research* 277/278, pp. 5–22.

Wilson, K.A. 2005. *The Campaign of Pharaoh Shoshenq I Into Palestine*. Forschungen zum Alten Testament, 9. Tübingen: Mohr Siebeck.

Winnett, F.V. 1965. "Re-Examining the Foundations", *Journal of Biblical Literature* 84, pp. 1–19.

Wolf, H.W. (ed.). 1971. *Probleme biblischer Theologie: Gerhard von Rad zum 70. Geburtstag*. München: Chr. Kaiser Verlag.

Wright, G.E. 1957. *Biblical Archaeology*. 2nd edn. London: Gerald Duckworth & Co Ltd.

—— 1958. "Archaeology and Old Testament Studies", *Journal of Biblical Literature* 77, pp. 39–51.

—— 1962. *God who Acts: Biblical Theology as Recital* (Studies in Biblical Theology, 8; London: SCM Press.

Wright, G.E. and R. Fuller. 1965. *The Book of the Acts of God*. Pelican A764. Harmondsworth: Penguin Books.

Yates, F. 2001 [1979]. *The Occult Philosophy in the Elizabethan Age*. London: Routledge, reprint edn.

Yadin, Y. 1960. "New Light on Solomon's Megiddo", *The Biblical Archaeologist* 23, pp. 62–68.

—— 1972. *Hazor: The Head of All Those Kingdoms*. The Schweich Lectures of the British Academy 1970. London: Published for the British Academy.

—— 1979. "Megiddo of the Kings of Israel", *The Biblical Archaeologist* 33, pp. 65–96.

Index of Scripture References

Genesis 15:2	86	1. Kings 9:15	115
Genesis 14	87, 144	1. Kings 10:26–29	115
Genesis 14:13	87	1. Kings 14:25–26	10
Genesis 15:2	143	2. Kings 11–12	5
Exodus 21:1–6	92	2. Kings 18–19	9
Deuteronomy 4:44–49; 5	144	2. Kings 18:13–16	9
Deuteronomy 26: 5–9	81	2. Kings 22–23	10, 11
Joshua 24	80	2. Kings 22:8–11	128
Judges 4	78	2. Kings 17	141
Judges 5	78	1. Chronicles 22	113
Judges 8:18–21	144	2. Chronicles 12:1–9	10
Judges 19–21	5, 78	2. Chronicles 34	10
2. Samuel 8; 10; 12:26–31	110		
2. Samuel 6	113	Matthew 1	20
2. Samuel 24	113	John 18: 38	40

Index of Modern Authors

Aharoni, Y. 115
Ahlström, G.W. 70, 83
Albertz, R. 37, 60, 81, 126
Albright, W.F. 2, 13, 25, 30, 33, 36, 37, 41, 48, 50, 51, 52, 53, 54, 56, 60, 69, 71, 80, 81, 83, 84, 85, 86, 87, 88, 90, 91, 93, 94, 96, 117, 121
Alt, A. 2, 12, 13, 15, 23, 30, 47, 49, 50, 56, 69, 71, 72, 91, 93, 138
Antoun, R.T. 97
Arnold, B.T. 23
Athas, G. 106, 107, 108, 109
Avalos, H. 94
Bächli, O. 75
Bahn, P. 94
Baker, D.W. 23
Barr, J. 24, 25, 26, 27, 29, 43, 44, 45, 46, 51
Barth, F. 58, 97, 98
Bates, D.G. 97
Beckman, G. 81
Ben-Tor, A. 96
Bezold, C. 28
Biggs, R.D. 132
Binger, T. 1, 81
Binford, L. 59
Biran, A. 22, 105
Blenkinsopp, J. 22
Bliss, F.J. 115
Bottéro, J. 87
Bright, J. 25, 49, 65, 66, 67, 68, 70, 71, 72, 77, 83, 84, 85, 87, 88, 90, 122
Broshi, M. 21
Brown, N.M. 116
Brown, W.P. 83, 84
Bruneau, P. 102
Brunner, H. 33
Bryce, T. 91
Buccellati, G. 88

Buhl, F. 29
Bultmann, R. 52
Burke, A.A. 89
Burrows, M. 52
Cantrell, D.O. 117
Carlson, R.A. 70
Carroll, R.P. 26, 44, 55
Cattell, M.G. 105
Causse, A. 95
Chadwick, H.M. 76
Chavalas, M.W. 23, 46
Charlesworth, J.H. 80
Childe, V.G. 115
Climo, J.J. 105
Cline, E.H. 36
Cody, A. 76
Cogan, M. 9
Cochavi-Rainey, Z. 92
Cole, D.P. 97
Cook, G. 109
Coote, R.B. 45
Cowley, C.E. 112
Cross, F.M. 25, 38, 54, 117, 128
Crowfoot, J.W. 56, 114
Cryer, F.H. 105, 105, 107, 108, 124
Cubitt, G. 15, 105
Dahood, M. 131, 132
Dassow, E. von 90
Davies, P.R. vii, 4, 16, 17, 26, 31, 33, 35, 38, 41, 43, 44, 62, 107, 108
Davis, T.W. 24, 37, 50
Delitzsch, F. 28
Derrida, J. 38
Dever, W.G. 14, 15, 18, 20, 23, 24, 25, 30, 31, 34, 36, 37, 38, 39, 40, 41, 42, 43, 45, 46, 47, 48, 50, 55, 57, 58, 59, 60, 79, 81, 90, 95, 96, 101, 106, 123
Dibelius, M. 52

Diebner, B.J. 4, 22, 67, 83, 122
Dietrich, W. 81, 128
Donner, H. 66
Dostoevsky, F.M. 39
Dothan, Moshe 34, 116
Dothan, Trude 34
Doughty, C.M. 95
Droysen, Johann Gustav 3, 22, 27
Durand, J,-M. 85
Edelman, D.V. 113
Ehmann, D. 97
Eichrodt, W. 80, 84
Eißfeldt, O. 74
Emerton, J. 87
Engel, H. 74, 101
English, P.W. 97
Engnell, I. 25, 70
Eriksen, T.H. 58
Ewald, G.H.A. 27, 35, 73
Fantalkin, A. 57
Fenton, S. 58
Ferdinand, K. 97
Finkelstein, I. 10, 14, 15, 22, 41, 56, 57, 100, 101, 113, 116, 117, 118, 119, 120, 123, 138
Fisher, C.S. 114
Fohrer, G. 74, 77, 90
Franklin, N. 117
Freedman, D.N. 25, 50, 54, 55, 132
Frerichs, E.S. 79
Frevel, Christian 5, 6, 7, 11
Fried, M. 103
Friedman, R.E. 124
Friedrich, J. 81
Galling, K. 33, 45, 73, 74, 87
Garbini, G. 78, 86, 102, 106, 111
Garfinkel, Y. 57
Garstang, J. 114
Gernot, W. 90
Geus, C.H.J. de. 75, 76
Gilbert, F. 3
Gmirkin, R. 107, 137
Gnuse, R. 137
Goff, J. le. 105
Goldman, S. 20
Goody, J. 121
Gottwald, Norman K. 13, 31, 95, 96

Grabbe, L.L. 6, 8
Graf, K.H. 27, 46
Greenfield, J. 132
Griffin, H.M. 3
Grønbæk, J.H. 110
Grotefend, G.Fr. 28
Gruen, E.S. 58
Grundtvig, N.F.S. 51
Gubser, P. 97
Gudme, A.K. de Hemmer 141
Guillaume, P. 5, 6, 7, 8, 109
Gulick, J.J. 97
Gunkel, H. 1, 64
Gunn, D.M. 44
Guthe, H. 68
Hagelia, H. 106, 109
Hallo, W.W. 9, 140
Halpern, B. 21, 22
Halsall, G. 116
Handy, L.K. 139
Harmanşah, Ö. 117
Hayes, J.H. 65, 66, 75, 111, 112
Heimpel, W. 85
Hempel, J. and L. Rost 157
Hendel, R.S. 117
Herrmann, S. 74
Herzog, Z. 118, 120
Hesse, F. 84
Hjelm, I. 101, 141, 143
Hodder, I. 58, 59
Hoffmeier, J.K. 36
Hoftijzer, J. 108
Holman, K. 131
Hommel, F. 28
Hoppe, L.J. 55
Hostetter, E.C. 23, 46
Hudson, S. 58, 59
Hutchinson, J. 58
Hütteroth, W.-D. 100
Hutton, P.H. 105
Jensen, P. 28
Jeremias, A. 28
Jongeling, K. 108
Kant, I. 103
Kartveit, M. 139, 141
Kaufmann, Y. 12, 13, 49
Kelle, B.E. 6, 7, 108

Kenyon, K.M. 56, 57, 85, 96, 114, 120
Kierkegaard, S. 39, 51
Kimbrough, S.T. 95
Kitchen, K.A. 29, 36, 130
Kittel, R. 68
Kletter, R. 114, 119, 120
Klopfenstein, M.A. 81
Knauf, E.A. 5, 6, 7, 8, 35, 108, 109
Knoppers, G.N. 139, 141
Knudtzon, J.A. 92
Koenen, K. 54
Kofoed, Jens Bruun 26, 46
König, J. 137
Kooij, G. van der 36
Korošec, V. 81
Kossinna, G. 115
Kratz, R.G. 4, 15, 135, 137, 141
Kraus, F.R. 138
Kuenen, A. 27, 46
Kuhn, T.S. 12, 75
Kupper, J.-R. 97
Lancaster, W. 14
Landsberger, B. 87
Larsen, M.T. 29
Leach, E. 59
Leinert, E. 116
Leonard-Fleckman, M. 22
Lesko, L.H. 79
Lessing, G.E. 63
Lévi-Strauss, C. 59
Liverani, Mario 4, 5, 11, 12, 40, 53, 55, 72, 78, 87, 89, 92, 93, 95, 143
Løgstrup, K.E. 51
Long, B. 2, 25, 50, 53, 60
Long, V.P. 6, 30, 45
Long, V.P., D.W. Baker and G.J. Wenham 163
Longman III, T. 6, 30, 45
Loretz, O. 65
Lowenthal, D. 127
Luckenbill, D.D. 9
Macalister, R.A. 57
McCarter, P.L. 23, 46
McCarthy, D.J. 82
McInerney, J. 58
MacLeod, R. 137
Maidman, M.P. 85, 90

Malamat, A. 44, 55
Mandell, S. 64
Ma'oz, M. 100
Marchetti, N. 114
Margalit, R. 117
Marx, E. 97
Masalha, Nur 21
Matthews, V.H. 97
Mayes, A.D.H. 75, 76
Mazar, A. 41, 57, 96, 115, 116, 118, 121, 122, 123
Mazar, B. 90, 92
Mazar, E. 57, 120
Mendels, D. 58
Mendenhall, G.E. 13, 50, 81, 82, 90, 91, 92, 93, 94, 95, 96, 123
Merlo, P. 81
Meyer, E. 73
Miller, J.M. 65, 66, 75, 111, 112
Moore, M.B. 6, 7, 108
Moran, W.L. 92, 103
Mowinckel, Sigmund 1, 64, 73, 74
Muceniecks, A. 116
Möhlenbrink, K. 54
Musil, A. 95
Na'aman, N. 92
Naveh, J. 22, 105
Nelson, R.A. 128
Nestor, D.A. 58, 115
Niebuhr, B.G. 3, 27
Nielsen, E. 29, 70
Nielsen, F.A.J. 134
Niemann, H.M. 5, 7, 8, 109, 121
Niesiołowski-Spanò, Ł. 53
Nigro, L. 36, 114
Noll, K.L. 6
Noth, M. 2, 12, 13, 14, 15, 23, 30, 31, 47, 48, 49, 50, 52, 53, 54, 56, 60, 65, 66, 67, 68, 69, 70, 71, 72, 73, 74, 75, 77, 84, 93, 111, 122, 128, 134
Nyberg, H.S. 70
Oeming, M. 121
Oestigaard, T. 114, 121
Östreicher, T. 128
Oikonomopoulou, K. 137
Olrik, A. 130

Olyan, S.M. 81
Ong, W.J. 122
Oppenheim, A. Leo 9
Oppenheim, M. Freiherr von 95
Orlinski, H. 74
Pappe, I. 18, 143
Parpola, S. 82
Pasto, J. 45
Pedersen, J. 29, 70
Perlitt, L. 28, 82
Pettinato, G. 131
Pfoh, E. vii, 104
Pioske, D.D. 22
Pitard, W.T. 86
Pollard, J. 127
Pritchard, J.B. 9
Provan, I. 6, 26, 30, 43, 45, 46, 62, 63, 130
Pury, A. de 108
Rad, G. von 81, 84, 128, 137
Radogan, Z. 107
Rainey, A.F. 17, 34, 91, 92
Ranke, Leopold von 3, 27
Redman, C. 59
Reid, H. 137
Reimarus, H.S. 63, 78
Reisner, G.A. 114
Rendsburg, G. 15, 16, 24, 25, 30, 34, 35, 37, 41, 42, 47
Renfrew, C. 94
Renz, J. 81
Richter, W. 75
Ricœur, P. 105
Robertson, R.G. 80
Röllig, W. 33
Römer, T. 108, 121, 128
Rose, M. 135
Rost, L. 4, 81, 110
Roth, M. 138
Rowton, M.B. 14, 97, 98
Running, L.G. 50
Said, E.W. 97
Salzman, P.C. 14
Sand, S. 20, 119
Sasson, Jack M. 171
Saxo Grammaticus 171
Schmid, H.H. 135

Schmid, K. 139, 140
Schmitt, R. 81
Schnidewind, W. 92
Schopenhauer, A. 39
Schumacher, G. 114
Sellin, E. 68, 114
Service, E.R. 94, 123
Shanks, H. 23, 33
Sherrard, B. 2, 25, 38, 50, 52
Shiloh, Y. 57, 120
Silberman, N.A. 11, 14, 20, 22, 33, 114, 119, 121
Silverman, J. 107
Singer-Avitz, L. 120
Smend, R. 25, 27, 28, 128
Smith, A.D. 58
Smith, S. 92
Smith, W. Robertson 29
Soggin, J.A. 111
Speiser, E.E. 91
Steiner, Margreet 57, 112, 120, 121
Stinespring, W. 49
Strange, J. 34, 139
Strootman, R. 137
Stucken, E. 28
Sweet, L.E. 97
Taha, H. 36, 114, 143
Thompson, R.J. 82
Thompson, T.L. vii, 16, 17, 21, 23, 26, 31, 32, 33, 34, 41, 42, 43, 45, 57, 62. 64, 87, 88, 89, 90, 101, 131, 143, 144, 145
Toll, C. 70
Tumblety, J. 105
Ulrich, Eugene 125
Ussishkin, D. 9, 57, 113, 116, 117, 118, 120
Van Seters, J. 18, 22, 45, 87, 88, 89, 90, 129, 130, 131, 132, 133, 135
Vaughan, A.G. and A.F. Killebrew 174
Vaux, Roland de 12, 13, 74
Veijola, T. 128
Wagemakers, B. 174
Wajdenbaum, P. 137
Watanabe, K. 82
Watzinger, C. 114

Weber, M. 104
Weidner, E.F. 81
Weinfeld, M. 82
Weinrich, H. 105
Weippert, H. 96
Weippert, M. 93
Weippert, M. and S. Tim 175
Wellhausen, Julius 27, 28, 29, 46, 68
Wesselius, J.-V. 137
West, J. vii
West, J. and J. Crossley 175
Wette, W.M.L. de 27, 68
Wheeler, R.E.M. 56
White, H. 127
Whitelam, K.W. vii, 16, 17, 30, 31, 41, 45, 62

Whiting, Robert M. 89
Whybray, R.N. 110
Wiggins, S.A. 81
Wightman, G.J. 118
Wilson, K.A. 176
Winckler, H. 28
Winnett, F.V. 124, 128, 129
Wolf, H.W. 176
Woodhead, J. 57
Woolf, G. 137
Wright, G.E. 25, 37, 41, 49, 50, 54, 55, 56, 96
Yates, F. 39
Yadin, Y. 115, 116, 117
Younger, K.L. 9, 140

Index of Subjects

Abdi-Ḫeba (ÌR-Ḫeba) 102, 103, 112
Abiathar 4
Abraham 20, 83, 84, 86, 87, 88, 119, 129, 131, 132, 144
Absence of evidence 28
Aj 52
Alalakh 89
Albright group 2, 12, 13, 15, 18, 23, 31, 36, 37, 47, 50, 81, 82, 94, 101, 117, 145
Aleppo 99
Aleppo Codex 54
Alexander the Great 38
Alexandria 79, 137
Amarna letters, archive 34, 92, 112
Amarna period 10, 101, 102
Ammon 110
Amorites 85, 88, 89, 99
Amphictyony 13, 14, 31, 32, 65, 66, 67, 68, 71, 72, 73, 74, 75, 76, 77, 83, 90, 105, 136, 137
Amurru 88
Ancient Israel 1, 4, 20
Anthropology 59
Antiquity 39
Anti-Semitism, anti-Semites 35, 41
Anti-Zionism 35
Arameans 110
Archaeological schools 56
Archaeology, biblical 36, 50, 59, 60, 71
Archaeology, Palestinian 36
Archaeology, political (national) 114
Archaeology, Syro-Palestinian 36
Archaeology in Israel 2, 20, 34, 47, 53, 56, 123
Archives 32
Aristotle 39, 40
Arrian 38
Artaxerxes I 113

Ashdod 34, 116
Asherah 81
Ashurbanipal 140
Assyrian treaties 82
Augustus 134

Babylon 137
Babylonian conquest(s) of Jerusalem 56, 140
Baltimore school 2, 25, 50
Bar-Kochba 72
Bathsheba 110
Beersheba 76
Benjaminites (Mari) 99
Beowulf 131
Bethel 76
Bethlehem 21
Biblical historiography 1, 127, 135
biblical narratives: rationalistic paraphrase 2
biblical Israel 6, 15
Biblical Theology Movement 41
Books of Chronicles 72
Book of Daniel 21
Book of Deuteronomy 82, 144
Books of Kings 3, 20, 72, 109
Book of Joshua 52, 69, 73
Book of Judges 52, 73, 78
Books of Samuel 3, 20, 43, 72, 91, 109
Byblos 86
Bytdwd 108

Canaan, Canaanites 76, 79, 85, 91, 92, 93, 121
Cancel culture 60
Central sanctuary 75, 76, 77
Centralism, centralist 60
Chaldeans 88, 129
Charlemagne 132

Chronicler 132
Chronicon Lethrense 22, 131
Clan system 104
Codex Hammurabi 137
Conquest of Canaan 5, 12, 13, 50, 52, 65, 67, 68, 69, 111
Conservative evangelical 82
Conservatism 51
Copenhagen, Faculty of Theology 31
Copenhagen School 1, 4, 46
Covenant, Book 137
Covenant theology, theory 75, 80, 81, 82, 91
Credo 81
Cultural evolutionism 95
Cultural (collective) memory 1, 15, 53, 105
Cuneiform 28

Damascus 86, 99, 109, 110, 112, 144
Damascus text 43
Damnatio memoriae, defamation 7, 8, 21, 37, 138
Dan 108
Dan'il 77
Darwin, Charles 63
David, 5, 14, 20, 21, 22, 32, 43, 44, 63, 70, 73, 77, 105, 106, 109, 110, 111, 112, 113, 116, 117, 118, 120, 123, 131, 136
David's empire 111, 136
David's palace 120
David's succession, history of 4
Dead Sea Scrolls/texts 33, 43, 54, 124, 125
Deconstruction 38
Delphic league 74
Denmark 22
Deuteronomistic historiography 141
Deuteronomistic history 134, 135
Deuteronomistic literature 11, 128
Deuteronomy, Book of 11, 128
Dielheimer Blätter 4
Dimorphic society 98
Dionysos II
Divided kingdom 65
Dostoevsky, F.M. 39

Ebla 131, 132
Edom 110
Egypt 10, 14, 28, 45, 65, 66, 68, 78, 79, 82, 84, 86, 89, 91, 92, 93, 111, 112, 114, 118, 127
Elephantine 112, 139
Elohist 128
Enlightenment, the 62
Enneateuch 135
Ethnicity 58, 121, 126
Ethnology 59, 101
Etiology 53
Euphrates 110
Euripides 110
Evangelical 24
Evangelical-Lutheran Church of Denmark 24
Evolutionary thinking 26
Exile 15
Exilic period 38
Exodus 36, 50, 63, 67, 68, 72, 78, 79, 111, 137
Ezekiel the Tragedian 79

Falsification 8
Fascism, fascist, 42
Folklore 76, 130
Formgeschichte 52
Freemasonry 127
Fundamentalism, fundamentalist 24, 25, 26, 28, 50, 127

Genesis, Book 90, 129, 137
Gerizim 102, 141
German Protestant Institute of Archaeology in Jerusalem 47, 48
Gestae Danorum 22, 116, 131
Gezer 34, 57, 86, 110, 115, 116
Gibeah 78
Gideon 144
Gilead 110
Gilgamesh 77, 144
Goliath 109
Göttinger Schule 25
Göttinger Sieben, 25
Greek historiographers 136
Grundtvig, N.F.S. 51

Index of Subjects

Ḫabiru 86, 87, 91, 92, 93, 118
Hamath 110
Hammurabi 88
Hasmonean 139, 141
Ḫatti 143
Hazael 109
Hazor 34, 52, 78, 115, 116
Hebrew(s) 91, 92
Hebrew Bible 21
Hebrew conquest 94
Hebrew monarchy
Hebron 76, 119
Hegel, Hegelianism 27, 28, 46, 63
Heimskringla 23
Hellenism 15
Hellenistic period 4, 15, 38, 62, 102, 113, 124, 137, 141
Heraclitus 63
Herodotus 36, 66, 79, 134, 135, 136, 142
Heroic age 76
Hesiod 76
Hezekiah 9, 14
High chronology 118
Historical–critical scholarship 3, 27, 48
Historical narrative, date 65
Historical negationism 18, 19
Historiographic tradition 65
Historiography 126
Hittite vassal treaties 81, 82, 91
Hollingshed's chronicle 39
Holocaust denial 20
Homeric epic 110
Homo mensura 39
Horeb 144
House of David 22, 105, 108, 109, 119
House of Omri 22, 138, 140
Hurrians, Hurritic 89
Hyksos 79

Identity creation 127
Ideology, ideologues 35, 40, 41, 43, 46, 62
Idrimi of Alalah 92
Iflatun pınarı (the well of Plato) 117
Iliad 78, 110

Intermediate Bronze Age 89
Isaac 82
Islamic tradition 70
Israel, historical, 4, 20
Israel, biblical 4, 6, 15, 20, 35
Israel, history 8, 47, 65, 124
Israel, Kingdom 10
Israel, idea of 15
Israel, in Egypt 68, 79, 91
Israel, modern 21, 35
Israel, name 139
Israel, origins 69, 77, 90, 96
Israel, settlement 72
Israel, tribes 11
Israel inscription 101, 102
Israeli archaeology 121
Israelites 121

Jacob 83
Jericho 52, 56, 113
Jeroboam II 117
Jerusalem 4, 9, 10, 11, 14, 22, 34, 56, 99, 110, 112, 113, 115, 117, 118, 119, 121, 138, 141
Jesus 63
Jewish rebellions 21
Joab 110
Joseph, story 91
Josephus 79
Joshua 114
Josiah 10, 14, 128
Josiah's reform 10, 124, 128, 139
Judah, Kingdom 10
Judges 5, 75
Judah 119

Kadesh Barnea 79
Kant, Emmanuel 39, 104
Khirbet Qeiyafa 57
Kierkegaard, Søren 39, 51
King Arthur 23, 116, 134
King Dan 22
Kirta 77
Konya 117

Lab'aya 10, 102, 103
Lachish 9, 52, 116

Lejre 130Leonardo da Vinci 40
Levites 76
Libya 79
Lineage 103
List of twelve tribes 75
Livy 22, 77, 134, 136
Løgstrup, K.E. 51
Luther 24
Lutheran evangelism 24

Maccabees 72
Major judges 76
Manetho 79
Mari 45, 85, 88, 99
Marxism, marxist 31, 41, 95
Masoretic tradition 125
Maximalism, maximalist 6, 7, 8, 11, 15, 21, 23, 24, 25, 26, 46, 51, 60, 73, 79, 110, 130, 141
Mea Shearim 35
Megiddo 52, 86, 114, 115, 116
Megiddo, Stables 117
Memory, memory studies 15, 70
Merneptah 101, 102
Mesha inscription 22
Messianism 21
Messianic tradition 64
Metahistory 127
Michelangelo 40
Middle position (in scholarship) 12
Minimalism, minimalist vii, 1, 2, 3, 6, 7, 8, 11, 13, 15, 16, 18, 19, 20, 21, 23, 24, 26, 29, 30, 31, 32, 33, 34, 35, 36, 37, 38, 39, 40, 41, 42, 43, 44, 45, 46, 47, 53, 55, 58, 59, 60, 62, 64, 67, 77, 94, 106, 107, 111, 112, 117, 118, 122, 123, 129, 130, 132, 141, 145
Minor judges 74, 76
Moab, Moabites 76, 110
Moses 20, 63, 68, 79, 91, 119
Moses group 91, 93
Mt. Sinai 79
Museion 137
Myth and Ritual School 25

Napoleon 78

Nation, National state, concept of 120, 121, 126
Nationalism 126
national history, national histories 134, 136
Near Eastern society 98
Nebuchadnezzar 72, 140
Negev Bedouins 103
Niebelungenlied 116
Nihilism, nihilist 30, 31, 36, 41, 42, 47, 48, 49, 73, 83
Nomads, Nomadism 97, 98, 100
Nomadization 99
Norse sagas 116
Nuzi, Nuzi archives 32 33, 34, 45, 85, 89, 90

Offenbarungsarchäologie 122
Og 144
Old Babylonian period 88
Old Testament, a Hellenistic Book 3
Old Testament theology 64
Oral tradition 69, 117, 130

Palestine 4, 6, 9, 10, 13, 20, 21, 34, 35, 36, 38, 45, 47, 48, 31, 52, 56, 66, 69, 69, 71, 73, 78, 81, 82, 85, 86, 87, 88, 89, 90, 81, 92, 100, 101, 102, 103, 109, 110, 112, 114, 115, 116, 117, 119, 120, 121, 124, 131, 136, 138, 140, 141, 143, 145 141, 143
Palestine, history of 38
Pan-Hellenism 61
Panbabylonism 28
Paradigms, changing 12, 75
Patriarchs 5, 12, 32, 50, 67, 68, 72, 77, 83, 84, 86, 87, 111
Patriarchal age 89
Patriarchal narratives 45, 65
Patronage 104
Peloponnesian War 142
Pentateuch 66, 76, 132, 135, 137
Period of the Judges 31, 48, 65, 73, 76, 82, 90, 111
Persian period 4, 15, 38, 62
Philistines 76

Philosophy 46, 47, 62
Plato 39, 40, 104, 137
Plutarch 38
poetic literature of the Old Testament 65
Polybius 136
Postmodernism, postmodernist 38, 39, 40, 43, 45, 57, 59
Post-processual archaeology 59, 123
Priestly writer 129
Prophets 65
Protocols of the Elders of Zion 21
Proto-Israelites 101

Qatna 85

Ragnar Lodbrog 131
Ramesside period 101
Raphael 40
Rationalistic paraphrase 6
Rehoboam 10
Renaissance 39
"Revelation archaeology" 4
Revisionism, revisionist 18, 19, 38
Revolution hypothesis (conquest) 13
Rolf Krake 130
Rome 22
Romulus 22

Salmanasser V 140
Samaria 11, 56, 113, 121, 138, 140
Samarina 138
Samari(t)ans 102
Samari(t)an studies 32
Sargon II 140
Saul 43
Saxo Grammaticus 22, 116, 130, 131, 134
Schopenhauer, Arthur 39
Sennacherib 9, 125, 138
Septuagint 21
Serapeion 137
"School of Athens" 40
Shaaraim 57
Shakespeare 39
Shechem 10, 76, 80, 93, 101, 102, 113
Shilo 76

Shishak 10, 125
Shivta 48
Shoshenq 10
Sihon 144
Sinai 67, 68, 72, 80, 81, 91, 93, 137, 144
Snorri Sturluson 23
Social anthropology 59, 50, 94, 95, 96, 97, 123
Sociology 14
Solomon 5, 14, 77, 105, 110, 111, 113, 116, 117, 123, 136
Song of Deborah 73, 78
Song of Roland 78
Source criticism 3, 66
Students' revolt 1968 32
Šuppiluliumaš I 91
Sutu 91
Šuwardata 112
Syria 36
Syro-Palestine 36
System theory (in sociology) 58, 59

Tall al-Fukhar 34
Tel Beersheva 115
Tel Dan inscription 22, 105, 106, 107, 108, 132
Telipinus 143
Tell Balata/Shechem excavations 36
Tell el-Hesi 115
Tell Sultan/Jericho excavations 36, 114
Tel Yizreel 20, 34, 57
Temple of Solomon 5
Ten Commandments 144
Theological history 84
Thucydides 142
Tiglathpileser III 140
Tiv 103
Torah 137
Traditions of early Israel 77
Tribe, tribal 136
Tribal borders 75
Tribal league, see Amphictyony
Tribal lists 76
Tribal society 103
Tribal wars 75
Turkish administration 99, 100

Twelve tribe league 14, 15
Twelve tribe ideology 105
Twelve-tribe system 3, 136

Ugarit 86, 89
Umm Qes-Gadara 34
United monarchy of David and Solomon 65, 117, 123
Uppsala school 25, 70
Ur in Chaldea 88, 129

Village culture 100

Weber, Max 104
Wie es eigentlich gewesen 3

Yahwist 128, 132, 135, 136
Yehudim 139

Zionism, Zionist 20, 25, 35, 119

www.ingramcontent.com/pod-product-compliance
Lightning Source LLC
Chambersburg PA
CBHW062044220426
43662CB00010B/1640